C000264892

ISSUES IN POLITICAL THEORY

Political Theory has undergone a remarkable development in recent years. From a state in which it was once declared dead, it has come to occupy a central place in the study of Politics. Both political ideas and the wide-ranging arguments to which they give rise are now treated in a rigorous, analytical fashion, and political theorists have contributed to disciplines as diverse as economics, sociology and law. These developments have made the subject more challenging and exciting, but they have also added to the difficulties of students and others coming to the subject for the first time. Much of the burgeoning literature in specialist books and journals is readily intelligible only to those who are already well-versed in the subject.

Issues in Political Theory is a series conceived in response to this situation. It consists of a number of detailed and comprehensive studies of issues central to Political Theory which take account of the latest developments in scholarly debate. While making original contributions to the subject, books in the series are written especially for those who are new to Political Theory. Each volume aims to introduce its readers to the intricacies of a fundamental political issue and to help them find their way through the detailed, and often complicated, argument that that issue has attracted.

PETER JONES
ALBERT WEALE

ISSUES IN POLITICAL THEORY

Series editors: PETER JONES and ALBERT WEALE

Published
David Beetham: **The Legitimation of Power**
Tom Campbell: **Justice** (2nd edition)
John Horton: **Political Obligation**
Peter Jones: **Rights**
Albert Weale: **Democracy**

Forthcoming
Raymond Plant: **Equality**
Hillel Steiner: **Utilitarianism**

Series Standing Order

If you would like to receive future titles in this series as they are published, you can make use of our standing order facility. To place a standing order please contact your bookseller or, in case of difficulty, write to us at the address below with your name and address and the name of the series. Please state with which title you wish to begin your standing order. (If you live outside the United Kingdom we may not have the rights for your area, in which case we will forward your order to the publisher concerned.)

Customer Services Department, Macmillan Distribution Ltd
Houndmills, Basingstoke, Hampshire RG21 6XS, England

The Legitimation of Power

David Beetham

© David Beetham 1991

All rights reserved. No reproduction, copy or transmission of
this publication may be made without written permission.

No paragraph of this publication may be reproduced, copied or
transmitted save with written permission or in accordance with
the provisions of the Copyright, Designs and Patents Act 1988,
or under the terms of any licence permitting limited copying
issued by the Copyright Licensing Agency, 90 Tottenham Court
Road, London W1T 4LP.

Any person who does any unauthorised act in relation to this
publication may be liable to criminal prosecution and civil
claims for damages.

The author has asserted his right to be identified as the author of this
work in accordance with the Copyright, Designs and Patents Act 1988.

Published by
PALGRAVE
Houndmills, Basingstoke, Hampshire RG21 6XS and
175 Fifth Avenue, New York, N. Y. 10010
Companies and representatives throughout the world

PALGRAVE is the new global academic imprint of
St. Martin's Press LLC Scholarly and Reference Division and
Palgrave Publishers Ltd (formerly Macmillan Press Ltd).

ISBN 0–333–37538–6 hardcover
ISBN 0–333–37539–4 paperback

This book is printed on paper suitable for recycling and
made from fully managed and sustained forest sources.

A catalogue record for this book is available
from the British Library.

Transferred to digital printing 2003

Printed and bound in Great Britain by
Antony Rowe Ltd, Eastbourne

Contents

Preface and Acknowledgements

Unlike other volumes in the series, this book is more a work of social science than of normative philosophy. Its ambition is to rescue the concept of legitimacy from the confusion into which it has sunk, so that its place in the analysis of power relations can be securely located. Fulfilling such an ambition is necessarily both a theoretical and a philosophical task. The first part of the book identifies the different components of legitimacy, and explores the processes of legitimation across the dimensions of gender, class and political power. The second part offers an account of legitimacy in relation to the contemporary state. The argument of the book is cumulative, so that each part is necessary to the other. I hope readers will forgive such a presumption on their continuing interest.

I have incurred many debts in writing the book, and learnt a lot from the comments of others. Draft chapters have been discussed by Diana Coole, Malcolm Harrison, Veronica Munoz, Ben Rogers and John Schwarzmantel. The bulk of the manuscript has been read by Zygmunt Bauman, Margaret Beetham, Diemut Bubeck, David Held, Steven Lukes, Peter Jones and Albert Weale, the last two in their capacity as editors of the series. I am grateful to them all for the trouble they have taken. Initial work on the project was made possible by a grant from the Economic and Social Research Council, and I acknowledge their support for research that is more interpretative than utilitarian in purpose. I must plead (who can't?) the pressure of administrative and teaching responsibilities for not having completed it sooner. Among the benefits of procrastination must be counted the fact that the manuscript was not ready when the European revolutions of 1989 took place, nor yet when the Iraqi army invaded Kuwait. Although details of my analysis will be further overtaken by events, the main thrust of the argument will, I hope, prove sound. Finally, as one who remains wilfully devoted to the pen in preference to the keyboard, I salute once more the skills of Jeanne Bellovics.

David Beetham

PART I
THE CRITERIA FOR LEGITIMACY

1 Towards a Social-scientific Concept of Legitimacy

The exercise of power by one person over others, or by one group over another, is a basic and recurrent feature of all societies. Those who are subordinate experience it as constraining, often humiliating and sometimes life-threatening; and many would escape it if they could. Those who hold power, or seek to do so, are themselves frequently at odds with one another over the scope of their power and the control over their subordinates, with potentially damaging consequences. Power, in other words, is a highly problematical, as well as recurrent feature of human societies. And because it is so problematical, societies will seek to subject it to justifiable rules, and the powerful themselves will seek to secure consent to their power from at least the most important among their subordinates. Where power is acquired and exercised according to justifiable rules, and with evidence of consent, we call it rightful or legitimate.

How far power is legitimate, what makes it so, and why it matters: these are all inherently difficult and contentious questions. They have at various times and places seriously exercised those involved in power relations, especially in periods of legal uncertainty, moral disagreement or intense social and political conflict. These questions have also been the special concern of different groups of professionals – legal experts, moral or political philosophers, social scientists, to name but three – who have each approached them from a different focus of interest, and have tended to employ different conceptions or definitions of legitimacy according to their respective professional standpoint. So in addition to the inherent difficulty of deciding what makes

3

power legitimate, there is the extra complication of divergent definitions offered by different groups of professionals. It is this double layer of complexity that makes the subject of legitimacy so confusing.

In unravelling this complexity, I shall begin with the different professionalisms, or academic specialisms as we could call them, since this will provide the best point of departure for understanding what the subject of legitimacy is about. To begin with, legal experts, and especially constitutional lawyers, are concerned with the resolution of legal disputes about power: how it is validly acquired, who is entitled to exercise it, within what limits, and so on. Their special expertise and focus of interest is with the definition and interpretation of legal rules, and with how these are initiated, revised and enforced. For them, power is legitimate where its acquisition and exercise conform to established law. For them legitimacy is equivalent to *legal validity*.

Now there is an obvious sense in which we would all recognise legal validity as an important aspect of legitimacy. A recurrent context in which the terms 'legitimate' and 'illegitimate' have traditionally been used has been in relation to children, and whether they have been conceived within a legally authorised marriage or not. This question has historically derived its significance from its relation to issues of power, and in particular to disputes about the succession to property and position. In societies where the chief mode of access to power is through birth, it becomes of supreme importance to determine who is the legitimate, i.e. legally valid, heir to an estate or a dynasty. And what applies to power based on heredity applies with equal force to any other system of power; the mode of access to it, as well as its scope and duration, require social regulation, and the characteristic means of doing so is through legal rules. To say that the power a person has was legally acquired and is exercised within the law, is a first condition of its legitimacy.

However, if legal validity is a recognisable element in legitimacy, it cannot by any means exhaust it. Disputes about the legitimacy, or rightfulness, of power are not just disputes about what someone is legally entitled to have or to do; they also involve disagreements about whether the law itself is justifiable, and whether it conforms to moral or political principles that are rationally defensible. Are the relations of power, of dominance and subordination, which the law sustains, are the rules that determine access to positions of power or the means of exercising it, themselves rightful? If not, are we obliged to obey them, or to cooperate with the powerful, on any other grounds than a prudent calculation of our own self-interest? These moral questions and practical dilemmas about power go deeper than the question of its legal validity; they concern the justification for the law itself. It is not what the law actually prescribes, but what it ought to prescribe, that is here the central issue of legitimacy.

Now, the question of how power relations within a society ought to be arranged, and what would count as a sufficient justification to require the support of the subordinate for them, has been the special concern of moral and political philosophy. Some philosophers have been primarily apologetic, seeking justifications for an existing structure of power; others have been critical, exposing its deficiencies, and advocating revisions or alternatives to it. Yet what they share is the project of elucidating the most general principles – of justice, of right, of social utility – necessary to the justification of power relations; and also, in the modern period at least, of specifying what conditions have to be met if those subject to power can be said to have consented to it, and so be morally obliged to obey or support it. For the moral and political philosopher, power is legitimate where the rules governing it are justifiable according to rationally defensible normative principles. And as with any moral principles, these embody a universalising claim; it is not the principles that happen to pertain in a given society that are sufficient, but those that any rational person, upon considered and unbiassed reflection, would have to agree to. What is 'legitimate' to the philosopher, then, is what is morally justifiable or rightful; legitimacy entails the *moral justifiability* of power relations.

If we turn, finally, to the social scientist, we see a different focus of interest from those of the legal expert or moral philosopher. The social scientist's concern is not with solving legal disputes or moral dilemmas about power, or helping others to do so; it is rather with identifying the empirical consequences that legitimacy has for the character of power relations, for the different ways in which they are organised, and for the extent to which the powerful can actually count on the obedience or support of those subordinate to them. The social scientist's purpose, in other words, is primarily an explanatory one. An understanding of legitimacy helps explain, for example, why people have the expectations they do about a power relationship, why institutions of power differ systematically from one type of society to another, why power is exercised more coercively in some contexts than in others. Above all, it helps explain the erosion of power relations, and those dramatic breaches of social and political order that occur as riots, revolts and revolutions. It is not just because these events are particularly dramatic and fateful that they interest the social scientist. As with so much else about society, it is only when legitimacy is absent that we can fully appreciate its significance where it is present, and where it is so often taken for granted.

What, then, is legitimacy for the social scientist? What makes power legitimate? Social scientists, unlike moral or political philosophers, are concerned with legitimacy in particular historial societies rather than universally; with legitimacy in given social contexts rather than independent of any particular context; with actual social relations rather than ideal ones. They are only too aware that what makes power legitimate in one society may differ from others, and that the criteria for legitimacy in one may be rejected by another. Moreover, they are trained to stand back from their own values and beliefs so as better to understand those of others. As individuals they may be convinced by philosophical anarchism, but this position will not help them understand the legitimacy of the modern state, or distinguish where it is, from where it is not, legitimate. As individuals they may regard all religious beliefs as rationally unfounded and indefensible, but such a judgement will not help them understand the legitimacy of the late Ayatollah Khomeini. What matters for an adequate understanding is not what they personally believe, but what is believed in the society they are studying. For this reason most social scientists in the twentieth century have followed Max Weber in defining legitimacy as the *belief in legitimacy* on the part of the relevant social agents; and power relations as legitimate where those involved in them, subordinate as well as dominant, believe them to be so (Weber, 1968, p.213).

At this point in the discussion it is important that I make clear what sort of book this is going to be. It is not intended as a work of legal theory or political philosophy, as I have characterised them above. In particular, it is not about political obligation as philosophers would treat it. My purpose is not to clarify the moral dilemmas of citizens faced with the choice of whether or not to break the law. This is not because I consider such issues unimportant or unamenable to rational argument. It is because my concern is with the different, social-scientific question: what are the causes and consequences of people's disobedience? That is to say, I am concerned with legitimacy as a problem for social science rather than for political philosophy.

There are a number of reasons for my choice. The first is that, although I am a political philosopher as well as a social scientist, I believe that the two activities have a different purpose and a different logic, and neither is best served by confusing it with the other. This is not to say that there is no significant connection between the two activities; but the connection can only properly be defined, as I hope to show, by first carefully observing the distinction between them. My second reason is that handling normative topics, which is the everyday business of the philosopher, provides the severest challenge to the social scientist, and confronts him or her with the most acute methodological difficulties. Nowhere is it more essential to overcome these difficulties than in the study of power relations, which because of their importance carry such a potential for obfuscation. On both methodological and substantive grounds, then, the subject of legitimacy must count as one of the central issues of social science. My third reason is that social scientists have in fact been thoroughly confused about legitimacy, and their confusion has its starting point in their failure to conceptualise it adequately, or to offer a coherent account of what makes power legitimate in particular societies. If that judgement sounds like arrogance on my part, it is also a confession: I have been thoroughly confused myself. The following discussion, which seeks to identify the confusion and offer a convincing resolution of it, is also the record of a personal journey out of the maze which this subject represents.

The source of the confusion lies with the work of Max Weber. It is one of the most remarkable features about the study of legitimacy in politics departments, at least in the Anglo-Saxon world, that it is suspended between two separate bodies of literature that have absolutely no connection with one another. If you are studying legitimacy as a subject in political philosophy you will probably start with Thomas Hobbes, if not earlier, and proceed through the great tradition which includes Locke, Rousseau, Hegel and others. If you are studying it as a subject in political science or political sociology you will most likely begin with Max Weber, and may not discuss other thinkers at all, but proceed to a series of empirical case studies of power relations and theoretical explanations for obedience and disobedience. I will return to the problems exposed by this extraordinary disjunction later; but for the moment my starting point as a social scientist has to be with Weber, rather than with the earlier theorists.

Max Weber is rightly regarded as one of the 'founding fathers' of twentieth-century social science, and his influence across a range of disciplines and subjects has been enormous, and usually beneficial, even where later thinkers have disagreed with him. On the subject of legitimacy, however, it has to be said that his influence has been an almost unqualified disaster. The starting point of what is wrong lies in his definition of legitimacy. For a social scientist to say that a given power relation is legitimate, Weber argues, is not to make a moral judgement about it in the manner of the philosopher; it is rather to make a report (which may be empirically true or false) about other people's *beliefs*. Power is legitimate where those involved in it believe it to be so; legitimacy derives from people's belief in legitimacy. So, he writes, legitimacy is equivalent to 'Legitimitätsglaube' (a belief in legitimacy); and legitimate power is power 'als legitim angesehen' (that is regarded as legitimate) (Weber, 1956, pp.23, 157, 659; 1958, p.493).

What is wrong with this formulation can be seen most clearly from what other social scientists have made of it. Social scientists are, by training, dismissive of universal truths and values; they are only too aware of the variety of beliefs held from one society to the next, and from one historical epoch to another. They become sceptical about the possibility of any rational grounding for normative ideas or value systems, which they frequently label as 'myths', 'prejudices' or 'ideologies'. Such scepticism leads them in turn to concentrate on the processes of socialisation, the structures of influence, the agencies of dissemination whereby ideas come to be acquired and reproduced. The beliefs people hold are thus explained as the product of the cumulative influences to which they have been exposed.

Such an explanation appears particularly plausible in an age of propaganda and public relations, when the public sphere is dominated by an emphasis on presentation over reality. If people believe in the legitimacy of power, is this not because the powerful have been successful in the public relations campaign, because they have managed to convince people that they are legitimate, because their 'legitimations' have been accepted? Is the question of their legitimacy not therefore in the hands of the powerful themselves? So S.M. Lipset, in typically Weberian vein, defines the legitimacy of a political system as its capacity 'to engender and maintain the belief that the existing political institutions are the most appropriate ones for the society' (1958, p.86). And R. Merelman calls legitimacy 'a quality attributed to a regime by a population. That quality is the *outcome* of the government's capacity to engender legitimacy' (1966, p.548). Taken to their logical conclusion, such definitions would imply that the reason for the collapse of the communist regimes in Eastern Europe in 1989 lay in a deficiency of public relations, rather than anything actually wrong with the system of rule itself.

At this point political philosophers become indignant with social scientists and their Weber-inspired definitions, which transform the issue of legitimacy from a question about the actual characteristics of a system of power into one concerning the beliefs people hold about it. In so doing, it is argued, they are emptying the concept of legitimacy of any objective reference or moral content, and in effect acquiescing in the very manipulations of the powerful that they are concerned to describe. 'The new definitions,' writes J.H. Schaar, 'all dissolve legitimacy into belief or opinion. If a people holds the belief that existing institutions are "appropriate" or "morally proper", then those institutions are legitimate. That's all there is to it.' (1969, p.284). Hannah Pitkin in turn draws attention to the epistemological consequences of such a definition: 'In seeking to insulate the sociologist from the context of judging and taking a position,' she writes, 'Weber in effect made it incomprehensible that anyone might judge legitimacy and illegitimacy according to rational, objective standards' (1972, p.283). And Robert Grafstein points to the abandonment of moral judgement entailed by the Weberian approach: 'The concept should properly signify a normative evaluation of a political regime: the correctness of its procedures, the justification for its decisions, and the fairness with which it treats its subjects. In Weber's hands, however, legitimacy no longer represents an evaluation of a regime; indeed it no longer refers directly to the regime itself' (1981 p.456).

These criticisms seem to me entirely justified in pointing to the reductionist conclusions that can be drawn from the Weberian definition of legitimacy. Yet they are also mistaken if they imply, as they seem to, that the social scientist ought to become a moral or political philosopher, and engage in evaluating a regime against independent normative standards. The problem with the Weberian definition is not that it fails to meet the criteria of normative philosophy, but that it encourages bad social science. And one reason it does so is that it leaves the social scientist with no adequate means of explaining why people acknowledge the legitimacy of power at one time or place and not another. The social scientist, it seems, is someone who must always be taken by surprise when people stop treating power as legitimate and take to the streets in protest.

Now it can be argued in Weber's defence that his social-scientific definition of legitimacy as the 'belief in legitimacy' need not have the reductionist and manipulative implications I have described above, and that all I have offered is a caricature of his position. What is mistaken, it could be said, is to divorce people's beliefs about legitimacy from their *grounds* or *reasons* for holding them; and these are to be found precisely in the actual characteristics of a regime, such as its conformity to their values, its ability to satisfy their interests, and so on. Did not Weber himself explore the different grounds for people's belief in legitimacy in his analysis of the rational–legal, traditional and charismatic principles of authority? And would not a social scientist who was alert to the actual inadequacies and processes of degeneration of a regime be able, if not to predict, then at least adequately to explain, the erosion of belief in its legitimacy? The mistake, in other words, is not Weber's, but that of those social scientists who have reduced the explanation of beliefs to the processes and agencies of their dissemination and internalisation, rather than an analysis of the factors which give people sufficient grounds or reasons for holding them.

I have some sympathy with such a reply. In particular, I shall, myself, at various points in this work be analysing people's beliefs and examining their reasons for holding them. Yet the above reply is still handicapped by the Weberian definition of legitimacy as the 'belief in legitimacy', within whose orbit it remains. What is wrong with this definition is, first, that it misrepresents the relationship between beliefs and legitimacy; and, secondly, that it takes no account of those aspects of legitimacy that have little to do with beliefs at all. This brings me now to the heart of the matter.

The first objection to the Weberian definition of legitimacy – which could be called the 'received' definition, since almost all social scientists have adopted it – is that it misrepresents the relationship between legitimacy and people's beliefs. A given power relationship is not legitimate because people believe in its legitimacy, but because it can be *justified in terms of* their beliefs. This may seem a fine distinction, but it is a fundamental one. When we seek to assess the legitimacy of a regime, a political system, or some other power relation, one thing we are doing is assessing how far it can be justified in terms of people's beliefs, how far it conforms to their values or standards, how far it satisfies the normative expectations they have of it. We are making an assessment of the degree of congruence, or lack of it, between a given system of power and the beliefs, values and expectations that provide its justification. We are not making a report on people's 'belief in its legitimacy'.

An example will clarify the point I am making. It is argued that the British electoral system, with its first-past-the-post rules determining who shall be elected in each constituency, is losing its legitimacy, and to an extent therefore also weakening that of the governments elected under it. This is not because of any shift in people's beliefs, but because the rules have increasingly delivered results that diverge, both regionally and nationally, from the proportion of votes cast, and hence from accepted notions about the representative purpose of elections in a democracy. It is the increasingly unrepresentative character of the electoral system, and its consequent vulnerability to attack in a society that believes in representation, that is the basis for the weakening legitimacy of governments appointed under it. The vulnerability was there before it was exploited, and the weaken-

ing of legitimacy took place before people publicly acknowledged
it. It may have taken the poll-tax legislation to bring the issue
to the forefront of public attention. But the potential for doing
so was already present in the growing discrepancy between the
rules and the beliefs or values underpinning them. It is this
discrepancy that is important to an analysis of legitimacy; what
has occurred cannot be made intelligible in terms of a shift in
people's beliefs about legitimacy or 'belief in legitimacy'.

The Weberian definition not only misrepresents the role that
beliefs play in legitimacy. In making legitimacy primarily a matter
of belief, it also ignores those elements which are not really to
do with beliefs at all. I have already mentioned legality as an
important component of legitimacy. Whether power is or is not
acquired and exercised within the law is a question quite independent of people's beliefs; it is a matter of judicial determination.
Or consider another element in legitimacy that I have so far only
touched on: that of consent. Despite the confusion that some
political philosophers have created with the notion of 'tacit consent' (e.g. Locke, 1967, pp.365–7), what is important for legitimacy is evidence of consent expressed through *actions* which
are understood as demonstrating consent within the conventions
of the particular society, such as: concluding an agreement or
entering into a contract with a superior party; swearing an oath
of allegiance; joining in acclamation; voting in an election or
plebiscite; and so on.

Why are such actions important? It is not that they provide
evidence of people's 'belief in legitimacy'. Consent can be given
from a variety of different motives, including considerations of
personal self-interest. What is important about these actions is
that they *confer* legitimacy; they contribute to making power
legitimate. They do this both through the public demonstration
of people's consent to the power relationship, and through the
resulting obligations that derive from them on the part of both
dominant and subordinate alike. They possess simultaneously a
symbolic and a normative force.

Contributing to legitimacy, then, are to be found a number of
different factors, operating at different levels. There is the legal
validity of the acquisition and exercise of power; there is the
justifiability of the rules governing a power relationship in terms
of the beliefs and values current in the given society; there is

the evidence of consent derived from actions expressive of it. These factors, successively and cumulatively, are what make power legitimate. To the extent that they are present, it will be legitimate; to the extent that they are absent, it will not. Together these criteria provide grounds, not for a 'belief in legitimacy', but for those subject to power to support and cooperate with its holders; grounds, that is to say, not for belief, but for obligation.

It follows that the social scientist, in concluding that a given power relationship is legitimate, is making a *judgement*, not delivering a *report* about people's belief in legitimacy. The Weberian definition not only misconceives the nature of legitimacy; it also proposes a quite misleading research strategy for determining whether power is legitimate: that of asking people whether they believe it is. Apart from the problem of expecting ordinary people to understand what legitimacy means, when social scientists have such difficulty themselves with the concept, this strategy involves looking in the wrong place. Is power valid in terms of the law? Is the law justifiable in terms of the beliefs and values established in the society? Is there demonstrable evidence of consent to the given relations of power? All these questions can in principle be answered from evidence in the public domain. This is not to say that the answers may not on occasion prove contradictory, or that the evidence will not need careful interpretation. But the point is that the evidence is available in the public sphere, not in the private recesses of people's minds. And when we have answered the questions given above, the further question 'do people believe in the legitimacy of a given power?' becomes redundant.

If the social scientist, then, in considering the legitimacy of a given power relation or system, is necessarily involved in offering an assessment, in making a judgement, what kind of judgement is it, and how does it differ from those of the lawyer and the philosopher? Unlike the lawyer, the social scientist is interested in much more than legal validity; he or she is interested in the normative standing of the power arrangements that the law validates. Unlike the moral or political philosopher, on the other hand, the social scientist assesses these arrangements not against independent or universal criteria of the right or the good, but against those that pertain within the society in question; he or she does not assess actions expressive of consent against ideal conditions or ideal criteria for consent, but in relation to the conventions of the particular society. Legitimacy for social scientists is always legitimacy-in-context, rather than absolutely, ideally or abstractly. It is this that enables them to give a coherent account of legitimate power in societies other than their own, and to assess the degree of legitimacy of political systems far removed in time and space (Lowenthal, 1979, pp.401–2).

However, although the criteria of legitimacy the social scientist employs are different from those of the lawyer and the philosopher, they are also connected to them, as the account I have given should make clear. The social scientist will need to extend the lawyer's criterion of legal validity in the same way as the philosopher does; he or she will in turn need to contextualise the criterion of normative justifiability used by the moral or political philosopher. Yet in each case it will be the same *kind* of criteria that will be looked for. Because of this, the account of legitimacy that I have offered, unlike that of Weberian social science, can where relevant draw upon different traditions of legal and political theorising respectively, rather than remain completely divorced from them. It will also be able to give a coherent account of the roles of the lawyer and the philosopher at key moments of uncertainty and dispute about the legal or moral bases of legitimacy in given historical societies.

Let me sum up the argument so far. The account I have given seeks to distinguish a properly social-scientific judgement about legitimacy-in-context from both the misleading Weberian strategy of reporting people's belief in legitimacy on the one side, and the normative–philosophical project of elucidating independent criteria of justifiability, or ideal conditions for consent on the other. The inadequacies I find in both, from the *social-scientific point of view*, are similar to those discussed by Habermas in his article 'Legitimation problems in the modern state', in which he rejects both what he calls 'the empiricist' and the 'normativist' concepts of legitimacy:

'The one can be employed in the social sciences but is unsatisfactory because it abstracts from the systematic weight of grounds for validity; the other would be satisfactory in this regard but is untenable because of the metaphysical context in which it is embedded.' (1979, p.204)

At the same time, he goes on, a Rawlsian approach which seeks to define the procedural conditions (or ideal speech context) necessary to a rational consensus cannot provide the basis for analysing legitimacy in given historical societies:

'Every general theory of justification remains peculiarly abstract in relation to the historical forms of legitimate domination. If one brings standards of discursive justification to bear on traditional societies, one behaves in an historically "unjust" manner. Is there an alternative to this historical injustice of general theories, on the one hand, and the standardlessness of mere historical understanding, on the other?' (ibid. p.205)

Habermas' own answer to this question – the key question about legitimacy for the social scientist – involves constructing a developmental sequence of historical forms of legitimation after the pattern of cognitive developmental psychology. I find his solution unsatisfactory, at least as a starting point for an analysis of legitimacy. This is because, in concentrating on the differences between different historical forms, rather than also on what they have in common, Habermas fails to give an account of the underlying structure and logic of legitimation in general, which must form the necessary basis for an exploration of what is historically variable and specific. My own starting point lies with this underlying structure of legitimacy, which I have already sketched out, and will consider more systematically in the section that follows. The reader who has experienced difficulty in following the discussion so far will, I hope, find the issues becoming progressively clearer as I proceed.

The different dimensions of legitimacy

The key to understanding the concept of legitimacy lies in the recognition that it is multi-dimensional in character. It embodies three distinct elements or levels, which are qualitatively different from one another. Power can be said to be legitimate to the extent that:

i) it conforms to established rules
ii) the rules can be justified by reference to beliefs shared by both dominant and subordinate, and
iii) there is evidence of consent by the subordinate to the particular power relation.

The first level is that of rules; the second that of justifications grounded on beliefs; the third that of actions. The three levels are not alternatives, since all contribute to legitimacy; all provide the subordinate with moral grounds for compliance or cooperation with the powerful. Each, however, is different, and has its own characteristic form of non-legitimacy. I shall say something further about each of them in turn.

i) The first and most basic level of legitimacy is that of rules, corresponding to the legal definition already discussed. Power can be said to be legitimate in the first instance if it is acquired and exercised in accordance with established rules. For convenience I shall call the rules governing the acquisition and exercise of power the 'rules of power'. These rules may be unwritten, as informal conventions, or they may be formalised in legal codes or judgements. Pressure towards formalisation arises in most societies from the need to resolve disputes about power by making the rules both precise and strictly enforceable, but there still remains a considerable role for convention, or 'custom and practice', even where legal formalisation is well advanced. There also remains considerable scope for dispute about the law, though a characteristic feature of legal systems is the presence of an ultimate authority whose rulings are acknowledged as final.

The opposite of legitimacy according to the rules is, simply, *illegitimacy*; power is illegitimate where it is either acquired in contravention of the rules (expropriation, usurpation, coup d'état), or exercised in a manner that contravenes or exceeds them. The illegal acquisition of power usually has more profound, because more all-pervasive, consequences for legitimacy than some breach or contravention in its exercise, though that depends upon the seriousness of the breach, and whether it is repeated. Where the rules of power are continually broken, we could speak of a condition of chronic illegitimacy.

ii) On its own, legal validity is insufficient to secure legitimacy, since the rules through which power is acquired and exercised themselves stand in need of justification. This is the second level of legitimacy: power is legitimate to the extent that the rules of power can be justified in terms of beliefs shared by both dominant and subordinate. What kinds of justification and what kinds of belief are needed? To be justified, power has to be derived from a valid source of authority (this is particularly true of political power); the rules must provide that those who come to hold power have the qualities appropriate to its exercise; and the structure of power must be seen to serve a recognisably general interest, rather than simply the interests of the powerful. These justifications in turn depend upon beliefs current in a given society about what is the rightful source of authority; about what qualities are appropriate to the exercise of power and how individuals come to possess them; and some conception of a common interest, reciprocal benefit, or societal need that the system of power satisfies.

No society is characterised by a complete uniformity of beliefs. Indeed, one of the distinctive features of power relations is the difference of circumstances, opportunities and values between dominant and subordinate groups. Yet without a minimum of the appropriate beliefs defined above being shared between the dominant and the subordinate, and indeed among the subordinate themselves, there can be no basis on which justifications for the rules of power can find a purchase. Naturally what counts as an adequate or sufficient justification will be more open to dispute than what is legally valid, and there is no ultimate authority to settle such questions; nevertheless clear limits are set by logic and the beliefs of a given society to what justifications are plausible or credible within it.

This second level or dimension of legitimacy has its corresponding negative or opposite. Rules of power will lack legitimacy to the extent that they cannot be justified in terms of shared beliefs: either because no basis of shared belief exists in the first place (e.g. slavery, 'artificial' or divided communities); or because changes in belief have deprived the rules of their supporting basis (e.g. hereditary rule or male power, in face of a declining belief in the superior qualities supposedly ascribed by birth or sex); or because changing circumstances have made

existing justifications for the rules implausible, despite beliefs
remaining constant (the example of the British electoral system
discussed on pages 11–12). These different situations clearly have
widely differing significance, but they can all be described as
examples, not so much of illegitimacy, as of *legitimacy deficit* or
weakness.

iii) The third level of legitimacy involves the demonstrable
expression of consent on the part of the subordinate to the
particular power relation in which they are involved, through
actions which provide evidence of consent. As I argued earlier,
the importance of actions such as concluding agreements with a
superior, swearing allegiance, or taking part in an election, is
the contribution they make *to* legitimacy. They do this in two
ways. The first is that they have a subjectively binding force for
those who have taken part in them, regardless of the motives
for which they have done so. Actions expressive of consent, even
if undertaken purely out of self-interest, will introduce a moral
component into a relationship, and create a normative commitment on the part of those engaging in them. Secondly, such
actions have a publicly symbolic or declaratory force, in that
they constitute an express acknowledgement on the part of the
subordinate of the position of the powerful, which the latter are
able to use as confirmation of their legitimacy to third parties
not involved in the relationship, or those who have not taken
part in any expressions of consent. They are thus often associated
with impressive forms of ceremonial.

Now some theorists would argue that consent is a distinctively
modern component or condition of legitimacy, and one that is
specific to the liberal or individualist tradition; it therefore cannot
be relevant to an understanding of legitimacy in other historical
societies. However, this is to narrow the concept of consent to
the criteria pertaining in an individualist culture: namely, that it
should be linked to an individual choice between alternatives
(e.g. between alternative possible husbands, employers or
governments), and that all adults are in principle qualified to give
consent. The fact that the criterion of choice between alternative
'superiors' does not necessarily pertain in other societies does
not mean that there are not other conventional forms of expressing consent appropriate to those societies. And in most historical

societies only some among the subordinate have been qualified to give consent; as I shall show later, the qualification is typically related to the category of the 'free' in the sphere of social and economic power relations, and to those who count as members of the political community in the sphere of politics. Moreover, in a pre-individualist age it was taken for granted that some adult males could give consent on behalf of other people (their wives, children, clients, tenants, even descendants) in a manner that would be unacceptable in a more individualist culture, unless those involved were acting in an explicitly representative capacity. What counts as consent, therefore, and from whom it is required to confer legitimacy on the powerful, is itself a culturally specific matter, determined by the conventions of a given society, rather than definable absolutely. What is common to legitimate power everywhere, however, is the need to 'bind in' at least the most significant members among the subordinate, through actions or ceremonies publicly expressive of consent, so as to establish or reinforce their obligation to a superior authority, and to demonstrate to a wider audience the legitimacy of the powerful.

It is in the sense of the public actions of the subordinate, expressive of consent, that we can properly talk about the 'legitimation' of power, not the propaganda or public relations campaigns, the 'legitimations' generated by the powerful themselves. And if the public expression of consent contributes to the legitimacy of the powerful, then the withdrawal or refusal of consent will by the same token detract from it. Actions ranging from non-cooperation and passive resistance to open disobedience and militant opposition on the part of those qualified to give consent will in different measure erode legitimacy, and the larger the numbers involved, the greater this erosion will be. At this level, the opposite or negative of legitimacy can be called *delegitimation*.

For power to be fully legitimate, then, three conditions are required: its conformity to established rules; the justifiability of the rules by reference to shared beliefs; the express consent of the subordinate, or of the most significant among them, to the particular relations of power. All three components contribute to legitimacy, though the extent to which they are realised in a given context will be a matter of degree. Legitimacy is not an all-or-nothing affair. For this reason I used the formula above: *power can be said to be legitimate to the extent that . . .* etc. Every power relation knows its breaches of the rules or conventions; in any society there will be some people who do not accept the norms underpinning the rules of power, and some who refuse to express their consent, or who do so only under manifest duress. What matters is how widespread these deviations are, and how substantial in relation to the underlying norms and conventions that determine the legitimacy of power in a given context. Legitimacy may be eroded, contested or incomplete; and judgements about it are usually judgements of degree, rather than all-or-nothing.

Above all, the analysis I have given above demonstrates that legitimacy is not a single quality that systems of power possess or not, but a set of distinct criteria, or multiple dimensions, operating at different levels, each of which provides moral grounds for compliance or cooperation on the part of those subordinate to a given power relation. By the same token, power can be non-legitimate in very different ways, which I have signalled by the different terms: illegitimacy, legitimacy deficit and delegitimation. The erosion of justificatory norms, slavery, conquest, dictatorship, coup d'état, separatist agitation, revolutionary mobilisation – all are examples where power lacks some element of legitimacy, but does so in very different ways. The accompanying diagram summarises in tabular form the different dimensions of legitimate and non-legitimate power that I have distinguished, to reinforce the argument of the text.

Table 1.1 The three dimensions of legitimacy

	Criteria of Legitimacy	Form of Non-legitimate Power
i	conformity to rules (legal validity)	illegitimacy (breach of rules)
ii	justifiability of rules in terms of shared beliefs	legitimacy deficit (discrepancy between rules and supporting beliefs, absence of shared beliefs)
iii	legitimation through expressed consent	delegitimation (withdrawal of consent)

In analysing legitimacy into its component elements, I am claiming that these constitute basic criteria for legitimacy in all historical societies, past and present. In other words, if we want to know what makes power legitimate anywhere, it is to these criteria that we must look. Such a claim can only ultimately be vindicated by the persuasiveness of the explanatory analysis that follows in the rest of the volume. Here it is important to clarify what this claim does, and does not, entail.

At first sight it might seem that the claim that there are criteria of legitimacy universally applicable must contradict what I said earlier about the social scientist's task being to assess the legitimacy of power in its context, i.e. against the norms and values of a given society. In fact there is no contradiction. The criteria distinguished above constitute only the most general framework, the specific content or substance of which has to be 'filled in' for each historical society. Is power valid according to the rules? The relevant rules have to be specified, their conventional or legal form established, the mode of adjudication pertinent to the given society determined, and so on. Are the rules justifiable in terms of the beliefs and norms of the particular society? Again the content of these beliefs will have to be specified; but the analysis given above, and elaborated later in Chapter 3, provides a guide to what we must look for: beliefs about a) the valid source of authority (tradition, the people, divine authorisation, etc.); b) how people come to possess the qualities appropriate to the exercise of power (heredity, achievement, etc.); c) the ends that power should serve (variable according to gender, class, political power, etc.). Moreover the form in which these beliefs are reproduced and authenticated will also vary systematically from one age or society to another: myths and story telling, divine revelation, philosophical argument, scientific 'proof'. Is there, finally, evidence of expressed consent on the part of those qualified to give it? Again, who counts as qualified, and what actions count as appropriate, will be determined by the conventions of the given society or system of power.

What we have, then, is a set of general criteria for legitimacy, the specific content of which is historically variable, and must therefore be determined for each type of society. This combination of a general category, with variable and historically specific forms, is a common feature of comparative analysis in the social sciences. Consider for example the Marxian concept of class. Marx was insistent that it was the historical differentiation between different forms of class society (slave, feudal, capitalist) that was crucial to understanding the specific dynamic of each. But the differentiation was only possible in the first place by being based upon a theoretically elaborated *general* concept of class, as a relationship between the direct producers and the owners of the means of production, in which the latter appropriated a surplus from the labour of the former. An understanding of this general category, according to Marx, provided the key to the analysis of class relations in each historically specific mode of production (Marx, 1966, vol.3, pp.790–2).

A closer parallel would be that provided by Barrington Moore in his book *Injustice*, where he identifies, beneath the variability of social norms and arrangements in different historical periods, 'recurring elements' in their moral codes (Moore, 1978, ch.1). In a similar manner I am proposing that there is an underlying structure of legitimacy common to all societies, however much its content will vary from one to the other. What explains this common structure? As I shall show more fully later, it has its origin in the different ways in which power that is not legitimate offends our moral sense; in an underlying logic common to moral argument everywhere, however diverse its actual content; and in the needs that are shared by all societies, however varied the social relations and organisational arrangements by means of which they are met. It is these common features – of human beings as rational moral agents seeking to ensure that their social relations and arrangements meet their needs and conform to their moral sense – that provide the underlying structure to legitimacy everywhere.

The structure that I have so far merely outlined, comprising rule-conformity, the justifiability of the rules in terms of shared norms and beliefs, expressed consent on the part of those qualified, provides the social scientist with the framework to undertake two different tasks. The first is a systematic comparison between different forms of legitimacy appropriate to different historical types of social and political system. The assumption made here is that rules or arrangements of power *embody* justificatory beliefs or norms, and conventions about consent, even if they may come to diverge from them over time, or the beliefs themselves become atrophied. Here is the second task which the above structure provides the basis for: that of assessing the degree of legitimacy-in-context of a given power relationship, as a necessary element in explaining the behaviour of those involved in it. This is the immanent judgement or assessment of the social scientist, as opposed to the normative philosopher's assessment of a power relationship against independent, external standards or criteria. And this judgement also becomes an immanent *critique* when the social scientist is able to show the features internal to a system of power that, on the one hand, sustain and reproduce its legitimating beliefs, or, on the other, systematically undermine them over time.

The value of the multi-dimensional conception of legitimacy in facilitating the fulfilment of such an agenda stands in marked contrast to the Weberian conception considered in the previous section. Although Weber himself made a modest contribution to the first part of the agenda outlined above, the conception of legitimacy that he bequeathed to twentieth-century social science was inadequate for the purpose, and quite useless for the second, more critical, task of analysis and explanation. This is because the conception that power is legitimate if people believe it to be so, is mistaken on a number of grounds, which can now be summarised. It reduces legitimacy from a complex of factors which give people good grounds for compliance, to a single dimension: their 'belief in legitimacy'. It misconceives the relationship between legitimacy and the beliefs that provide the justificatory basis for rules of power. It fails to recognise that, although prudential and normative reasons for obedience are indeed distinct, nevertheless, people's interests can be harnessed to legitimacy through actions expressive of consent. Finally, it leaves the social scientist helpless in the critical task of analysing an erosion of legitimacy in power relations, by proposing a report on people's 'belief in legitimacy' rather than identifying a developing discrepancy between rules of power and the norms that provide their justification.

I said earlier that Weber's definition of legitimacy was only the starting point of what was wrong with his theory. The problem of his definition works through into his threefold typology of legitimate authority: traditional, rational–legal and charismatic (Weber, 1968, pp.215–16). If I also continue my critique of

Weber at this point it is not because of any unreasoned animus on my part, but because of my conviction that it is necessary for social science to be freed from the whole Weberian legacy if it is to make sense of the subject of legitimacy. Social scientists since Weber have, if anything, been even more transfixed by his threefold typology than by his definition of legitimacy itself; indeed it has become a straightjacket into which, either singly or in combination, every example of legitimate power has, willy-nilly, to be forced.

True to his definition of legitimacy as the 'belief in legitimacy', Weber makes each of his types of legitimate authority – traditional, rational–legal, charismatic – dependent upon a different type of belief: in the sanctity of tradition, in rule-conformity and procedural correctness, and in the charismatic qualities of the individual leader, respectively. What is wrong with this, to put a complex matter briefly, is that it elevates each of the three contributory components of legitimacy, that I have distinguished above, into a separate and fully self-sufficient *type* of legitimacy (see Beetham, 1991). Thus, the first level of legal validity becomes a 'rational–legal' type, based upon a belief in rule-conformity and procedural correctness; in the process it becomes detached from any substantive beliefs or principles in relation to which the legal rules and procedures can be justified. Weber's traditional type, on the other hand, represents *one* example of a second level basis for the justification of rules (belief in the sanctity of the past); but the contrast with the rational–legal type obscures its true status, and conveys the misleading impression that power in a traditional order is not validated in terms of rules at all. At the same time the typology offers no account of the beliefs that have replaced traditionalism as a second-level basis for justifying rules of power in the modern world. The charismatic type, thirdly, represents the rare case of a legitimacy deriving solely from consent, in the absence of rules or justifying beliefs, a consent expressed in the act of acknowledging and following a leader. However, Weber's typology once more obscures its character, by making the basis of legitimacy not the act of recognition by a following, but their subjective belief in the 'charisma' of the leader, a concept that has had a particularly confused and unfortunate career.

In each case, Weber's typology represents the elevation of a different level of legitimacy into a self-sufficient type, in a way that obscures the status of each as but one element in a totality. Once this process is understood, it becomes clear why the typology has proved both plausible to later social scientists, and at the same time such a potent source of confusion. Its plausibility derives from the fact that the typology embodies three genuine components of legitimacy; the confusion from the fact that it does so in a distorted form, whereby the proper status of each component has become obscured. True to Weber's conception of legitimacy as constituted by subjective beliefs, each element with its distinctive characteristics has been transposed into a different type of *belief*: in rules and procedures, in tradition, and in charisma respectively.

Other critics of Weber have had a sense of unease about his threefold typology, and the concept of charismatic authority in particular has met with repeated objections (e.g. Friedrich, 1961; Wolpe, 1968; Bensman and Givant, 1975). Yet the typology continues to hold the field, with or without qualification, because the source of Weber's error has not been clearly identified, and no convincing alternative has been proposed. I hope I have said enough, if not more than enough, to convince the reader that there is indeed an alternative approach to the subject; and that the whole Weberian theory of legitimacy has to be left behind as one of the blindest of blind alleys in the history of social science, notable only for the impressiveness of the name that it bears, not for the direction in which it leads. That at any rate is the course that I propose to follow in the remainder of this book, in which the name of Weber will hardly be mentioned again. The final introductory task will be to explain more fully why the analysis of legitimacy, such as I have offered, is so important to an understanding of power relations.

The significance of legitimacy

Legitimacy, as we have seen, comprises the moral or normative aspect of power relationships; or, more correctly, the sum of these aspects. A social-scientific analysis of legitimacy is concerned with the effect it has on the character of a given relationship, and on the behaviour of those involved in it. It is the importance of legitimacy – its character and degree – to explaining people's *behaviour* that concerns the social scientist.

To consider first the behaviour of those subordinate within a power relationship: its legitimacy provides them with moral grounds for cooperation and obedience. Legitimate power or authority has the right to expect obedience from subordinates, even where they may disagree with the content of a particular law or instruction; and subordinates have a corresponding obligation to obey. This obligation is not absolute – hence the dilemmas that occur when people are required by a legitimate superior to do things that are morally objectionable to them, as opposed to inconvenient or merely stupid. But it is the right that legitimacy gives those in authority to require obedience in principle, regardless of the content of any particular law or instruction, that makes it so important to the coordination of people's behaviour in all spheres of social life.

The legitimacy or rightfulness of power, then, provides an explanation for obedience through the obligation it imposes on people to obey, and through the *grounds or reasons* it gives for their obedience. I emphasise 'grounds or reasons', because there are numerous psychological studies of obedience which explain it in terms of acquired attitudes and characteristics, such as the internalisation of a respect for authority, which is confirmed by continuous symbolic reinforcement (e.g. Merelman, 1966; Milgram, 1974). The problem with such explanations, which reduce obedience to the sum of attitudes and characteristics developed and internalised over time, is that they fail to explain why people stop obeying, whenever they do so; or else they have recourse to considerations of the psychological 'stress' or 'dissonance' to which people are subjected. Yet people only disobey because they have sufficient and compelling reasons for disobedience in particular contexts; and such reasons will turn out to be precisely the counterpart to the reasons they have for *not* stepping out of line in normal times or situations. Psychological explanations for obedience only carry plausibility when they are in fact disguised accounts of people's reasons; or when we are driven to appeal to non-rational factors because rational ones will not suffice on their own.

However, normative grounds or reasons are not the only reasons people have for obedience. As I shall set out more fully in the next chapter, power relations are almost always constituted by a framework of incentives and sanctions, implicit if not always explicit, which align the behaviour of the subordinate with the wishes of the powerful. They do so by giving people good reasons of a different kind, those of self-interest or prudence, for not stepping out of line. Obedience is therefore to be explained by a complex of reasons, moral as well as prudential, normative as well as self-interested, that legitimate power provides for those who are subject to it. This complexity may make it difficult to determine the precise balance of reasons in any one situation; but it is important to distinguish them analytically, since each makes a very different kind of contribution to obedience.

The fact that power relations typically involve a framework of incentives and sanctions gives plausibilty to a 'realist' or 'organisational' view of power, which holds that obedience is *only* a matter of the resources available to the powerful to ensure compliance with their wishes, and that legitimacy is irrelevant: an issue to be debated by moral philosophers, perhaps, but of no importance to an explanatory account of obedience, and therefore of no interest to the social scientist (Skocpol, 1979; Mann, 1986). This sceptical view is also to be found in the currently fashionable 'rational choice' approach, whose explanatory force depends upon the assumption that social action is to be explained by the agents' calculations of their own self-interest (e.g. Taylor, 1988). What such an account leaves out is obvious to all but the most hardened exponents of the theory: that people are also moral agents, who recognise the validity of rules, have some notion of a common interest, and acknowledge the binding force of promises they have made – all elements involved in legitimate power. To explain all action conforming to rules as the product of a self-interested calculation of the consequences of breaching them, is to elevate the attributes of the criminal into the standard for the whole of humankind, and to make a prison regime into the paradigm case of power. People relate to the powerful as moral agents as well as self-interested actors; they are cooperative and obedient on grounds of legitimacy as well as for reasons of prudence and advantage. It is the task of a theory of legitimacy to identify as clearly as possible what its distinctive place in this complex is.

One way of doing this is to see what happens to a power

relationship when legitimacy is eroded or absent. In such a case, power does not necessarily collapse, or obedience cease, since it can continue to be kept in place by incentives and sanctions. However, coercion has to be much more extensive and omnipresent, and that is costly to maintain. Moreover, the system of power now has only one line of defence, that of force; and it can therefore collapse very rapidly if coercion is insufficient or people believe that those in power have lost the will to use it. Once Gorbachev made clear that the USSR would no longer intervene militarily in Eastern Europe, the writing was on the wall for the communist regimes there, since they were only kept in place by the ultimate threat of Soviet invasion. Only the timing and manner of their demise was unpredictable. To admit the role of force in this situation is not to acknowledge the validity of the 'realist' theory of power. What has to be explained is the *prior* loss of legitimacy of communist rule in Eastern Europe, which made it so reliant on coercion, and therefore so vulnerable once sufficient coercion could no longer be guaranteed.

The collapse of authority where legitimacy is eroded, and coercive force is insufficient to maintain power on its own, provides only the most dramatic evidence for the significance of legitimacy to the obedience of subordinates. Less dramatic, but equally important, is the effect a lack of legitimacy has on the *degree* of cooperation, and the *quality* of performance, that can be secured from them, and therefore on the ability of the powerful to achieve goals other than simply the maintenance of their position. Where the powerful have to concentrate most of their efforts on maintaining order, they are less able to achieve other goals; their power is to that extent less effective. The classroom teacher provides a typical example. If pupils do not share a belief in the value of education, on which the justification for the teacher's power is based, or have no respect for the individual teacher, he or she will have to devote correspondingly greater energies to maintaining order than to teaching. To that extent the purposes for which power is held will not be achieved, and this may lead in turn to a further erosion of legitimacy.

The kind of vicious circle in which the powerful can become trapped when their legitimacy is eroded is well illustrated from the attempts at economic reform under communist rule in Eastern Europe. These repeatedly failed, in part at least because governments had insufficient legitimacy to demand the short term sacrifices, or risk instituting the price rises, necessary to the development of a more market-oriented system (Lewis, 1982, pp.137–8; MacFarlane, 1984, pp.177 ff.). And the failure of economic reform in turn further eroded the system's legitimacy. The point was well made by President Jaruzelski in an interview in May 1990:

'The party could not mobilise Polish forces into constructive channels . . . We tried economic reforms time and time again. But they always met with public resistance and explosions. It is very different now. Now with a government that enjoys public confidence, it is possible to demand sacrifices.' (*The Guardian*, 7 May 1990)

Without the legitimacy to demand sacrifices, the ruling party's power over society became a largely negative one: able to control the population in the sense of preventing them doing what they wanted, but not in the sense of securing the cooperation necessary to the achievement of the government's policies.

These examples of the loss of moral authority, from the classroom to the state, indicate that legitimacy is significant not only for the maintenance of order, but also for the degree of cooperation and quality of performance that the powerful can secure from the subordinate; it is important not only for whether they remain 'in power', but for what their power can be used to achieve. Passive non-cooperation, work to rule, feigned incompetence, 'looting', and so on: these attributes of the Good Soldier Schweik and the 'worker in a workers' state' are typical of subordinates where legitimacy has become eroded, and will to that extent reduce the capacity of those in power to achieve their goals (Hasek, 1973; Haraszti, 1977). The effectiveness of the powerful, in other words, is not just a matter of resources and organisation, as the 'realists' would contend, but also of their legitimacy. The realists are at this point simply not realistic enough; they do not take people seriously as moral agents, or recognise that what the powerful can get others to do depends upon normative considerations as well as upon the resources and organisational capacities at their command.

Wherever the goals of the powerful are dependent upon the

degree of cooperation and the quality of performance on the part of subordinates, therefore, to that extent is legitimacy important for what they can achieve as well as for the maintenance of their power. It follows that legitimacy is more crucial to some kinds of power relationship than to others. It is worth exploring in a preliminary way what these might be. We could distinguish two different kinds of situation where the legitimacy of a power relationship is *un*necessary to the goals of the powerful.

The first is a labour regime where continuous work is required from subordinates, but the quality of their performance is unimportant, and they can be treated as dispensable because there is a ready supply of replacements available. Such was the position in most historical examples of slavery, where the supply of slaves was repeatedly replenished through conquest and trade. A close parallel was early industrial capitalism, where the work required little skill from the worker, and an unlimited supply of new recruits was available from the labour market to expand production or replace those incapacitated by illness, accident or death. Both these examples of coercive labour regimes lacked legitimacy from the outset, though the source of their coercion differed (physical force, economic duress). In the case of capitalism, the increasing need to secure quality of performance, on the one side, and the pressure of self-organisation by the workers, on the other, necessitated the development over time of a more legitimate relationship, based upon the employers' recognition of collective bargaining rights and the negotiation of collective agreements over the terms and conditions of work (Fox, 1985, ch.4).

In the examples of slavery and early industrial capitalism the absence of legitimacy in the relationship was irrelevant to the performance of subordinates. At this point, however, we need to observe an important distinction. The fact that the relationship depended on coercion did not mean that the powerful did not have a legal basis for their power, or that they did not seek to justify it to themselves. Indeed, both slavery and early capitalism witnessed the most elaborate justifications, derived, in the one case, from Aristotelian notions of a slave 'nature' (Aristotle, 1962, pp.32–4) which was elaborated by later racial theories, and, in the other, from the doctrines of classical political economy. Such 'legitimations', however, were addressed to the conscience of the powerful, not at all to their subordinates. To address the latter was not only practically difficult, given that they often shared no common language. It was also logically impossible, since the justification for treating slaves and early industrial workers in the way they were treated was that they belonged to a category of objects, and were therefore by definition incapable of being addressed 'as persons'. Slaves were chattels, wholly owned by the slaveowner (Aristotle, 1954, p.212). Industrial workers were 'hands', whose labour power was owned as a commodity, and, like any other commodity, obeyed the laws of supply and demand in the marketplace; if it was overproduced, the numbers would simply be cut by the necessary forces of want, disease and starvation (Smith, 1976, pp.89–90; J.S. Mill, 1909, pp.343–60). In other words, we must distinguish between the 'legitimations' that the powerful develop to reconcile their consciences to the treatment (and maltreatment) of their subordinates, and a legitimate *relationship*, justified in terms of shared beliefs, regulated according to understood conventions and confirmed through the expression of consent.

If the characteristic of coercive labour regimes was that they did not require legitimacy for the level of performance needed in the context, we could contrast them with other labour regimes where quality of performance is crucial. An example from the other end of the spectrum is that of gender relations in most historical periods, where women's domestic work has demanded qualities of skill, dedication and independent initiative that could only be obtained from subordinates within a legitimate relationship. Here the beliefs that provide the justification for the hierarchical division of labour and the definition of a common interest have been shared between men and women, and the legitimacy of the individual relationship has been confirmed by express consent. In the case of gender relations the distinction between the legitimacy of the respective roles and the motivation necessary to perform them is a fine one, and the account of legitimacy will need supplementing with reference to the socio-psychical processes whereby attitudes appropriate to given roles become so deeply internalised that they appear as 'natural' (see below, pp.78–9). Important to note here, however, is simply the point that the quality of performance needed from the subordinate party in a relationship, and the degree of legitimacy the relationship requires, are closely connected.

One kind of situation, then, where the legitimacy of a power relationship does not matter is where the quality of work performed by subordinates is unimportant. A second is where the relationship between dominant and subordinate is so distant, or indirect, that little is required by the one of the other. In many pre-modern states it made little difference what the beliefs of the vast majority of the population were, and their consent to the state was irrelevant, since their obligations were to purely local chiefs or superiors; it was the relationship between the central state and local power-brokers that was all-important. The contemporary state, in contrast, requires of its whole adult population a general obligation to pay taxes and be available for military service if needed; and there is a variety of situations in which the cooperation of different sections of the population is essential to the realisation of government policy. The legitimacy of the relationship becomes even more critical where, as in a command economy, the state is also the main employer of labour, and economic performance itself is directly dependent upon the state's legitimacy. One of the chief weaknesses of the communist system has been that the state's requirement for legitimacy has been correspondingly greater than that of the capitalist state, but at the same time it has been less able to sustain it than states in at least the advanced capitalist societies, for reasons that will be explored later in the book. Here it will be sufficient to emphasise the qualitative difference between the *erosion* of legitimacy where it matters, as in a communist regime, and the *absence* of legitimacy where it doesn't, as in the slave systems discussed above. One consequent difference is the repeated attempt to reestablish a basis of legitimacy in the former; and the danger of regime collapse, as opposed to merely revolt or rebellion, in the event of failure to do so.

In considering the different levels of performance that are required from those in different subordinate positions, an obvious distinction can be drawn between those who staff the administrative and coercive apparatuses of the state, and the population as a whole. In view of the quality of performance and degree of commitment required from the former if the state organisation is to function effectively, considerable pains will be taken to reinforce their support for the norms of the regime, and to bind them to it with special contractual commitments and oaths of allegiance. However, it is mistaken to conclude from this, as some writers have done, that the legitimacy of government is therefore chiefly of consequence for the members of the state apparatus, or the political élite, and has little relevance for the population as a whole (Therborn, 1980, p.109; Bialer, 1980, pp.194–5). In the modern period, at least, it has been repeatedly shown that the state apparatus cannot be immunised from an erosion of regime legitimacy that has affected the attitudes and behaviour of the rest of the population; and that the refusal of the masses to do as they are told will provoke a corresponding crisis of obedience among the armed forces that are ordered to discipline or crush them. The collapse of the Shah's regime in Iran in 1979 is only the most spectacular recent example of the erosion of an army's loyalty in the face of repeated mass protest. It provides convincing evidence that the legitimacy of a regime is as crucial to its effectiveness as the competence of its administrators or the firepower of its armies, and that the strength of an organised power structure is dependent in the last analysis upon the readiness of subordinates to obey orders under pressure.

Enhanced order, stability, effectiveness – these are the typical advantages that accrue to a legitimate system of power as a result of the obligations upon subordinates that derive from its legitimacy. 'Order' depends upon people obeying rather than disobeying. 'Stability' is not mere longevity, but a system's ability to withstand shock and failure because a solid level of support from its subordinates can be guaranteed. 'Effectiveness' includes the ability of the powerful to achieve their goals because of the quality of performance they can secure from those subordinate to them. Legitimacy is not the only factor contributing to the order, stability and effectiveness of a system of power; organisational capacities and resources are obviously crucial as well. Moreover, as we have seen, it is possible in certain situations for the goals of the powerful to be realised on the basis of coercion alone. Yet legitimacy makes its distinctive contribution to achieving these other qualities through the effects it has on the attitudes and behaviour of the subordinate as moral agents, not just as self-interested actors.

I have spent a good deal of time identifying the effects of legitimacy, because there are so many different elements involved in a power relationship, and the interaction between them is enormously complex and easy to misread. Many political scientists confuse legitimacy with regime-stability, or define it as simply a by-product of effective system-functioning (e.g. Luhmann, 1969). This conceptual conflation, which equates legitimacy with the consequences it produces, can only be avoided if we are able to give a clear account, not only of what legitimacy is, but of how it produces the consequences it does through the obligations that subordinates derive from it. The accompanying diagram (Figure 1.1) sets out in summary form the different steps I have distinguished in my account of the consequences of legitimacy, first for the behaviour of subordinates, and then in turn for other characteristics of the system of power.

Figure 1.1 Characteristics of a power system or relationship

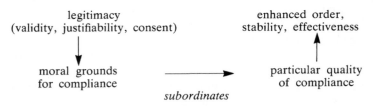

So far I have discussed the consequences of legitimacy for the behaviour of the subordinate within a power relationship. I now turn more briefly to consider its consequences for the powerful. If legitimacy, as I have argued, enhances the order, stability and effectiveness of a system of power, then we should expect that the powerful will seek to secure and maintain the legitimacy of their power, in view of its advantages to them. Here again, however, we must be careful to avoid drawing the wrong conclusions from a mistaken definition of legitimacy. If we reduce it to people's 'belief in legitimacy', then we are likely to conclude that the way in which the powerful maintain their legitimacy is primarily by means of ideological work, and through the influence they have over the beliefs and ideas of the subordinate. 'Every power seeks to establish and cultivate a belief in its legitimacy,' wrote Weber; and many have drawn the conclusion from this statement that it is precisely by cultivating beliefs that legitimacy is maintained (Weber, 1956, p.157; 1968, p.213).

I do not wish to discount altogether the role of ideological work, particularly in reinforcing the basic norms that underpin a given system of power, though I shall want to argue later that the processes involved are complex ones, and have been oversimplified in much of the relevant literature. What I would emphasise at this point, however, is that we need to look quite elsewhere for the effect of legitimacy on the behaviour of the powerful. If legitimate power is, as I have argued, power that is valid according to rules, and where the rules themselves are justifiable by and in conformity with underlying norms and beliefs, then the main way in which the powerful will maintain their legitimacy is by respecting the intrinsic limits set to their power by the rules and the underlying principles on which they are grounded. Legitimate power, that is to say, is limited power; and one of the ways in which it loses legitimacy is when the powerful fail to observe its inherent limits.

What are these limits? I would draw attention to two different kinds. One kind of limit is set by the rules which determine what the powers of the powerful are, and what they can rightly expect those subordinate to them to do – which specify, in other words, the respective duties and obligations of those involved in a power relationship. These rules may be largely conventional, or they may be legally defined. A feature of the modern world is the increasingly precise legal specification of the respective powers, or 'sphere of competence', of each powerholder. Even today, however, there is still considerable room left for 'custom and practice', for conventional understandings built up over time through processes of struggle and compromise, which govern the expectations of the powerful and the subordinate about what is, and is not, required of them; what can, and cannot, legitimately be demanded.

For the powerful to breach these rules in a substantial way, say by imposing some new or additional obligation on subordinates without warning or consultation, is either to invite action for legal redress, or, where the law is silent, to provoke informal protests which may develop into a more widespread crisis of legitimacy for the system of power. Unless they are arrogant or stupid, powerholders will only take such action when it is essential to some important purpose, or if they are driven to it by a serious predicament of their own. The fact that mostly they do not do so, and that they mostly respect the rules and conventions governing their relations with those subordinate to them, makes it easy to overlook an essential feature of legitimacy: that it sets limits to the behaviour of the powerful as well as imposing obligations on the subordinate. Because we more readily notice what the powerful do than what they refrain from doing, this essential feature of legitimacy tends to go unremarked.

The other kind of constraint which their need to maintain legitimacy imposes on the powerful is a more fundamental one: to respect the basic principles that underpin the rules or system of power, and to protect them from challenge. Rulers who derive their legitimacy from a divine source must respect religious traditions and defer to religious authorities; they will regard any threat to religion or religious belief as among the most serious they face. Those who derive their authority from the people will ignore at their peril any insistent and widespread popular current of opinion; to be seen to favour foreign interests at the expense of national ones will do more damage to their standing than almost anything else. Those who claim a monopoly of representation of the working class by virtue of a privileged knowledge of their interests cannot afford to allow independent sources of working-class opinion to find expression, or alternative institutions of representation to develop, which might challenge their monopoly. The legitimating ideas and justificatory principles that underpin the given institutions of power define which challenges the ruler has to take most seriously, because they strike at the basis of the system of rule itself (Rothschild, 1977, pp.490–1).

To understand the limits inherent in a system of legitimate power, and the conditions necessary to its maintenance, is to identify the distinctive character of the rules governing it, and the justificatory principles which underpin them. Here we find that the study of legitimacy is not only a study of the difference that it makes to the behaviour of the people involved, by its presence or absence, or according to its degree. It is also a study of the consequences that the particular *form* of legitimacy – its source or principle of justification, its criteria of consent, and so on – has for the character of power relations. Whether access to power is determined by birth or merit, by ascription or achievement, whether the ultimate source of rules is located in tradition or the 'people', whether consent is defined in individualistic or more collective terms: all these have important implications for the character, the organisation and the institutions of power.

A basic assumption I shall make is that rules and institutions of power embody legitimating ideas or justificatory principles within them, whether this happens because they are consciously created at a particular moment, or develop through a lengthy process of historical evolution. This assumption does not imply an 'idealist' theory about the logical or historical priority of ideas. As I shall argue in the succeeding chapters, analysing power involves understanding the interaction between three different elements: the material and other means of power; the rules of its social organisation; its justificatory principles or ideas. Rules of power are shaped by both material means and legitimating principles or purposes, albeit in a historically variable manner; any opposition therefore between an 'idealist' and a 'materialist' theory of power is in my view misconceived.

If it is correct that systems of power embody justificatory principles or assumptions within them, then it is possible to develop typologies of power systems according to the main differences of principle they embody. One axis of differentiation concerns the distinctive social purposes they serve, which will differ for gender, class and political power respectively. A second line of differentiation concerns the different principles governing access to property or political power, and the form of consent appropriate to each, which will differ between different historical periods and different types of economic and political system. Besides an analysis of legitimacy in general, therefore, and of its consequences for people's behaviour, this book will also concern itself with a comparative study of the justificatory principles and conventions of consent embodied in different rules or systems of power.

Conclusion: a social or political concept?

In this chapter I have argued for a social-scientific conception of legitimacy that differs, on the one side, from the normative philosopher's search for independent criteria of legitimacy or

ideal conditions for consent; and, on the other, from a mistaken
Weberian conception which reduces the legitimacy of power to
people's belief in its legitimacy. It differs from the latter in that
it involves a judgement about a given system of power, not a
report on what people believe about it; it differs from the former
in that the judgement is a judgement of legitimacy-in-context,
assessed against the relevant norms, principles and criteria for
consent pertaining in the given society. In identifying what is
relevant, and therefore what to look for in the particular society,
the social scientist is guided by the general criteria I have elucidated, which together provide sufficient grounds for obedience.

Legitimacy is important, I have argued, because of its consequences for behaviour, and for the character of power relations.
Against those who hold that the obedience of the subordinate
can be sufficiently procured by incentives and sanctions, I maintain that the normative commitments that derive from legitimacy
ensure a distinctive level and quality of compliance and cooperation, though this level is more essential in some contexts than
others. Against those who equate legitimacy with stability or
efficiency, I argue that legitimacy should not be confused with the
effects it produces on a system of power through the enhanced
obedience of its subordinates. Finally I have shown that legitimate power sets limits to the powerful through the normative
expectations and principles it embodies, and that an analysis
of these norms and principles is essential to understanding the
distinctive character and institutions of a given system of power.

Throughout I have been critical of realist or sceptical theories
of power, which I have shown to be based on either a faulty
analysis of power, or an impoverished conception of human
nature. If power is one person's ability to achieve their purposes
through others, then it cannot be a matter of capacities and
resources alone, but also depends on the degree of the others'
willingness to cooperate. And that willingness cannot be sufficiently created by incentives and sanctions on their own; it
depends on the normative status of the power holder, and on
normative considerations that engage us as moral agents. This
normative status derives from the character of a legitimate power
relationship as legally valid, justifiable according to shared norms
and beliefs, and confirmed through actions expressing consent.
Above all, therefore, I have been critical of accounts which

reduce legitimacy to the sum of 'legitimations' that the powerful can get the subordinate to accept. Legitimacy is not the icing on the cake of power, which is applied after baking is complete, and leaves the cake itself essentially unchanged. It is more like the yeast that permeates the dough, and makes the bread what it is.

A final question remains to be answered in this introductory chapter. Is legitimacy a specifically political concept, which should properly only be applied to political power? So some theorists have argued (e.g. Habermas, 1979, p.179), while others have sought to narrow its application still further, to the sphere of post-medieval politics, on the grounds that only in the modern state have the issue of political obedience and the contestability of legitimacy become persistent features of public life (e.g. Hennis, 1976, pp.26–7). I would argue against both attempts at narrowing the applicability of the concept. Political philosophy may only flourish where legitimacy is contested, and social science may only appreciate its importance from the experience of situations where it is absent or under challenge. Disruptions of order provide a necessary stimulus to both kinds of intellectual activity. It does not follow, however, that legitimacy is only significant *where* it is most noticeable and most contested. Indeed it is precisely disorder and instability that demonstrate its necessary contribution to order in more settled, not to say stagnant, times.

If the concept of legitimacy cannot be restricted to the post-medieval world, neither can it be limited to the sphere of politics as such. It should be evident from everything that I have said in this chapter that it is power itself that morally stands in need of legitimation, though not every form of power requires it in practice, and by no means all achieve it. All societies find it necessary to regulate the access to and exercise of power; and wherever power is organised and distributed in accordance with social rules – in the spheres of production and reproduction, in the family and the economy, as well as the polity – these rules stand in need of legitimation. Legitimacy is an important aspect of power in all these spheres. How we define what is 'political' is a matter of convenience and focus of interest. In so far as the power of gender and property are the subject of legitimation, involving reference to law and convention, the public justification of rules and the organisation of consent, these forms of power are eminently 'political' in the broadest sense of the word.

It is undeniable, however, that legitimacy also has a special significance for the more narrowly political sphere, the sphere of the polity, for a number of reasons. The political domain is responsible for the legal formulation, adjudication and enforcement of society's rules, and thereby legitimates all other social powers. At the same time there is no law-making authority beyond itself to legitimate its own rules of power. Moreover, the form of power which is distinctive to it – organised physical coercion – is one that both supremely stands in need of legitimation, yet is also uniquely able to breach all legitimacy. The legitimation of the state's power is thus both specially urgent and fateful in its consequences.

The fact that legitimacy is significant for power relations in general, while also having a particular urgency for the state, has determined a two-part structure to this book. The first part will consider legitimacy across the three dimensions of gender, class and political power together, while also identifying significant differences between them. Chapter 2 will analyse what exactly power is, and the respects in which it requires legitimation. Chapter 3 will explore further the basic normative structure of legitimacy, as already outlined. Chapter 4 will draw out the implications of the fact that legitimacy in historical societies is typically constructed and reproduced within established power relations, rather than outside or beyond them. The second part of the book will examine legitimacy in the contemporary state; it will consider the internal dynamics and crisis tendencies of different political systems, explore the different modes of non-legitimate power, and explain why the contemporary state has such difficulty in attaining the legitimacy it needs.

Underlying the substance of my analysis will be a deeper methodological purpose: to arrive at a valid understanding of the relation between social science and normative philosophy. Although I have argued that the point of each activity is different and should not be confused, by Chapter 4 it will have become clear that an adequate explanatory account of legitimacy can only be obtained by adopting the independent standpoint of the normative philosopher. And by the end of the book the necessity of unifying the two activities in a common enterprise will have been reached, as the culminating point of the enquiry. What I shall show is that a complete understandng of legitimacy can only be attained through an adequate specification of the relation in which social science and normative philosophy stand to each other. For that reason the subject of legitimacy can claim to constitute, not merely an important topic, but the central issue in social and political theory.

2 Power and its Need of Legitimation

In the first chapter I wrote about 'power' as if it were self-evident what it meant. But what is power, and why does it stand in need of legitimation? To answer these questions it will be necessary to make a clear separation between the concept of power and that of legitimacy. In practice such a separation will be artificial, since the interplay between power, rules and legitimating norms and actions typically constitutes a complex interrelationship, in which each element is affected by the others. Yet it is only by distinguishing them conceptually that we can come to understand the connection between them. Where the first chapter approached the subject of power through an analysis of legitimacy, the present one will provide an approach to legitimacy through the analysis of power. In doing so I shall aim to identify precisely what it is about power that calls for legitimation, which in turn explains the underlying structure of legitimacy that I outlined in the previous chapter.

Two caveats are in order before I proceed. First, although I do not believe that the concept of power is an essentially or necessarily contestable concept, as some have argued (e.g. Lukes, 1974), there is no doubt that it has in fact been the subject of considerable disagreement and contestation. In what follows I shall simply set out what seems to me the most convincing way of analysing it, but it would require too much space to defend my analysis against alternatives at every point.

Secondly, the account of power I give, like that of legitimacy in the first chapter, is not intended to be historically limited, in the sense of applying to only one society or historical period. It is therefore couched at a level of generality which may require qualification, and certainly elaboration, in particular contexts, but which is nevertheless appropriate to my purpose. The first part of the chapter will seek to clarify what power is, and what having power over someone entails. The second part will move from the conceptual to the more sociological mode of enquiry, by analysing the way power is socially organised into systematic relations of dominance and subordination. The third part will identify precisely what it is about power that requires legitimacy, and why legitimations take the form they do.

The concept of power

In its widest sense the power a person has indicates their ability to produce intended effects upon the world around them, to realise their purposes within it, whatever these purposes happen to be (Morriss, 1987). Power in this general sense depends upon certain preconditions: the presence of personal capacities or 'powers' such as health, strength, knowledge and skill; the possession of material resources; and space or scope, in the sense of freedom from control, obstruction or subservience to the purposes of others. Power and freedom are closely related, but not identical, concepts. Without freedom, even the strongest individual may be rendered powerless (Samson in chains); but without resources of a personal or material kind even the most free person will remain impotent (the physically incapacitated in an open space, the penniless in a free market). Freedom is necessary if we are to utilise our powers to achieve our purposes; but without such powers in the first place, freedom will be worthless to us.

Power, in this most general sense of the ability to achieve our purposes, is unequally distributed; some people have greater power than others. We can thus speak of its relative distribution within a society. But there is a familiar and more specific sense of power which is also relational: the ability to influence or control the actions of others, to get them to do what we want them to, and what they would otherwise not have done (Wrong, 1979). This sense is linked to the first partly as means to end: one of the ways in which we are able to achieve our purposes is through influencing or controlling the actions of others. At the same time one of the typical means of attaining such power is through the possession of superior capacities or resources, whether of strength, knowledge, material goods, or a combination of these. I can come to influence or control your actions through greater strength (physical coercion or the threat of it), through superior knowledge (persuasion or manipulation), or through the promise to grant or the threat to withhold some resource or service you desire or need (inducement or threatened deprivation). Relative differences in capacity or resources between people thus also tend to become relational, the means to influence or control them.

Not all such relations involve an exercise of power by one person *over* another. If I get you to change your behaviour by means of persuasion, this does not affect your freedom, since persuasion requires agreement. Nor does it affect your freedom if I offer an inducement which you can readily refuse. In such cases I cannot be said to have power over you. But if I can threaten you with physical coercion if you do not comply, or with the deprivation of some resource or service that is necessary to you, or if I take advantage of your ignorance of psychological vulnerability (manipulation rather than persuasion), then my power is exercised at the expense of your freedom. I can be said to have power over you.

Some philosophers would argue that only the actual application of physical force inhibits a person's freedom; short of that he or she is still free to act. Even if I point a loaded gun at your head, they say, you can still refuse to sign the confession (Steiner, 1974; Parent, 1974). But this is a very heroic conception of freedom, which will not serve for everyday purposes. Most legal systems treat a confession obtained under such circumstances as invalid, because it is extracted under duress. However, it is precisely the actions of heroes, who place honour or ideals above life, that can subvert a system of power through their example, since they challenge the normal scale of values on which power is based. It is because most of us for most of the time value life above all else, that threats to deprive us of it limit our freedom, and constitute an effective basis of power over us.

The above example suggests that the restriction of freedom is not an all-or-nothing affair, but is greater or less according to the seriousness of the deprivation that can be inflicted. To speak of 'having power over' someone usually implies a continuous relationship, in which a substantial sanction is always present. One reason why sanctions are much more effective than inducements as the basis for a continuous power relationship is that they do not have to be continually used, or even explicitly threatened, to be effective in modifying behaviour. It is sufficient that people 'know their place'. Moreover, the possibility that they may anticipate the wishes of a superior without having to be explicitly instructed (the so-called 'law of anticipated reactions') may make the nature of the relationship difficult to read at first glance (Friedrich, 1963, pp.199–215; Nagel, 1975, pp.15–19).

This is particularly true of relations of dependency. These derive from a situation of relative powerlessness which leads the weak to seek the protection of the strong, the propertyless to seek service with the propertied, and so on. The awareness of their impotence outside the relationship can itself be sufficient to keep the dependent party submissive to the wishes of the superior, without any threats needing to be made. To possess superior physical power or resources is not only to be able to compel others; it is also to be able to offer protection against physical coercion or destitution, and hence to establish relations of dependency. Here an initial inducement can become the basis of a continuous power relationship, through the vulnerability of the dependent party to the withdrawal of the essential resource on which they rely.

To say that having power over someone involves a restriction of their freedom, a subordination of their purposes to one's own, is not necessarily to say that these purposes are self-seeking, or are always pursued at the expense of the subordinate. Otherwise we could have no concept of paternalism. The restriction of the freedom of children by their parents is often in their interests; it enables their parents to realise their purposes for them. However, the subordination of children is a temporary condition, and one whose end is the expansion of their own powers, of their capacity to realise their purposes in the future. And it is precisely because of the value that we place upon realising our purposes that in general we regard the restriction involved in power relations, and the subordination of one person's will to another, in a negative light, and something that therefore requires justification. It is just here, as I shall show later, that legitimacy, or at least one key dimension of it, has its point.

The social organisation of power

So far, to assist conceptual clarification, I have treated power as
if it were simply an attribute of individuals. Yet the relative
differences of power between people are largely the result of
social arrangements. And the relations of power between them
are typically the product of collective organisation. Sociological
theories are often distinguished according to whether they
emphasise one or other of two different aspects of the collective
organisations of power, which are extrapolated into two different
definitions of power itself. One is the power of the dominant
over the subordinate, and its collective organisation to achieve
the purposes of the powerful. The other is the power of the
society or collectivity as a whole – over the forces of nature and
the environment, and in relation to other societies – and its
collective organisation to achieve common purposes (Parsons,
1960, pp.219–25; Wrong, 1979, pp.237–47).

To emphasise one of these aspects to the exclusion of the
other is erroneous, since they are interrelated. The manner in
which a society's internal power relations are organised has obvious consequences for the power of the society as a whole. And
the limitations of freedom and subordination of purposes
involved in power over others constitute an important means of
social coordination. Power is not the only means of coordinating
social activity; voluntary agreement, market arrangements and
socialisation into common values are all familiar ways in which
people's purposes are aligned with one another to make collective purposes attainable. But power relations constitute a crucial
element in this process, both in themselves and as an underpinning to the other means of coordination.

However, it is important not to confuse the analysis of power
with the question of its legitimacy. One of the most common
justifications for the power of any dominant group over a subordinate one is that it enables the collective purposes or general
interests of the society as a whole to be realised. Such justifications are rarely all they seem. A characteristic attribute of the
powerful is their ability to define what the goals of the collective
as a whole should be, i.e. to achieve their purposes for the
collective in preference to others'. And a recurrent feature of
the social organisation of power is that general interests can only

be met in ways which also serve the particular interests of the powerful, since the means of realising them are under their control. To treat any collective as an undifferentiated whole, as a single entity with definable purposes and interests, is to overlook the way these purposes and interests are both constructed by and mediated through its internal relations of power.

It is with these internal relations of power within societies that this book is primarily concerned. It is not concerned with differences of power between societies, except in so far as these come to affect the legitimacy of power relations within them (see Part II). It is not even concerned with differences or inequalities of power between groups or individuals within societies, except in so far as these become the means to exercise power *over* others. The subject is large enough without extending it to cover all forms of inequality. More importantly, it is precisely relations of power over others that raise the most central question of legitimacy for normative philosophy and social science alike: that of cooperation with, or obedience to, the powerful.

In order to indicate that it is power relationships that I am concerned with, I shall use the terms 'dominance' and 'subordination' to specify those systematic and continuous relations of power that occur between groups of people, or between individuals in so far as they represent social categories. Two questions are crucial to understanding the social organisation of these relations. First, what are the typical means of power whereby one social group is able to dominate another? Secondly, what are the basic groups or categories between which relations of dominance and subordination recur in most historical societies, and what explains this recurrence?

To begin with the first question, it is useful to distinguish a number of different means of power, which can provide the basis for relations of dominance and subordination. Although they are often found together, mutually reinforcing one another, it is helpful to separate them analytically for the sake of clarity. First is the possession of material resources, of which the means of production and subsistence on one side, and the means of physical force on the other, are the most significant. A common feature of such resources is that they only become a means of social power in so far as people can be systematically excluded from access to them. If we all had access to the means of production and subsistence (land, tools, the fruits of the earth) or to the instruments of physical force (weapons, armour, etc.), they could not constitute a basis for power relations. Central to the social organisation of power, therefore, are processes of exclusion, typically embodied in rules, which prohibit general access to key resources, and which determine who may acquire the use or possession of them, and by what means. These are usually called rules of property; and it is through the possession of, or the privileged access to, property that some people acquire and maintain power over others who lack or are denied such access (Parkin, 1974; Cohen, 1981).

As forms of property, the means of production or subsistence and the means of physical force obviously differ in the way they operate as agencies of power. The means of physical force give those who possess them the ability to obstruct, constrain, hurt, harm or destroy those who lack them, and to compel them to action or inaction through the threat of such inflictions. The possession of the means of production or subsistence, on the other hand, works through the need of the excluded to have access to the use of these resources, and through an exchange relationship whereby their services (usually labour services) are required in return for such use. The fact that power in this context is exercised through an exchange relationship both complicates and obscures its character, since exchange relations can also occur between equals. By comparison, physical coercion seems stark and uncomplicated, and for that reason is often used as the paradigm example of power. Yet the means of physical coercion are also a means of physical protection, and as such can provide the basis for a power relation through exchange, because of the need of the defenceless for protection against third parties, and their consequent dependency upon those who can provide them with it. In whatever form it occurs, however, what is common to both the means of physical force and the means of production and subsistence is that in each case relations of dominance and subordination are constituted in the first place through the possession of, and exclusion from, a key material resource, and by the rules that determine these respective conditions (property rules).

A second basis or means of power lies in the control of socially necessary activities, and the possession of the skills associated with their performance. Here too, such activities and skills only become a source of power through rules of exclusion and access, which limit the number of those who may acquire the skills and take part in the activities, and define who is entitled to do so. These rules are usually referred to as the division of labour. At first sight the division of labour looks like the basis for a mutual dependence and reciprocal benefit through the specialisation of social tasks and functions. However, in most societies the division of labour is hierarchically ordered, in that some activities and skills are defined as being more socially important and valuable than others, and the majority are prevented from engaging in them either by formal rules of exclusion, or because they are unable in practice to acquire the skills necessary to their performance. As with the ownership of key resources, the degree of power is determined by the extent of the exclusion, and by the importance of the activity to the excluded. It is further enhanced by the association of a given skill or practice with an esoteric body of knowledge, couched in a language removed from everyday discourse and comprehensible only to the initiated.

A third means of power consists in the occupancy of positions which carry with them the power of command over others. Such positions, in which the power of command is constituted, defined and circumscribed by rules, are called positions of authority. Authority is often said to be 'legitimate power', but this is an inadequate formulation because of the ambiguity inherent in the concept of legitimacy. All the means of social power mentioned above possess a primary legitimacy in so far as they are determined by rules. What distinguishes authority from the power over others that derives from the possession of property or the control of some necessary social activity or skill is that, in the case of authority, it is the *relationship* between the dominant and subordinate itself that is specified by the rules. At this point the distinction between the different means of power becomes at best an analytical one, since most relations of dominance and subordination embody an element of authority, i.e. the rule-governed specification of the relationship. In this sense authority constitutes both an aspect of power relations *and* a means of power in its own right (power deriving from positions of command).

The same point could be expressed differently by saying that

most historical examples of authority have in practice been
associated with a hierarchical division of labour or the possession
of key resources, whether because an initial power relation based
upon the control of a resource such as land led to a formalisation
of the relationship with the landless in rule-governed terms
(authority); or because holding a position of authority enabled
its occupants to acquire such resources; or because their possession was necessary to the enforcement of its commands (as is
true particularly of the means of physical coercion). In whichever
manner the connection may historically have occurred, authority
has typically comprised a part of most systematic relations of
dominance and subordination, even though an analysis of these
relations cannot by any means be exhausted by an account of
their formal authority rules.

Before leaving the discussion of authority, it is worth noting
its importance as a means of coordinating and organising the
power of the dominant in face of the subordinate. Military
power, for example, is as much dependent upon the coordinating
role of authority as it is upon the possession of the physical
means of coercion. It is rare for subordinate groups to lack any
means of power of their own, even if this only takes the defensive
form of a power of limitation or veto in face of the power of
initiative exercised by the dominant. The subordinate are often
more numerous, and their own contribution within the social
division of labour makes them indispensable, as a group, to the
dominant. However, even a defensive power requires coordination for it to be effective, and it is precisely one of the purposes
of the organisation of power on the part of the dominant, e.g.
through their authority over an administrative staff, to ensure
the disorganisation among, as well as their control over, the
subordinate.

The main bases or means of power, then, underlying relations
of dominance and subordination, involve exclusion from and
access to necessary material resources, activities or skills and
positions of command, i.e. property, the division of labour and
authority respectively. A distinctive feature of the account I have
just given is the emphasis I have placed upon rules (whether
conventional or legal in form), and in particular upon rules of
exclusion, as both the source of social power and the means of
maintaining it. Here we should distinguish between two different

types of exclusion rule. Primary rules of exclusion are those which turn key resources, activities and skills into a means of power, and protect the authority of those who hold positions of command. These are the basic 'keep out' signs, which exclude the majority, and determine their relative powerlessness. Secondary exclusion rules are those which determine who can come to hold the means of power thus constituted and protected, and which may exclude whole categories of people from attaining them, as, for example, women have at various times and places been excluded from owning property, engaging in socially important activities or holding positions of authority. Such rules may operate indirectly as well as directly, in that a person's position within the division of labour may prevent them in practice from obtaining access to key resources or positions of authority to which they are formally eligible. Taken together, I shall call the rules of exclusion and access discussed above the 'rules of power', in view of their significance for the way that power is socially organised.

Now that the main bases of social power have been identified in the possession of key resources, in the division of labour and in authority positions, and in the rules of exclusion and access underpinning them, we need to explain why it is that the division of societies into dominant and subordinate groups takes historically recurrent forms. In theory, the different means of power could be distributed or combined in an almost infinite variety of ways. In practice, three lines of division are historically recurrent: those of class, gender and political power. The reason for their recurrence is that relations of dominance and subordination are organised around the most fundamental social activities – of production, reproduction, physical protection and rule determination respectively. While each of the three dimensions involves all the different means of power identified above, one of these has historically had a central place in each.

The dominance and subordination of classes is constituted in the process of material production. The primary basis of class power has historically lain in the private ownership of the means of production, and in the compulsion of the propertyless to work for the propertied as a condition of obtaining their own subsistence. Marx's theory draws attention to the different types of ownership – of the person of the worker, of land, of capital

– which form the basis of different systems of class dominance (Marx and Engels, 1968, pp.181–5). His theory of surplus appropriation also shows how the labour of the direct producers has freed dominant classes to engage in a whole variety of activities from which the direct producers have been excluded. The ownership of property can thus provide the basis for a social division of labour, as well as access to the means of physical coercion, whether formally through the linkage of property to political functions, or informally through the purchase of weapons and the acquisition of the skills necessary to use them (military aristocracies).

The significance of Marx's analysis of class is that it emphasises the control over labour and its product as the central feature of class relations. Other theories of class look at class relations in a different way. Weberian theory, for instance, defines classes by the different kinds of resource they possess (e.g. property, skill, collective organisation) in competing for differential shares of the social product. Its concern, in other words, is more to analyse the inequality between classes than the dominance of one over another (Parkin, 1979, pt.1). From the standpoint of analysing power relations, however, Marx's approach is preferable (even if one does not accept his labour theory of value), because it draws attention to the way in which the power of ownership secures control over labour.

Under contemporary capitalism the power of property is increasingly exercised through impersonal institutions, rather than as a direct personal relationship between owner and worker; and the typical capitalist is as much the company director who acquires a personal share stake in the business by virtue of position, as the owner of a family firm or the wealthy rentier whose claim on the product is only indirect (J. Scott, 1982, ch.6). In command economies of the Soviet type (now almost a historical phenomenon), in which private ownership was largely divorced from power over the means of production, control over the labour of others was determined wholly by authority position within state-owned institutions. What these economies exemplified was not so much the end of control over the means of production as the basis of class dominance and subordination, as its reconstitution under a different form, i.e. under different rules of power, with correspondingly different principles of legitimacy (Djilas, 1958).

Where the dominance and subordination of classes is constituted in the process of material production and by the power deriving from control over key productive resources, that of gender is organised around the activities of reproduction, and determined by the social division of labour. Although only women are capable of giving birth and suckling children, the sexual division of labour has historically gone well beyond these physiological differences, in two respects. First, the conventional assignment to women of key domestic tasks such as child-rearing, care of the home, servicing the personal needs of men and women, has in practice discouraged, if not always prevented, them from engaging in activities accessible to males who do not have these responsibilities. Secondly, these disabilities have been reinforced by formal exclusions, debarring women from certain activities and positions, and creating a sharp separation between 'public' and 'private' spheres. It is these exclusions established by the division of labour that have been primarily responsible for women's physical and economic dependency upon men, albeit varying in degree according to historical circumstance (Rosaldo and Lamphere, 1974; Friedl, 1975).

The above account, which derives the dominance and subordination of gender from the division of labour, is at odds with accounts which explain women's subordination in terms of male physical power or sexual aggression. It is true that physical force has had a part to play in gender relations, whether as direct coercion or as the protection of women from the coercion of other men. Yet anthropological evidence suggests that male aggression against women is not universal. And it tends to be associated with a division of labour that removes men from any involvement in child-rearing or caring roles, and assigns them exclusive control of activities involving the means of violence, such as hunting dangerous animals or fighting against other societies. It is this joint division of labour which creates a particular type of male physical power on the one side, and women's vulnerability to it on the other (Harris, 1977; Sanday, 1981).

If the sexual division of labour is responsible for women's vulnerability to male coercion and their consequent physical dependency, the same division of labour also produces women's dependency on men for the means of subsistence. The extent of this dependency has varied historically according to the role that women have played in production, and this in turn has depended on whether production has been organised within the domestic economy or outside it. The same process that 'freed' the worker from the soil in modern Europe, and created wage labour, also 'freed' married women from any substantial role in production and left them economically dependent upon men. Although the legal rules excluding women as a whole from many spheres of paid employment have now largely been abolished in Western societies, the persistence of the sexual division of labour in the family, combined with a dual labour market in the economy, tends to restrict married women to lower-paid, part-time, less secure types of employment. What we see is the power of conventional rules to sustain informal processes of exclusion and inequality, and so to perpetuate women's economic dependency within the home and their subordination to men outside it (Barrett, 1980; Whitelegg *et al.*, 1982).

A third dimension of dominance and subordination, the political, is organised around two interconnected social activities, and two complementary means of power. The first activity is that of physical defence, and the power associated with it is that which derives from control over the means of physical force. The second activity is that involved in deciding and giving legal expression to the rules of the society, which provides a crucial means of power for those who control it, since it gives them the ability to determine the 'rules of power' for the society as a whole. If, as I have argued, the social organisation of dominance and subordination in its different dimensions is effected through rules of exclusion and access, then the ability to shape or determine such rules is a particularly important power. What links this distinctively 'political' activity of rule-determination with that of physical defence is the key part that the organisation and control of the means of force plays in both. Organised physical coercion provides the most effective means of enforcing society's legal rules, as well as protecting it against attack. As a consequence the two activities have usually been connected, and the two means of power combined in the same group or institution to form a potent basis of dominance and subordination.

In conclusion, it is the organisation of power relations around the most fundamental social activities that makes the dimensions of class, gender and political dominance and subordination recurrent features of societies throughout history. There are of course other recurring bases of inequality, of which race, ethnicity and religion are the most persistent historically. However, these only become structured as forms of dominance and subordination when associated either with political power, through conquest, or with the ownership of property, or with both, as in slave or caste societies. Of course the political or economic dimension does not exhaust the significance of such relations; but the ideas of superiority and inferiority associated with them belong as much to the sphere of legitimacy as to power itself, and will be considered at the appropriate point in the final section of the chapter.

In this section I have sought to identify the main dimensions of dominance and subordination, to distinguish the typical means of power associated with each, and to explain their historical recurrence. The fact that they are recurrent does not of course mean that the forms they take may not also vary considerably from one society to another, e.g. according to the environment, technology and historical legacy available to each. Variable also are the ways in which the different dimensions of class, gender and political dominance interrelate with one another, and in particular whether they are mutually reinforcing or cross-cutting. Marxist theories, as is well known, assign primacy among them to the dimension of class. If this priority is based upon the assumption that the activity of production is socially more important than the activities of reproduction, defence or rule-determination, or that the power deriving from control over the means of production is inherently superior to other means of power, then such a conclusion is simply untenable. More plausible is a different argument to the effect that the history of the expansion of human powers can most convincingly be written in terms of the expansion of productive forces, though even such a history is only explicable as a response to predicaments arising from military competition between societies, as well as to problems of material production within them. In any case such an argument could provide no grounds for assigning priority to the dominance of class within any particular society, the pattern of each of whose power relations has to be analysed separately, and on its own terms.

If the dimensions of dominance and subordination vary in form between societies, they are not immutable within them either. As I have already indicated, the subordinate are rarely ever powerless in face of the dominant and relations between them contain elements of tension and struggle: between classes over the rights of property and the extent of the surplus product; between men and women over the sexual division of labour; between the holders of political power and their subordinates over the power to influence rule-determination and the use of the means of coercion. Such struggles rarely challenge the relationship itself, as opposed to the terms on which it is conducted; and the outcome is necessarily a matter of context and circumstance, to be investigated in each particular case. My concern here has simply been to identify the main bases on which such relations of dominance and subordination have historically been constructed.

Power and legitimacy

In the previous section I argued that relations of dominance and subordination are determined by rules of exclusion and access, which make key resources, activities and positions into a means of power, and regulate who may gain access to them and upon what conditions. Yet in the first chapter I also argued that a primary ground for the legitimacy of power was that it was obtained and exercised according to established rules. Why does legality confer a *prima facie* legitimacy, and does it follow therefore that all power is by definition legitimate?

The basic point about social rules, whether conventional or legal, is that they have a normative force, not only in prohibiting us from certain actions, but in defining our duties and obligations towards others, and in conferring rights and entitlements that we can require others to respect in turn. In as much as power is itself constituted by rules of exclusion, therefore, it is also legitimated by them, since they confer the right on the powerful to require others to respect the exclusiveness which is the basis of their power. In other words, the very rules that constitute resources, activities and positions as a means of power in the first place also serve to legitimate them as forms of power.

Is this process circular? Does it follow that all power is necessarily legitimate? This is not so, for two reasons. One is that the occupancy of property, the development of a hierarchical division of labour, or the establishment of a command structure can occur, and historically frequently has occurred, through acts of forcible appropriation, exclusion or subjection which take place in violation of existing rules or outside of them. Such usurpations cannot be legitimate. However, the resulting power relations typically become consolidated and perpetuated through the establishment of rules which underpin and give legal form to the original usurpation. From that time on, subsequent positions of power come to be derived from the rules, in the same way as those whose rules originate through custom or agreement. Although the memory of the original usurpation may be kept alive, with the passage of time the issue of the rules' legitimacy becomes less a question of their origin than one of the ongoing character of the relationships they embody, and the nature of the requirements they impose.

Here lies the second reason why power is not necessarily legitimate, even when it is legally valid, and that is, as I argued in the first chapter, that legality constitutes only one dimension of legitimacy; it is a necessary but not a sufficient condition for it. The rules of power themselves require justification, however they may have originated. There is an important distinction to be observed, in other words, between the legitimacy of an individual power-holder, which is a matter of validity according to the rules, and the legitimacy of the power system as such, with its particular relations of dominance and subordination, its characteristic mode of access to power, and so on. Where the legitimacy of the individual derives from the rules, the rules themselves, and the power arrangements they define, can only be justified by moral considerations that go beyond them. Why is such justification necessary at all? The simple answer is that power relations involve negative features – of exclusion, restriction, compulsion, etc. – which stand in need of justification if the powerful are to enjoy moral authority as opposed to merely *de facto* power, or validity under a given system of law.

An examination of these negative features present in any

system of dominance and subordination will reveal why the justifications for power relations take the historically recurrent form that they do. Such relations involve, first, a marked difference of fates between dominant and subordinate, in the character and quality of their lives, in their respective powers, to use the language of the first section; i.e. their capacity to achieve their purposes, and the kinds of purposes they can achieve. They are distanced from one another by various forms of inequality. Secondly, these differences or inequalities are systematically connected, in that the expanded powers of the dominant are dependent upon the limitation of powers of the subordinate, and are achieved primarily at their expense, for instance because they are able to appropriate the product of the others' labour, or because the labour of others frees them to engage in activities that expand their own powers. The respective inequalities of condition are not a disconnected, but a causally related, phenomenon. Thirdly, the relationship involves the subordinate in a restriction of their freedom, through their direct subordination to the purposes of the powerful in a relation of command and obedience, or of submission to the wishes of another. Each of these three components of dominance and subordination carries a *prima facie* negative connotation, as evidenced by the terms in which they can be described. Thus the difference of fates of life chances can be termed inequality. The transfer of powers (resources or opportunities) from subordinate to dominant can be called exploitation or parasitism. The loss of freedom is termed subjection, subservience, or compulsion.

Now it is possible to avoid such negative connotations in the first place by simply removing the rules of power from the sphere of human agency and treating them as part of the natural world, whose allocations, like the weather, are morally blind and beyond the possibility of human control. The idea of fate, chance, fortune, is a commonplace one. However, these concepts are much more readily applicable to the unpredictabilities of life, the sudden shifts in fortune, than to the regularities of social relations and their rules of power. Here, appeals to the idea of nature take the form much more of nature as 'natural order' or 'natural law'. While it may be conceived as an order that is unchanging and beyond human control, nevertheless it is one that is also seen to make moral sense, either because it is intrinsically purposive, or because it is the creation of a purposive divine will.

Whether the social order and its power relations are conceived as having a natural, divine or human origin, then, there is a common expectation that they should satisfy certain moral requirements, and that the negative features of dominance and subordination should be amenable to moral justification. Although the content of such justifications is historically variable, the recurrent form they take is logically related to the negative features distinguished above.

Thus, first, the inequality of circumstance between dominant and subordinate is justified by a principle of differentiation, which reveals the dominant as specially qualified, suited or deserving to possess the resource, pursue the activity or hold the position which forms the basis of their power, and the subordinate as correspondingly unsuited or unfitted to do so, and hence rightly excluded from it. The inequality, in other words, is not arbitrary or fortuitous, but is based upon a normative distinction of superiority and inferiority, whether determined by birth, or developed and demonstrated over time. One feature of such normative distinctions is that they tend to carry over into all social relations between dominant and subordinate groups, beyond the site where the relationship is primarily constituted (e.g. class relations outside the workplace, gender relations outside the family); and also that they have a capacity for historical survival beyond the collapse of the power system which they served to justify (e.g. racial stereotypes after the end of slavery and colonialism).

Secondly, the systematic transfer of powers (of resources and opportunities) from subordinate to dominant is justified when it can be shown to serve not merely the interests of the powerful, but those of the subordinate also, or else to make possible the realisation of larger social purposes in which they have a concern. Legitimacy requires the demonstration of a common interest which unites, as well as a principle of differentiation which divides, dominant and subordinate. Where the subordinate are not conceived as having any interests of their own meriting attention, independent of their utility to the dominant, as a slave is equated with a domestic animal, there can be no moral community between them, and no legitimacy to the relationship.

Thirdly, the limitations of freedom involved in subservience to the requirements or purposes of the dominant are given moral acceptability by evidence of consent on the part of those qualified to give it. The free acceptance of subordination cancels out the restrictions on freedom involved in the relationship. Who counts as qualified to give consent varies according to the conventions of the given society, but, as I have already suggested, it is typically related to the category of those who count as free or independent. To be able to give consent a person has to be treated as free or independent in the first place, or at least as capable of freedom or independence. In the case of political power, consent is related to membership of the political community, which can be a more restricted category than that of the free.

To each of the negative characteristics of power relations, therefore, there stands a corresponding form of justification or rectification, which renders it morally acceptable. The inequality of powers and life chances is justified when it can be seen to correspond to the respective qualities of the dominant and subordinate; the difference is not one of power, merely, but of superiority and inferiority in some relevant respect. The transfer of resources and opportunities from subordinate to dominant is justified when it can be seen to serve not merely the interests of the powerful, but those of the subordinate also, or larger social purposes in which they have a stake. The restrictions on freedom are rectified when those who qualify as independent agents freely consent to them. The different dimensions of legitimacy, in other words, are not themselves arbitrary, but derive from the negative characteristics intrinsic to power relations as such, which arouse our concern as moral agents.

To say that, for a power relationship to be legitimate, it has to be justified in the ways outlined, is not to say that convincing justifications will always be provided, or that they will find acceptance among the subordinate. However, it is a notable feature of power relations that they are themselves capable of generating the evidence needed for their own legitimation. Thus the evidence of superiority and inferiority which justifies the inequality of condition between dominant and subordinate is itself largely the product of that condition. Those who are excluded from key positions, activities or resources are thereby denied the opportunity to acquire or demonstrate the capacities and characteristics appropriate to their occupation or exercise, so justifying their subordinate position. This is true even where relatively open processes of selection are at work, once the selection is performed by an education system which is given the task of preparing children differentially for their respective future roles. Evidence about the fitness or appropriateness of people to exercise power thus tends to be structured by the relations of power themselves, and therefore to have a self-fulfilling quality about it.

The same holds true for demonstrations of the general interest. Once some necessary social resource or activity comes to be controlled by a particular group, it follows that the interests of society at large can only be met through satisfying the interests of that group, and on terms acceptable to them. Those who have historically controlled the means of production or subsistence, of violence or administration, have been in a position to ensure that general needs for welfare, employment or security could only be met through the power relations that simultaneously secured their own privileges. The link between these relations and the performance of necessary social tasks, already described, ensures this legitimating connection. Marxist accounts which insist that power serves the particular interests of the powerful alone in a zero-sum manner, and that all claims to satisfy general needs are spurious, overlook the way that social relations are so arranged that general interests can in practice only be secured through satisfying the particular interests of the powerful. Functionalist accounts, on the other hand, which hold that any given distribution of power has evolved as the one most suited to carrying out necessary social functions, overlook the role that power itself plays in the construction of social relations, and the alternative patterns of distribution that could be equally 'functional' to the satisfaction of given social needs. That society at large should need the capacities and resources of the powerful is plain evidence of their public utility; that the utility might be realised without their power requires a perspective which goes beyond, and stands outside, the existing relations of power.

If we look, finally, at consent, then we find that it is precisely the lack of some key resource or skill deriving from the rules of power themselves that leads the subordinate to voluntary acceptance of their dependency upon the powerful. Arrangements made under the direct threat of physical coercion are usually held not to be morally binding, because they are extracted under duress. So too are those made from a condition of need or insufficiency, which is the intended outcome of actions by those who will benefit from any consequent agreement (e.g. driving people off their land so that they will be forced into dependency). But those conditions of need or insufficiency which are the systematic product of established rules of power have all the appearance of 'naturalness', since they are not the result of intentional human agency; and agreements arising from them are commonly held to be morally binding. The consent of the subordinate thus both derives from the rules which have determined their initial powerlessness, and also serves to reinforce them.

The capacity of power structures to generate the evidence necessary to their own justification, and to reproduce the conditions of dependency from which consent to subordination is freely given, helps to explain how it is that their legitimacy can come to be widely acknowledged by those involved in them, the subordinate included. 'Dominant ideology' theories tend to put far too much emphasis upon the determining influence exercised by the powerful over the ideas of the subordinate, through their preferential access to the means of ideological construction and dissemination (Abercrombie and Turner, 1978). The account offered here suggests a different kind of explanation: that both the evidence and the interests of the subordinate are so structured that the justifications advanced for the rules of power prove plausible to them within the given social context. Their plausibility can only be challenged from a position or standpoint outside that context, e.g. by comparison with alternative rules of power, or when social changes have come to undermine from within the evidence on which they are based. It is a characteristic of the modern period that such comparisons are more readily available, and substantial social change is more continuous, than in the pre-modern world. It follows that the legitimacy of any society's power rules is now more open to question, and its legitimating principles and procedures have to be more capable of withstanding comparison and challenge, if they are to provide a credible support for the rules of power.

In conclusion, I have attempted in this chapter to define what power is, to analyse what is involved in power relations, and to identify the negative features which require justification, and which in turn provide the normative structure of legitimacy. I have argued that the basis for systematic relations of dominance and subordination lies in what I have called the 'rules of power', the rules governing exclusion from and access to key resources, activities and positions of command. Such rules also provide the first dimension of legitimacy, though they may come to be infringed, and in any case stand in need of justification themselves. What is required for their justification can be demonstrated from an analysis of the negative aspects of power: the inequality of fates or life chances has to be shown to be appropriate to the differential characteristics of dominant and subordinate; the expanded powers of the dominant have to be seen to serve a general and not merely a particular interest; the limitations of freedom of the subordinate have to be made good by actions expressive of consent. As I have also suggested, a society's rules of power are typically capable of generating the evidence, and of structuring the interests of the subordinate, in a manner conducive to their own legitimation. The task of the next chapter will be to explore the underlying normative structure of legitimacy more fully, and the different forms it can take in different societies and periods; and to elucidate further what I have called the self-legitimating character of power rules.

3 The Normative Structure of Legitimacy

This chapter has a number of purposes which it will be as well to distinguish at the outset. Most basic is to elaborate the threefold structure of legitimacy as rule-derived validity, the justifiability of power rules, and expressed consent; and to consider some problems relating to them that I have not so far addressed. Within this structure, secondly, I propose to explore some of the main differences between legitimating principles, beliefs and forms of consent that characterise different historical epochs and types of legitimate power relations. If my treatment here appears overly schematic, it is because this is the only way to achieve a manageable grasp of such a diverse range of material. My final purpose will be to exemplify at appropriate points what I have called the self-fulfilling character of legitimate power: the way in which systems of power themselves structure many of the beliefs, interests and conditions of consent that provide for their legitimation; and to identify the kinds of circumstance in which this self-reinforcing cycle tends to break down. Since this last theme forms the subject of Chapter 4, my treatment of it here will not be systematic.

Legitimacy derived from rules

That any form of power should be acquired and exercised in accordance with established rules, whether the power be derived from property, position or social function, is the first condition of its legitimacy. 'I obtained it by the rules, and am therefore entitled to it,' is a standard claim in all societies. Rules form a basic component of social life. It is only through their presence that we are able to predict the behaviour of others, and introduce any settled expectations into our lives. Without rules we could make no plans for the future, or entertain any projects beyond the merest hand-to-mouth survival. Such settled expectations have a very different basis from the predictabilities of the natural order, with its circulation of the seasons, and succession of night and day. Social rules ensure predictability through their normative or prescriptive force; they impose obligations and create corresponding entitlements, which are publicly acknowledged and collectively enforced. As such they both serve to regulate behaviour in a predictable fashion, and provide the reference point for entitlement claims which people can expect to have recognised by others.

It follows from the nature of social rules that in any rule-governed social order the existence and acquisition of power cannot be separated from the normative expectations and entitlements by reference to which its possession is also justified. The rules of exclusion which make necessary resources into property, and therefore a means of power, are rules which lay obligations on the excluded to keep off or keep out; the social recognition of the obligation is essential to the power of those who possess such resources. So too, the rules which determine who shall come to acquire the power of property, position or function, and by what means, confer the right to its exercise and the corresponding duty to acknowledge and respect it on the part of others. In a rule-governed social order we cannot separate power from legitimacy, since both occur simultaneously; in acquiring power according to the rules a person also acquires the right to exercise it.

Social rules may be customary and conventional in form, or be part of a legal order. The drawback to custom and convention, particularly with regard to important and potentially contested issues, is that they carry with them no means of adjudicating disputes about their precise reference and scope, and they rely on diffuse means of enforcement applied by society as a whole. The distinctive features of a legal order, as H.L.A. Hart has shown, are the existence of second-order rules prescribing the means whereby primary rules are to be recognised and adjudicated, and the presence of a specialised agency to enforce them (Hart, 1961, pp.77–96). In most societies the basic rules determining access to the means of power come to be defined in legal form, even where they may have originated in convention, because of the disputes that arise among the powerful themselves over women, property and position. Among the characteristic features of the modern world are the extent to which its power structures are subject to precise legal regulation; and the flexibility of its procedures of legal enactment which enable the disadvantage of customary rules in the context of a rapidly changing environment to be overcome (Weber, 1968, pp.217–19).

However, even in the contemporary world the force of convention still persists, whether to qualify and subvert a status of formal legal equality, or to limit the power of the powerful in areas where the law itself is silent. The ability of conventional rules sustaining a hierarchical division of labour between the sexes to survive when no longer legally enforced is not only the result of the deep-seated assumptions and structured incentives supporting them. It is also related to distinctive characteristics of the rules in question which make them eminently sustainable in conventional form: the lack of contestability about which sex a person belongs to, and the effectiveness of dispersed means of enforcement, such as disapproval within the family and the peer group. On the other side, modern power relations of all kinds retain substantial scope for convention in the regulation of relations between dominant and subordinate. The almost absolute formal power of a UK Prime Minister with a guaranteed parliamentary majority constitutes a particularly striking example where the limitations on power are conventional rather than legally prescribed.

Throughout history, in fact, the limitations on power which the subordinate have been able to secure, and which they understand as constituting rights for themselves, have usually been conventional rather than legal in form, in contrast to the rules securing the power of the dominant. Such rights as those of peasants to a portion of the crop sufficient for subsistence, of industrial workers to control aspects of the work process, of women to a sphere of activity from which men are excluded, are typically the product of historical struggles between dominant and subordinate, and represent the crystallisation of a particular balance of forces at a given moment of time. Like rights of way, they become confirmed by repeated use, and established as customary rules governing the relations between the respective parties. The breach of such rules by the dominant constitutes one of the most frequent sources of grievance on the part of the subordinate, though one which does not necessarily undermine the legitimacy of the power structure as a whole (J.C. Scott, 1976, ch.6; Moore, 1978, pp.18–31). Where the powerful are able to secure legal validation for their action, the grievance becomes a dispute over which type of rule should have priority: that of law or custom; statutory rights or the 'rights of free-born Englishmen' (Thompson, 1975).

The much readier access of the powerful to the law, and the fact that it provides both the source and protection of their power, makes appeal to the law as the ground of legitimacy a particularly favoured strategy for dominant groups. Indeed, respect for the law is insisted on as the first duty of the subordinate, and legal validity is made to appear not only as the necessary, but also the sufficient, condition of legitimacy: its ultimate, rather than merely its proximate, source. Moreover, there are features inherent in most legal systems that serve not only to encourage respect for the law in general, but to put the particular content of existing law beyond question, and make it difficult to challenge. The sanctity that surrounds the law itself comes to impart its aura to the contingency of the law's content.

What are these features? Most deeply embedded are those terms used in everyday language which serve to distinguish the lawful from the unlawful in the achievement and exercise of power, and which demarcate, for example, theft, violence and murder from legally permitted forms of acquisition, compulsion and deprivation of life or livelihood. Such linguistic distinctions are reinforced by the solemn rituals and imposing figures associated with the conduct of the law, and by the weighty anathemas pronounced against those who infringe it. Associated with the presentation of the law as a morally edifying spectacle or theatre is the idea of the law as a seamless web, such that to challenge one element is to threaten the whole. In similar vein, the rules of power, which could well be other than they happen to be, are accorded the same moral status as those rules without which social life would be impossible at all. While societies could not exist without some property, division of labour, or authority position, the particular rules governing these could well be differently arranged. The necessity of the one serves to conceal the contingency of the other, and gives any challenge to them the character of a moral transgression.

Such features combine to set the existing rules of power beyond question, and turn legal validity into the ultimate, rather than simply the proximate, criterion of legitimacy, to the advantage of those who derive their power from established law. However, the more that the powerful appeal to the law as the self-sufficient justification for their power, the more they have to respect it themselves for their legitimacy to be sustained. The absolutist idea that those who make the law are themselves above it is historically exceptional. Much more usual is some version, however embryonic, of the idea of the 'rule of law': the idea that the powerful and their agents, whatever influence they may exercise over the formulation of the law, are themselves subject to it, and have to conform to recognised procedures if they wish to change it. What is distinctive about the modern concept of the rule of law is the development of institutional arrangements, such as the strict separation of powers between legislative, executive and judiciary, to give it practical effect. Although such a separation cannot of itself guarantee to the subordinate any control over the content of law, it can at least secure them against the arbitrary exercise of power, and provide the protection of due process when they fall foul of the powerful. The idea of the rule of law thus serves as a limitation on power as well as a guarantor of it, and as a resource available to the subordinate as well as the dominant, albeit to a lesser degree (Thompson, 1975, pp.258–69).

On its own, however, legality cannot provide a fully adequate or self-sufficient criterion of legitimacy. Despite all the features mentioned above which conspire to set the law beyond question, circumstances will always occur which expose a more fundamental issue: why these particular laws, and what gives them their legitimacy? Such occasions arise, for example, when there is a conflict over the interpretation of existing law, which can only be resolved by reference to some basic principle. Or social changes take place which provoke demands for reform of the law, thereby exposing its contingency. Or there occurs some infringement of the law by the powerful, which they seek to justify by reference to norms or an authoritative source that lies beyond existing rules. Such occasions expose a general truth, that appeal to the law can never provide more than a primary, and therefore provisional, ground for legitimacy. That such an appeal is a *necessary* first step is ensured by the fact that established rules provide the recognised source of entitlements, and because a generalised respect for rules is the condition for any social order or settled expectations. That it is *no more* than a first step follows from the fact that rules cannot justify themselves simply by being rules, but require justification by reference to considerations which lie beyond them. These considerations will be explored in the following section.

Legitimacy as justifiability of rules

The stipulation that power is legitimate to the extent that its rules are justifiable in terms of shared beliefs raises a number of questions. Justifiable to whom? What are the criteria for justifiability? What kinds of belief are relevant? The answer to the first question is already contained in the specification that the relevant beliefs be shared between dominant and subordinate. Without a common framework of belief, the rules from which the powerful derive their power cannot be justifiable to the subordinate; the powerful can enjoy no moral authority for the exercise of their power, whatever its legal validity; and their requirements cannot be normatively binding, though they may be successfully enforced. If the point of legitimacy is its significance for the character of power relationships, and its effect on the behaviour of the subordinate, then it follows that the rules of power must be justifiable to them.

The answer to the second question, about the criteria for justifiability, is largely contained in the answer to the third. Although such criteria are not as tight as those for legal validity, once we know what the relevant beliefs for the justification of power rules are, these will set limits to the range of possible disputes about them, and will identify what sort of disputes they will be. It is with the third question, therefore, about the kinds of justificatory belief, that this section will be primarily concerned.

In the previous chapter I distinguished a number of considerations relevant to the justification of power rules – for instance
that they should be based upon a principle of normative differentiation between dominant and subordinate, and that they should
satisfy some general interest or social purpose in which the subordinate have a concern. However, there is a different, and
arguably prior, way in which rules must be justified, and that is
by identifying an authoritative source from which they stem. It
is the impressiveness of the source from which they derive as
well as the moral persuasiveness of their content that gives social
rules their justifiability. This distinction between *source* and *content* is an important one, and I shall treat these considerations
separately in what follows, although in practice they are complementary.

i) legitimacy deriving from an authoritative source

What is the ultimate source of law and social rules, from whence
do they derive their authority, what provides the guarantee of
their authenticity or validity – these are questions that concern
the most fundamental of a society's beliefs, its metaphysical
basis, if you like, which cannot itself be questioned (except by
philosophers!), since it provides the terms in which all other
questions are settled. Whether it be tradition, divine command,
scientific doctrine, popular will, or whatever, this constitutes the
ultimate source which validates society's rules and system of law.
It also has a special significance for the legitimacy of political
power, for an important but simple reason. Where all other
power relations in society are validated in the first instance by
the law, the political sphere is itself the institutional source and
guardian of that law; and there is no positive law beyond it to
which it can appeal for its own validation. As institutional creator
and guardian of the law, therefore, the political sphere is
especially bound up with the ultimate source of normative
validity that is acknowledged within the society. And since there
is no positive law beyond it, it is uniquely dependent upon that
source for its own legitimacy.

In identifying the ultimate source of authority and validating
basis acknowledged within a society, therefore, we shall find the
legitimating principle for its system of political power as well as

for its body of law in general. These sources will differ in different types of society, and each will have its respective guardians and interpreters who enjoy a special prestige because of their connection with it. At the expense of seeming unduly schematic, I shall distinguish between sources that are external to the society, and those that are internal to it. I should emphasise that these different sources are not necessarily mutually exclusive, since some can coexist within the same society; however, it is useful to distinguish them for analytical purposes (see Figure 3.1, page 72).

a) external sources
For most of history, societies have derived the legitimacy of their rules of power from a transcendent source: a divine being or beings, belief in whose wisdom and power makes all rules that can be shown to emanate from them binding on behaviour. The divine will, however, requires definitive human interpretation; and most systems of religious belief are mediated through priests, prophets, or jurists, whose authority provides an essential underpinning to secular forms of power. Religious ideas are well suited to the legitimation of hierarchical social relations, since the rule of one God or many over the world they have created provides a definitive model for earthly authority, whether of rulers over subjects, masters over servants and employers, or husbands over wives (the German word for authority, Herrschaft, links all of these with the rule of a masculine deity). Although more egalitarian interpretations of religious doctrine are possible, their exponents have usually found themselves pitted against the religious as well as secular authorities, and been forced into schism. Today the processes of secularisation on the one side, and the multiplication of faiths on the other have made religious belief largely incapable of providing a single coherent source of legitimacy for a society, though there are notable exceptions within the Islamic world (see below, pp.191–204).

An external source of legitimacy of a secular kind has been provided at particular periods of history by natural law doctrines, which derive society's rules of power from universal normative principles grounded in nature and appropriate to an unchanging human condition. Although such doctrines can be linked with religious belief, such linkage is not necessary, and in the Euro-

72

Figure 3.1 Legitimacy as justifiability of power rules

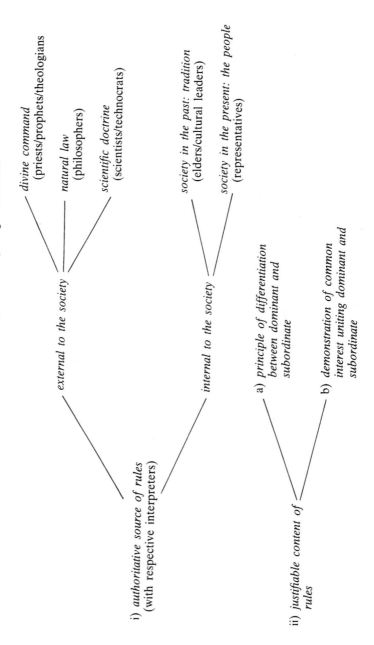

pean Enlightenment they took a strongly anti-religious form, involving the replacement of the moral and intellectual influence of the priest or theologian by that of the secular philosopher. Natural law doctrines played an important part in the assault on the feudal order in modern Europe, but they are not necessarily egalitarian; that depends upon how human nature itself is defined, and in particular whether differentiation is made between different types of nature. The Aristotelian version of natural law justified slavery as well as aristocracy, while most Enlightenment versions postulated a radical difference between the nature of men and women. Theories of human nature, its needs and capacities, still have an important part to play in philosophical debates about legitimacy, but the idea of an eternal moral law independent of human creation is difficult to sustain in a world in which a multiplicity of different beliefs and practices is so evident.

A further possible external source of legitimacy for a society's rules of power is provided by the laws of science. Scientific theories are logically incapable of generating normative principles on their own yet the prestige of science in the modern world is such that it is often appealed to as an authoritative source for rules of social organisation. So *laissez-faire* was justified in the first half of the nineteenth century by the science of political economy, and in the second half by the theory of Social Darwinism, though the latter was also appealed to by social imperialists to justify collectivist organisation at home and the 'survival of the fittest' abroad (Semmel, 1960, ch.2). In the twentieth century, science has provided Soviet-type societies with a legitimating basis in the form of Marxism–Leninism, with its claim to be able to guide society according to a scientific understanding of the historical process, knowledge of which is vested in the party as the representative of the most historically advanced class. More generally, a belief in the validity of science sustains the authority of experts in many fields, and justifies rules of organisation for a whole range of activities where technical decisions have been made paramount, to the exclusion of normative or political choices. Wherever science serves as a source of legitimacy, it works in an anti-democratic direction, by assigning the power of decision-making to the expert at the expense of the citizen, and to the professional at the expense of the lay person.

The evolution of intellectual epochs from religion through philosophy or metaphysics to science, first charted by Saint-Simon, represents a major shift in the belief systems of societies, in the character of their leading intellectuals, and in the mode of discourse in which social rules have been legitimated: from myth and cosmogeny, through philosophical argument to scientific proof. However, the Saint-Simonian belief that science could provide a definitive and non-controversial basis to social rules of power was premised on the assumption that all issues of social organisation in the industrial age could be reduced to technical questions of production. For all the prestige of science today, this conception of a wholly de-politicised social and legal order is in principle unattainable, despite the frequent recurrence of technocratic illusions to this effect (Saint-Simon, 1975).

b) internal sources
Whatever the main intellectual forms of reasoning and criteria of validity in different historical societies, none have relied on these external sources alone for their ultimate basis of authority. All have been complemented by sources internal to the society. Of these there are two major variants capable of providing a source of legitimacy: society in the past (tradition) and society in the present (the people). The first derives the rules of power from the society's own past, through the sanctification of tradition. There is a fine but important distinction to be drawn between accepting rules because they have always been there (habit) and the idea that those rules are the best for society which have been tried and tested over time, and embody the accumulated wisdom of successive generations (belief in tradition). Tradition by its nature conveys authority upon 'elders', and those whose role is to study and perpetuate a society's cultural legacy. It also favours rules of succession, such as heredity, which embody continuity with the past. The traditionalist principle makes changing rules difficult though not impossible; traditions are usually rich and complex enough to allow precedents for most things to be discovered. Yet the traditionalist principle tends to be incompatible with continuous rule change, such as is required by modern industrial economies. And its way of privileging society's past is inconsistent with a conception of history as one of unilinear development towards a more progress-

ive future. For these, a source of legitimacy in the present society is needed.

The most common source of legitimacy in contemporary societies is the 'people'. This source offers a highly generalised basis of legitimacy for the political domain, from which the rest of society's rules can in turn derive their legitimacy via the legislative process, freed from the limitations of tradition. Although the characteristic institution of popular origin is the representative assembly, the actual form of political arrangements can vary widely according to the precise definition of the people, and the type of representation adopted. Until the twentieth century the concept of the 'people' usually excluded propertyless males and all women. In Marxist–Leninist regimes the people have been defined primarily as the working class, to be represented through the monopolistic class party. And in all societies the definition of the people as the 'nation' has carried both inclusive and exclusive connotations, which have had important implications for the territorial boundaries of the state and for different citizenship statuses within it.

These various sources of legitimacy, both external and internal to societies, are rooted in clearly distinguishable types of belief system, each with its own respective interpreters and mode of discourse. Among the most profound social changes are those marked by a shift in these belief systems that determine the source of legitimacy for a society's rules of power: from religious to secular; from external and universalistic to internal and particularistic; from society as past, to society as its people in the present. Such shifts in belief, as gradual as they are also fundamental, will leave a society's established power rules intellectually unsupported, like a bridge whose foundations have been weakened by the slow processes of erosion. Thus the power of a hereditary monarchy becomes vulnerable to a decline in the belief in tradition, or the power of a theocratic order to the onset of secularisation. A similar gap between rules and beliefs can develop, conversely, through the attempt to introduce or impose new rules of power in a context where the appropriate beliefs are lacking: a representative democracy in a society that is highly traditionalist in orientation, or a Marxist–Leninist regime in a deeply religious society. All these are examples of what can be termed a legitimacy gap or deficit, in contrast to illegitimacy, i.e. a breach in the rules themselves. Whereas the latter is relatively clear-cut, the former requires careful analysis to elucidate, though one of its distinctive symptoms will be fundamental contestation between different groups of intellectuals.

Now although such disjunctions can develop between rules of power and the beliefs necessary to support them, it is also important to insist that any particular legitimating source does not deliver an unequivocal set of power rules. The authority of religion, for example, has historically been called in aid of a wide variety of social and political arrangements, from individual to collective property ownership, from absolute monarchy to a Calvinist republic. Such a belief system will only exclude certain possibilities, rather than unequivocally determine their form. By the same token, it is possible for similar power rules to derive their legitimacy from widely differing intellectual sources, as, for example, gender rules have claimed validation successively from religious doctrine, natural law and scientific argument. The belief systems which provide the source of legitimacy thus constitute only the most general intellectual framework within which legitimation of rules of power, and also challenges to them, may take place. They serve to define the boundaries of possible belief and debate, and the terms in which any debate must be conducted. It is important therefore to underline that the belief systems we have been considering at most locate an ultimate *source of authority* for power rules, rather than determine the particular form they should take. To justify the *content* of such rules, i.e. who should have access to the means of power, on what terms, etc., an appeal to more specific and substantive principles is needed.

ii) legitimacy as justifiable rule-content

As I have indicated above, the demonstration of an authoritative source for the rules of power does not suffice to answer the question: why these rules? Why this particular arrangement of the division of labour, of property, of political power? Behind the variety of answers that can be given to this question, it is possible to identify a common structure of argument. This structure comprises two distinct elements. The first is a principle of differentiation or separation, which *distinguishes* the dominant from the subordinate, and justifies their respective access to and exclusion from essential resources, activities and positions. The second is a principle of community or common interest, which *links* dominant and subordinate, and demonstrates the advantage the latter derive along with the former from the rules of power in question (see Figure 3.1, 72). As I shall argue, the first of these principles, that of differentiation, may be sufficient for the dominant to justify their power to themselves. But for their power to be justified to the subordinate, the second principle is required as well.

a) principles of differentiation
All social relations of power, and the rules of access and exclusion on which they are based, presuppose the differentiation or separation of the dominant from the subordinate. This separation is justified on the grounds that those who hold power possess qualities lacking in those subordinate to them, and that these qualities are appropriate to the particular form of power that is exercised. Rules of power, in other words, are considered rightful in so far as they select the qualified and exclude the unqualified, and ensure the dominance of the superior and the subordination of the inferior. How these qualities are defined will vary according to the particular form of dominance and subordination, but a broad distinction can be made between those justifying principles which assume that the qualities are assigned to and detectable in people at birth (so-called 'ascriptive' theories), and those which hold that they are demonstrated only through performance and achievement ('meritocratic' theories).

Among theories of ascription, the principle of aristocracy has been prevalent for much of human history. Its central idea is that of noble birth: the superior qualities appropriate to the possession of wealth and the exercise of power are supposedly inherited at birth, and the more surely so, the longer the line of noble ancestry that can be traced. It is the family into which a person is born that determines his or her natural position in society, and that confers the qualities appropriate to that position. Such a belief is associated with land as the major source of wealth, with traditionalism as the ultimate source of legitimacy, and, for all the tensions between the two, with a hereditary monarchy deriving its justification from the same aristocratic principle. Aristocratic societies generally provide scope for new talent, whether in political service or mercantile activity; but the achievements are only publicly recognised once they are translated into titles and estates through gift or purchase. Even then it takes a generation or two for a new family to become accepted, since it is inheritance, not achievement, that provides the guarantee of genuine quality. As with fine wine, so with breeding: only the passage of time can confer excellence (Powis, 1984).

While the principle of heredity has provided a historically important justifying ground for the differentiation of power and life-chances, that of gender has been even more universal. Here the distinguishing element is not the family into which a person is born, but the physical characteristics of sex that are supposed to reveal the naturally determined qualities appropriate to given social roles. The idea of women as the 'weaker sex' justifies their exclusion from a range of activities that involve the exercise of power, or lead to its acquisition. The definition of women as natural nurturers justifies their confinement to caring and servicing roles, for which men in turn are considered unsuited. The concept of the 'feminine' represents women as a passive adornment, rather than endowed with active intellectual or deliberative capacities, such as could be exercised in a public realm. These supposedly innate characteristics are typically combined into an ideal of womanhood, which is more positive than simply the absence of masculine qualities. Such an ideal does more than justify the sexual division of labour. It serves to obscure the power relationship between the sexes under the rubric of 'different but equal', and to reconcile women to the limitations of their condition by offering them a positive image to which to aspire, and a domain of their own, the domestic, within which to exercise a carefully circumscribed power (Millett, 1971, pp.88–108; Okin, 1980, pt.3).

The example of gender demonstrates clearly, however, that what is at issue in the legitimation of power rules is not only the development and dissemination of an appropriate body of ideas, or ideology, but the construction of a social identity by a complex set of often unconscious processes, which make that identity seem 'natural', and give the justifying ideas their plausibility. The processes whereby a differentiated gender identity is constructed in girls and boys take place through various stages from infancy to adolescence. They are ones through which children develop qualities, attitudes and capacities, learn patterns of behaviour, form desires and expectations, that are appropriate to their adult gender roles and relationships with the opposite sex. Although different theories in the fields of sociology and social psychology stress different mechanisms responsible for the construction of such an identity, few see it as the product simply of conscious instruction on the part of parents and other authority figures. More important is the exemplary effect of relationships between parents themselves; their less conscious assumptions and expectations for their children; the role-models to which the children are exposed both within the home and outside it; the reinforcement of attitudes and behaviour by siblings and peer-group pressure; the stereotypes presented in stories, books and other media. The cumulative effect of these influences is the construction of a social identity within the personality which, while by no means uniform within each sex, is systematically different between them (Oakley, 1972; Chodorow, 1978).

What has this to do with legitimacy? Central to the justification of gender roles, as of a hereditary aristocracy, is the demonstration that those assigned to their respective roles and hierarchically ordered positions are justly so assigned, because they are naturally endowed with the qualities and capacities appropriate to them. Yet the very 'naturalness' of this endowment is itself socially constructed, not only in the realm of intellectual doctrine or ideology, but by the complex set of processes whereby different groups from birth onwards develop the characteristics appropriate to their future roles in such a way that they appear as naturally given. An ascriptive principle of social differentiation, in other words, by requiring from birth the development of differential qualities in different groups, and excluding the development of other characteristics, itself generates the evidence necessary to its own justification.

The significance of such evidence can be grasped by asking what would be required for people to make the crucial but difficult distinction between naturally determined and socially acquired attributes and capacities. Either there has to be external evidence provided from other societies in which social roles are organised differently. Or there has to be a process of social change at work internal to the society, which allows or requires the supposedly ill-endowed by nature to assume roles involving the acquisition and exercise of power. The erosion of the aristocratic principle in Europe resulted from the expansion of new roles of this kind in economy and state, to the point where the capacities of the ignobly born could no longer be regarded as exceptions to be accommodated within the aristocratic principle. Such a process was a necessary condition for political philosophers from Hobbes onwards to make the critical distinction between 'natural' and 'political' (i.e. socially constructed) inequalities. Even though gender differences were still assigned to the 'natural' sphere, the distinction, once made, was available as a weapon to be used by later advocates of women's equality (Wollstonecraft, 1970; Mill, 1970). But it has taken the evidence of women successfully occupying supposedly 'masculine' roles for an effective challenge to be mounted upon the assumed naturalness of gender characteristics. The same social changes, in other words, which open up roles of power to the previously excluded, are also necessary to weaken the evidence that justifies their exclusion.

It is one of the basic contentions of a society which makes access to key resources, activities and authority positions subject to open competition, that it avoids the self-fulfilling cycle of closed societies and structures of power, whereby characters are moulded to fit the future roles they must necessarily occupy. The superiority claimed for meritocratic over ascriptive rules is that the processes of open competition, whether operated through the market, the education system, or appointment procedures, ensure that those who gain access to the means of power in any sphere are indeed the most suited to it, and have demonstrated evidence of achievement as a condition for attaining it. Moreover, for these processes to be effective, there must be equality of opportunity, and a principle of non-discrimination on grounds of irrelevant characteristics; i.e. a basic presumption of equality. In practice, however, the meritocratic principle is substantially restricted in its operation by the disposal rights of property ownership (doing what you want with your own) and the kinship claims of the family (doing what you can for your own). Together these ensure that the material and cultural resources enjoyed by the powerful in one generation are transmitted to the next, so that the acquisition of the means of power is as much the result of good fortune as it is of personal effort, of social advantage as of relevant ability.

There is a considerable divergence, therefore, between the principle of meritocracy and the social arrangements which it is required to justify, though the extent of that divergence will vary from one society to the next (Payne, 1987). Such discrepancy is obscured by the fact of competition itself, which serves to validate the qualities of the successful, however these have been acquired. And the celebration of impressive examples of ascent from base to summit of the social order provides evidence that access to power is in principle open to anyone, though not everyone, whatever the odds that may be stacked against them in practice. Furthermore, as far as the losers in the competition for power are concerned, the transmission of appropriate expectations and attitudes along with an impoverished cultural and material legacy suffices to reconcile them to their subordinate position. In this respect the open or meritocratic society is not altogether as different as it appears from the closed or ascriptive one in the manner in which children develop the characteristics and expectations appropriate to their future social roles, or in the agencies through which they do so. Studies of socialisation among the manual working class closely parallel those of gender in their demonstration of the way in which attitudes and ideas appropriate to their more limited future expectations are reproduced within the family and peer group (Willis, 1977). To this extent 'meritocratic' societies are unable, in practice, wholly to break out of the self-fulfilling cycle of legitimation, characteristic of ascriptive societies, whereby natural-seeming qualities are socially created.

Such a restriction of the meritocratic principle in practice is the result of an inability to prevent the intergenerational transmission of social advantage. To overcome this limitation would require either the abolition of the family, or the removal of the very inequalities whose allocation to particular individuals it is the purpose of the principle to justify. Yet even if, *per impossible*, a pure meritocracy could be attained, it would still operate as a principle of differentiation or selection, justifying the access of certain individuals to power, and the exclusion of others from it (Young, 1961). Like any principle of differentiation, what it could not justify would be why this particular distribution of power was necessary in the first place. Why this particular distribution of resources, division of labour, or position of authority? A principle of differentiation, in other words, can serve to justify why individuals of a particular kind should have access to power or be excluded from it, but not why the division itself should exist. For that, some argument from social necessity or social utility is required.

b) ideas of the common interest
One part of the justification of power-rules lies in the principle of differentiation, which distinguishes the qualified from the unqualified. It emphasises the difference in personal capacities, so as to justify the separation between the lives and powers of the dominant and those of the subordinate. Its necessary counterpart, however, is the belief that the dominant and the subordinate, however much they may differ, are also linked by a community of interest; and that the distribution of power serves the interests of the subordinate, and not those of the powerful alone. A sense of justified superiority may well suffice to reconcile the dominant to their power, its advantages and its impositions on others, with an easy conscience. But in the absence of any idea of community linking themselves with the subordinate, or of the latter as having any interests of their own worth protecting, even if those of inferiors, then that power can have no justification for the subordinate; the latter will be excluded not only from power itself, but from participation in a shared moral order within which alone, any justification could make sense to them.

A characteristic feature of power which seeks to justify itself to the subordinate, therefore, is the claim to serve a common interest. Feudal power justified itself in terms of the provision of law and protection to the peasantry subject to it, and the exactions on their labour as necessary to the fulfilment of these functions. In a different age, capitalist property and profits, and the accompanying authority of management, justify themselves in terms of their necessity to expanded production and employment, and the satisfaction of consumer wants. In state-socialist societies, the power of the bureaucracy has been justified as necessary to the effective organisation of production, distribution and most other essential social activities. Sceptics may regard such claims as spurious, serving merely as a cloak for the particular interests of the powerful. In doing so they pose a mistaken dichotomy between general and particular interests. As I have already argued, it is typical of the way social power is organised that general interests, including those of the subordinate, can only be met *through* satisfying the particular interests of the powerful; and therefore their claim to serve general interests is rarely an empty one. It only becomes so when a dominant group loses its social function, or fails to satisfy vital interests of the subordinate.

As I pointed out in the previous chapter, once some necessary social resource or activity is controlled by a particular group, it follows that the wider needs of society can only be met by satisfying the interests of that group, and on terms acceptable to them. Provided the resource or skill they command has been acquired according to the rules, making it available to others for a consideration will seem less like an extortion racket than a public service, and the price demanded as their legitimate reward for performing it. Where landowners rent out their land to a peasantry, the return they can command in kind or labour is the due reward for providing the peasants with the means of subsistence. 'If the landlords did not let us rent the land, we would starve,' said the peasants in William Hinton's account of discussions in the village of Fanshen during the Chinese revolution (Hinton, 1966, pp.128–31). As the relationship presented itself to the peasantry, their existence depended upon the landlords, rather than the existence of the landlords upon their labour, and therefore the rent exacted was acknowledged as morally justified.

From such a perspective, it is the failure to guarantee subsistence and the means of livelihood that is destructive to legitimacy, rather than the extent of any exactions made, since it infringes the basic interests that are presupposed in the relationship. This is a point made in many studies of peasant economies. James Scott, for example, argues that it is not the proportion of the crop, but its effect on subsistence that is crucial to the perception of exploitation:

'If the balance of exchange is deteriorating but the material situation of the cultivator's family is stable or even improving, discontent may be evident, but it is unlikely to provoke massive unrest. It is when a worsening balance of exchange menaces crucial elements of subsistence routines, when it stretches existing subsistence patterns to breaking point, that we expect explosions of rage or anger.' (1976, p.177)

As he goes on to show, the basic peasant interest in subsistence becomes part of a settled pattern of expectations, a 'norm of reciprocity', which imposes obligations on those who monopolise the scarce resource of land, and which is infringed when exactions are made, or continued, to the point where they threaten subsistence. The historical circumstances in which this can happen, and in which the legitimacy of landed property become eroded have been enormously varied.

The distinctive characteristic of industrial capitalism in its early stages in Europe, especially in comparison with systems of rural tenancy, was that from the standpoint of the workers it was a power relationship in which their interests were systematically disregarded. The capitalist undertook no responsibility for the livelihood of the workers, who could be employed at a wage insufficient for subsistence, and could be dismissed at will into a situation where they had no means of livelihood at all. The worker was simply an instrument for serving capitalist profit, on terms and conditions dictated by the capitalist, and without any security of subsistence. The argument that capitalist property and profit served a general interest could only be made at the level of the market economy as a whole, and in terms of the abstract constructions of theoretical political economy: viz., that the worker's insecurity was necessary to ensuring efficiency of production and its responsiveness to consumer needs in a competitive market; and that the accumulation of profit ensured expanded investment and production, and enabled an ever-increasing population to be employed (Smith, 1976, bk.2, ch.3). None of these arguments addressed the immediate interests of the workers as producers. At the point where the power relations of capitalism were experienced directly, in the individual factory, their interests went unattended. The public benefits of the system, such as they were, could only be demonstrated through the working of the economy as a whole, and in the theoretical terms of a political economy whose purpose was to prove the intuitively implausible proposition, that the unrestrained pursuit of private advantage by the capitalist served the public interest by way of its unintended consequences via the 'hidden hand' of the market.

In the light of this disjunction between the official justification for capitalist profit and the actual experience of the workers it is hardly surprising that many of them were attracted to an alternative, socialist-oriented political economy, which directly addressed their experience as producers, and promised the humane working conditions, the security of employment and the right to the product of their labour that capitalism denied them. Capitalism itself was only able to attain a measure of legitimacy as, on the one hand, the workers were able to secure a share of expanded profits in improved wages and working conditions through the pressure of collective organisation at the workplace; and, on the other, as the state came to guarantee the means of subsistence to them when unemployed, and in general compensated for the inadequacies of the market. It has been Marxism's insistence that these necessary conditions for capitalism's legitimation could not be achieved without a chronic crisis of profitability that has proved to be the central weakness of its theory, for all its impressive analysis of the condition of labour under the capitalist mode of production.

Whereas capitalist legitimacy has proved weakest in the early stages of industrialisation, and stronger in the later stages as workers have secured a share of expanded profits, and the state has alleviated the conditions of insecurity inseparable from the market economy, the record of state socialism has proved to be the reverse. Its claim to be able to satisfy the public interest directly, through the planned organisation of production, rather than abandoning it to the vicissitudes of the market, seemed initially vindicated in the USSR by its impressive achievements in industrialisation and the development of the necessary human and material infrastructure. For this reason state socialism has offered an attractive model to other developing societies. However, the central planning system has proved far too insensitive for the more intensive stages of economic development, and its producer-goods bias has left basic consumer wants chronically unsatisfied, to the point where bureaucratic power and privilege have become divorced from the effective performance of the economic purpose that has provided their rationale (Bahro, 1978; Feher *et al.*, 1983). What we have witnessed is the classic erosion of legitimacy of a power structure through its inability to satisfy the basic interests it claims to serve. The comparison offered by capitalism at its most successful stage of stimulating and satisfying consumer wants has no doubt contributed to this erosion.

The upshot of these examples drawn from different systems of production is that the control exercised by dominant classes over essential resources and activities, which ensures that general social needs or interests, including those of the subordinate, can only be met on terms acceptable to them, achieves justification provided that these interests continue to be satisfied, and that the claim to this effect is validated by the experience of the subordinate themselves. However, there is an important distinction to be observed, as I remarked earlier, between the failure of a system of power to serve the interests it claims, and the absence of any such claim in the first place. The distinctive feature of most slave systems is that they did not accord any place to the interests of the subordinate whatsoever, nor see them as part of a common moral order. Slave-owners certainly justified the institution of slavery to themselves, and to third parties whose cooperation was needed for its survival. In this sense slavery constitutes a paradox for legitimacy. If we are interested in explaining the rise and fall of slavery as an institution, then we will want to talk about the 'legitimacy' of slave-owning within a given society, and examine the history of its justifications. But if we are concerned to analyse the character of the power relationship between slave-owner and slave, then the important thing is that the form these justifications took posited such a radical differentiation of status between the two that no considerations of common interest between them were possible; nor could there be any basis of right or morality in the *relationship*. As the eighteenth-century historian Bryan Edwards, himself a slave-owner, wrote:

'In countries where slavery is established, the leading principle on which the government is supported is fear: or a sense of that absolute coercive necessity which . . . supersedes all questions of right.' (Genovese, 1970, p.162).

For the analysis of legitimate power relations, then, slavery constitutes the limiting case: the example of purely coercive, unlimited, arbitrary power of one group over another, where legitimacy is absent. 'All slaves are enemies' went the Roman proverb; they were indeed recruited through conquest, and the relationship formed a perpetuation of the conditions of warfare within the society (Hopkins, 1978, pp.118–23). As with all coercive regimes, power would dissolve when coercion slackened, as was demonstrated by the spectacular examples of mass slave desertions in the ancient world when their owners were away fighting (De Sainte Croix, 1981, p.147). However, even such a regime would need incentives as well as sanctions as a means of getting tasks done, and to lighten the weight borne by physical coercion in maintaining discipline. Yet it is important to distinguish between the use of incentives to encourage cooperation, within a predominantly coercive regime, and the claim that a power structure is justified because it serves the interests of the subordinate. The first is a purely instrumental means to promote the interests of the powerful; the second involves the recognition that the subordinate have interests of their own which merit consideration.

In this context the differences that Eugene Genovese identifies between different historical types of slavery are relevant. He draws attention, for instance, to a shift that occurred in the pattern of slavery in the southern states of the USA after the end of the slave trade, when the supply of slaves could only be maintained through reproduction. This entailed allowing a certain independence of family life to slaves, usually on estates where the slave-owner was also resident, and acknowledging that they had interests of their own meriting attention. Here the justification of slavery took a distinctively paternalist turn: slaves occupied the status of 'permanent children' within an extended family, where they were said to enjoy a greater degree of both physical and economic security than outside the institution of slavery, under a system of supposedly 'free' labour. In other words, slavery was in their own best interests! Genovese contrasts this situation with the slave regimes of the West Indies, with absentee landlords and dependence upon the slave trade for new recruitment, where the relationship was the historically more typical one of coercion rather than dependency (Genovese, 1970; 1975, pt.1).

Genovese's distinction between different types of slave regime, the paternalistic and the purely coercive, is important for marking one of the boundaries between a legitimate and a non-legitimate relationship: between one based on a recognition of the interests of the subordinate (and, therefore, with some corresponding limitation on the exercise of power) and one where no such recognition exists. In the practice of slavery in the southern states of the USA no doubt this distinction was more blurred than I have presented it, but the distinction is an important one, analytically. Genovese's example of paternalism also raises a final question to be considered here, and that concerns the different ways in which the interests of the subordinate are treated in a power relationship, and the correspondingly different types of relationship this treatment implies.

A paternalist form of power involves a relationship in which the subordinate are defined as wholly or partially, temporarily or permanently, incapable of recognising and defending their own interests, and these therefore have to be defined and advanced by the powerful on their behalf. It can be contrasted with a form of power in which the subordinate are defined as fully capable of identifying their interests, and therefore as entitled to be consulted in any decision that may affect them; in which, therefore, processes of consultation are formally or informally built into the relationship. The paradigm case of a paternalist relation is of course that between parents and children. Here the principle of differentiation that justifies the power dimension of the relationship (adult–child) specifies a relative incapacity in the child that requires the parent or guardian to make provision, take decisions and secure obedience in the child's own interests. Yet the incapacity is only a temporary one. In the case of women, the principle of differentiation between the sexes that has historically justified male supremacy has defined them as permanently weaker, less capable, less rational, and so on, and their interests as therefore having to be determined and protected on their behalf by men. The logic of racial differentiation has been similar. In each case it is some presumed weakness or incapacity inscribed in the principle of differentiation that defines the subordinate as necessarily dependent, and their interests as requiring interpretation and protection by a superior.

There is a different form of paternalism which is to be found in the political domain, and which should be distinguished from the above, because it is not necessarily based upon any differentiation of inherent status between categories of people. This is where the fundamental belief system that specifies the ultimate source of authority for the political domain has implied in it the premise that decisions about the public interest, the common good, etc., must be matters of special knowledge, and that those who have attained this knowledge are thereby entitled to determine policy, decide laws, etc., on behalf of those who haven't. If the ultimate source lies in tradition, then it will be the elders, or those whose families have privileged access to traditional wisdom, who will acquire the right to decide. If it lies in divine command, then it will be spiritual leaders, or those qualified in religious law, as in a theocracy. If it lies in science, then it will be those who have access to scientifically determined principles or expertise about the proper organisation of society, or the necessary course of history (as in Marxist–Leninism). In each case the underlying principle of authority entails that some people are entitled to take public decisions on behalf of others by virtue of some special knowledge they have acquired about the public good, and which others do not have. All such principles by definition entail a paternalist relationship between governors and governed: 'trust us, because we must know best'.

The only principle of government that is non-paternalist is one where the ultimate source of authority is located wholly in the people, because only here is the criterion for the public good to be found not in some special wisdom, revelation or expert knowledge, but in what the people, freely organised, determine it to be, whether directly or through their representatives. Only here are those subordinate to government recognised as the ultimate judge of what their interests are. I say 'wholly' in the people, because the distinctions I have made are typological only, and there are mixed sources of authority where, say, a representative assembly has limited rights of decision or consultation in relation to a hereditary monarch or religious ruler. The principle of popular sovereignty can be qualified formally, in this and other ways, by a traditionalist, religious or scientific source of authority. It can also be qualified informally, when those who are popularly elected claim access to a privileged source of truth that others do not have, and where consultation with the subordinate becomes thereby irrelevant or a charade. There are, finally, other kinds of mixed system where government is constituted on paternalist lines with one section of the society, and on non-paternalist lines with another, as when voting rights are limited on grounds of property qualification, gender or race. (Here it is the differentiation of inherent characteristics that is the determinant).

The problem intrinsic to all paternalism is that, in denying the subordinate all independent means of expressing or defending their interests, there is nothing to stop it degenerating into the exercise of power in the interests merely of the powerful, except the latter's own integrity; and even integrity is no guarantee against self-deception or ignorance. Moreover, for its legitimacy, paternalist power depends upon the continued belief on the part of the subordinate in the principle of differentiation, or the source of authority, that provides its justification. Among the complex of factors contributing to the erosion of such beliefs, not the least is the experience of interests systematically neglected or impaired because they are subject to paternalistic definition by the powerful.

In this section I have briefly considered the way in which different systems of production meet the interests of subordinate classes, or fail to do so; the limiting case of slavery which makes no such claim; and the link between different types of paternalist power and the different sources of authority and principles of differentiation that define the subordinate, for one reason or another, as incapable either of determining their own interests or of having a valid conception of the public interest for themselves. The final section will discuss problems relating to consent.

Legitimacy through expressed consent

The subject of consent is a confusing one, and its relationship with legitimacy makes it doubly so. If by consent to power we mean a condition of voluntary agreement to it, then what counts as voluntary, and what sort of evidence is needed to demonstrate such agreement? Simply obeying the requirements of the power-ful, or keeping to the law is not enough, since obedience can be maintained by coercion. The view that people consent to power if they are not openly protesting against it is therefore quite inadequate. What sort of evidence, then, do we need?

These questions become even more difficult when we try and relate consent to legitimacy. If we equate legitimacy with the 'belief in legitimacy', then do we say that the belief in legitimacy is something different from consent, because more normative? Or that it is part of consent, because it helps produce it? Or that consent provides us with evidence of people's belief in legit-imacy? If the last of these, then again what sort of evidence will count?

Most of these problems disappear once we free ourselves of the mistaken view that legitimacy is to be equated with people's belief in it. Then we are able to see that what is important about consent is not the condition of voluntary agreement, but the specific *actions* that publicly express it; and that these are impor-tant because they *confer* legitimacy on the powerful, not because they provide evidence about people's beliefs. They confer legit-imacy because they constitute public expressions by the sub-ordinate of their consent to the power relationship and their subordinate position within it; of their voluntary agreement to the limitation of their freedom by the requirements of a superior. Such actions are not the only source of legitimacy for the power-ful; but they make a distinctive contribution to it, along with validity according to justifiable rules, by demonstrating the con-sent of the subordinate to the relationship.

What sort of actions, then, will carry this significance? The answer of the liberal, individualist tradition, which has become embodied in the practice of Western societies, has typically been that consent is given to a condition of subordination only by a specific and voluntary promise, agreement or contract on the part of each individual in person: e.g. of the worker to the employer at the time of employment, of the woman to her husband at the point of marriage (I am referring here to the promise of obedience contained in the traditional form of mar-riage ceremony). Necessary conditions for the voluntariness of such an agreement are not only that it should not be coerced, but that there should be a choice available between potential employers and husbands respectively. One of the classical liberal objections to feudal society was that the worker had no choice between employers, and to arranged marriages that the woman had no choice of husband.

As regards the political sphere, the early liberal approach to consent was to develop the contract model into the idea of a social contract, whether historical or hypothetical, made by all individuals at the original establishment of government (Lessnoff, 1986, ch.4). However, the problematical status of this fictional social contract has led to a different approach today, which focuses instead on elections as the source of legitimacy. The convention within contemporary liberal democracies is that it is the act of taking part in elections that legitimates government and secures the obligation of citizens in principle to obey it. Here again, it is the existence of choice that is crucial – between candidates, programmes and parties. In other words, in the sphere of government as in that of employment or marriage, it is making an agreement to subordination under conditions of choice between alternatives that confers legitimacy on the exercise of power, and a corresponding obligation to obey.

I have begun with the liberal or individualist model of consent because it is familiar and paradigmatic for our society. However, it does not follow that this is the only form of action that can demonstrate consent or confer legitimacy on the powerful, or that there are not other types of action which, while failing to meet the liberal criteria for voluntary agreement, may not have or have had a legitimating force within the conventions of different social systems. Let me mention three such types of action that have historically been seen as conferring or confirming legitimacy, and which continue even within a liberal society, albeit in a subordinate role.

First is swearing an oath of allegiance. This of course is a form of promise, but differs from the liberal model in that typically there is no choice about whom a person is to obey. However, in societies where such oaths are required of subordinates, the lack of choice has not been regarded as making the promise any the less binding (Bloch, 1961, ch.11); nor has it in the case of a bride in circumstances of an arranged marriage. Even today when members of armed forces swear an oath of loyalty to the commander in chief the oath is not associated with any choice about whom the commander is to be. In traditional systems of rule such an oath given by the most important figures within the society was a significant element in the legitimation of the leader, chief or monarch. It carried an exemplary force for others, as well as a binding one for those who took part; for the ruler to show that he or she had the consent of those who carried weight in the society or in its different localities was an important and necessarily public aspect of legitimacy. By the same token, in countries subject to conquest, the ceremonies in which the established leaders of the conquered paid homage and swore allegiance to the conqueror, were an important element in the legitimation of alien rule (see, for example, the institution of the *durbar* or the *indaba* under the British Empire) (Cohn, 1983).

A second type of action expressive of consent is that of taking part in consultations or negotiations with the powerful, either about aspects of policy or about the terms on which a particular service is rendered, which culminate in agreement. In some respects this resembles a contract, but it does not entail any choice about who the superior will be, does not take place at the outset of the relationship, and may only affect certain aspects of it. Yet it carries with it, not only a commitment on the part of the subordinate to support the policy or observe the terms agreed, but an implication that they acknowledge the authority of the powerful more generally, and this act of public recognition itself confers legitimacy. In traditional societies the regular consultation between a ruler and other powerful figures provided a reinforcement to an original oath or agreement of allegiance. In early modern political systems the point of parliamentary elections was not to choose the head of government, but to select representatives who would negotiate with the monarch the terms on which taxation was to be levied and for what purposes. In present-day society, collective bargaining by trade unions with an employer or employers over the terms of the labour contract confirms the latter's legitimacy much more than any individual contract of employment (which is one reason why trade union leaders are so much the butt of attack by critics of capitalism).

A third type of action expressive of consent, which differs from the others in that it does not carry any connotations of promising, is the public acclamation whether of a monarch upon coronation or of a popular leader at a rally or other notable

event. The history of the twentieth century has made us deeply
suspicious of such occasions, especially where the organisers have
offered inducements to the masses to attend, or sanctions for
non-attendance. However, there is no denying that demonstrations of popular support and mass mobilisation confer a distinctive legitimacy in the age of popular sovereignty; and that a
party or movement that can harness the enthusiasm and commitment of a mass following thereby enhances the prestige and
authority of those who lead it. The most impressive example is
a revolutionary movement in which the people are ready to
sacrifice their lives to overthrow a discredited government, or to
support the one that replaces it. Such commitment confers enormous moral authority on a new regime; and the continued mobilisation of the people to help carry out its policies can prove an
effective alternative to the electoral process as a means of popular legitimation. This is the expression of consent through mass
participation in activity manifestly supportive of a regime.

As I shall argue in Part II, the general acceptance of the
principle of popular sovereignty in the modern world has meant
that, whatever the precise form of political system, and however
qualified the principle may be in the rules of appointment to
office, political legitimation has to be *mass* legitimation; but it
does not necessarily have to take the form of the liberal contract,
or be exercised through the electoral choice of government. It
is this requirement of mass legitimation that forms the decisive
point of difference from a traditional order, in which the right
to express consent (equivalent to membership of the political
community) was limited to the privileged or propertied section
of society, whose consent was both exemplary and binding for
everyone else. For political legitimation to be effective in the
modern world, the expression of consent has in principle to be
available to all, whether they take advantage of it or not, and
whether it takes place in the electoral mode or the mobilisation
mode, as I shall call it.

There is, however, a crucial difference to be observed between
the electoral and the mobilisation modes of consent, or the contractual and expressive modes, to give them a more general
characterisation, in respect of the *way* they confer moral authority upon the powerful. A contract confers moral authority
through the promise that is made and the commitment that is

undertaken for the future. It matters not at all for what reason or motive the promise is made. Indeed, it can be made purely out of self-interest. If I judge it in my interest to enter into a particular contract, then I may do so regardless of my attitude in general to the authority concerned; but my action carries its obligatory force and legitimating effect regardless, because of the kind of action it is. In other words, contracts can harness people's self-interest to the cause of legitimacy through the normative force of promising. (This still leaves intact the distinction between the prudential and moral grounds for obeying a particular requirement of an authority.)

The expressive mode of consent, on the other hand, whereby the subordinate demonstrate their commitment to a regime by voluntary actions supportive of its policies, carries no obligation with it, since it involves *no undertaking in respect of the future*. This means not only that it has continually to be demonstrated, but that its normative or legitimating effect depends entirely upon the quality of the action undertaken. If performed purely for self-advancement, because, say, it is the means to further one's career, rather than for the promotion of a cause or a collective project, then its expressive or normative impact will be diminished. This distinction may be difficult to judge from outside, but it will be evident enough to people within the society. The expressive or mobilisation form of consent, therefore, is typically effective when linked to an ideological programme or cause; and it tends to degenerate once enthusiasm for the cause wanes, unless it is revived through some form of cultural revolution or revivalist campaign. A degeneration into mere self-interest does not undermine legitimation in the contractual mode, in contrast, since its normative force stems from the action itself, not from the quality of the motives, or the degree of enthusiasm, with which it is undertaken. For this reason popular legitimation in the contractual mode can survive in societies where self-interest is paramount, and where the population is widely de-politicised, except at election time.

The fact that the expressive or mobilisation mode of consent is open to manipulation by the powerful, and to the abuse of people's commitment, when it is associated, as it typically is, with paternalist and unaccountable forms of power – all that is evident enough from the history of the communist systems. Less obvious, because more subtle, is the way in which power relations structure the expression of consent in the liberal or contractual mode. To explain this, let me return for a moment to the liberal criterion for the voluntariness of an agreement to accept a position involving subordination: that people should have a choice between those to whom they are to be subordinate. What they have much less of a choice about, however, is whether to make that choice in the first place, because the situation is such that their interests and therefore their choices are already pre-structured.

This is most obviously true of the wage-labourer. Once workers were 'freed' from any control over their own means of production, they had the Hobson's choice of submitting to given conditions of subordination under whatever employer, or starvation. The fact that today's alternative to subordination is the dole does not alter the position that the choice is already structured by the existing rules of power determining access to, and the use of, property. For most of the modern period women have had the choice of being subordinate to their fathers or their husbands; or, if they achieved independence through remaining unmarried, of forgoing the possibility of having children. And today the choice of who undertakes childcare is structured by the relative opportunities and wage levels in the labour market, as well as by the socially developed desires and capacities of men and women respectively. For this reason women within a supposedly equal relationship may have a strong incentive to agree to a strategy that perpetuates their disadvantage and dependency. In the political sphere, finally, citizens who do not vote may forfeit any influence on the outcome, and in any case will not avoid subordination to government by abstaining. The alternative to expressing consent by participating in the ballot, and thereby legitimating the government, is hardly a serious one (Pateman, 1980; 1985, ch.5).

There is a further point to be made. In agreeing to a particular condition of subordination, people are also thereby confirming the rules of power that underpin it. In strict logic this does not follow. For a person to agree to a particular condition of subordination is not to agree to the rules that determine the necessity of their subordination in the first place. Yet in practice and by social convention it is exceedingly difficult to separate the two. Is there any doubt that, when regularly in a society, women agree to obey their husbands in marriage, or workers their employers, or citizens their government, they thereby confirm the relations of dominance and subordination in general, of which their agreement is a part? We thus see once more the self-confirmatory circle at work between rules of power and the process of their legitimation. The existing rules of power themselves structure the condition of relative powerlessness, disadvantage or dependency that gives people the incentive to make agreements of subordination which in turn confirm the existing rules of power.

At this point, defenders of the liberal democratic system will insist that, in a society where freedom of speech and association pertain, it is open to anyone to campaign with others for a change in the rules; and the fact that they persist can only be because people in general do not want to change them. Such a claim points to an important principle, as I shall argue later. Yet what it overlooks in practice is the way in which the structures of gender and class power are themselves reproduced within the political domain, and the political domain is itself structured, in a manner that is weighted against such change. The self-confirmatory circle is less closed, to be sure, in the liberal democratic system than in others, just as it is less closed in an avowedly meritocratic than in an ascriptive order; and this reveals something significant about the principles that underpin these forms of power. For the moment, however, what I wish to draw attention to is the way in which the processes that reproduce legitimacy in practice occur within these types of power relation also.

Conclusion

In this chapter I have explored the threefold normative structure of legitimacy as validity according to rules, the justifiability of rules in terms of shared beliefs, and expressed consent on the part of those qualified to give it; and I have elucidated the inner rationale of each, as well as the different forms each can take. Of the three, the second is the most complex, involving in turn an authoritative source for the rules, a principle of differentiation between dominant and subordinate, and a common interest that

the system of power serves. All these are cumulative and complementary, rather than alternative, requirements for legitimacy.
By reference to them slavery through conquest can be seen as
the limiting case of a non-legitimate order, because no common
interest between dominant and subordinate is allowed by the
principle of differentiation between them. Caste systems and
serfdom constitute historical examples of orders that were legitimate without being legitimated, since the subordinate belonged
to the category of the unfree, and were hence unqualified to give
consent (though in the case of serfdom the fiction was observed
that consent to subordination had been given by the ancestors
of those enserfed.) Even in these examples the character of
their power relation can be elucidated by means of the threefold
structure of legitimacy I have outlined. Although I have presented the different components of legitimacy as separable
elements for purposes of analysis, for any given structure of
power it is the ensemble that is important, and the internal
connections between them, as I shall demonstrate in the account
of political systems offered in Part II.

In the process of explicating the normative structure of legitimacy, I have uncovered the features for two different kinds of
'story'. One is a story of developmental stages within each of
the components of legitimacy: from conventional to legal regulation of power relations, especially in securing rights for the
subordinate; from the traditional to the popular source of authority, and with it the expansion of those qualified to give consent
to include the whole adult population; from the ascriptive to the
meritocratic principle of access to the means and positions of
power; from the paternalist to the consultative determination of
subordinate or common interests; from the expressive to the
contractual mode of consent. These shifts under each aspect of
legitimacy do not coincide neatly with historical epochs, since
the shifts occur at different times, cut across one another, and
coexist in the same period within different societies. They cannot
therefore constitute a supposedly value-neutral or unequivocal
set of criteria for 'modernisation'. Yet in each case they represent
what can be seen as a developmental shift, in the sense that once
the later stage or level is reached in each case it is impossible
to regress to the earlier. It is this criterion of irreversibility that
entitles us to consider them as a hierarchy of higher and lower

stages, not as the product of some unanchored value judgement. This does not mean that legitimacy cannot be infringed or forfeited once a higher level has been reached; only that it cannot be restored on the basis of an earlier or lower principle. Working out the implications of this 'story' is premature at the present point of my enquiry, though it will concern me towards the end of the next chapter, and in the second part of the book.

The second kind of 'story' concerns the way in which, within any settled or established power relations, self-confirming processes are at work to reproduce and consolidate their legitimacy. This is because the legitimation of power takes place within and not outside established power relationships – in given social contexts, not in the sphere of abstract argument or ideal conditions for consent. That is to say, the impressiveness of the law, the evidence necessary for belief, the interests conducive to consent are all structured by existing rules of power, not independently of them. This self-confirming cycle is never perfect or complete. But we need to analyse how it is constructed in the first place before we can understand how and why it breaks down where it does. No social-scientific account of the normative structure of legitimacy can therefore be complete without an account of how that legitimacy is socially constructed. Drawing together the different strands of that account will be the task of a brief concluding chapter to this part of the work.

4 The Social Construction of Legitimacy

Let me begin by recalling that the social scientist's primary interest or purpose in the analysis of legitimacy is an explanatory one. In the first instance this purpose is, through understanding the distinctive rules, the justificatory principles and beliefs, and the conventions about consent that underpin a given system of power, to explain the behaviour of people within it, and the kinds of relationship that it involves. Such an understanding also provides the basis for a judgement about the degree of legitimacy of a particular authority figure, power relationship or system of power as a whole, when measured against its own criteria; this judgement will help identify its potential points of vulnerability, and explain any erosion of its ability to secure cooperation from the subordinate when under pressure. In making such a judgement the social scientist is not imposing extraneous or *a*historical criteria, but employing those internal to the society or system of power itself, against which it requires to be judged; he or she is, as it were, reproducing the reasoning of people within that society, and reconstructing the logic of their own judgements. However, in doing so, the social scientist is also guided by a general understanding of what legitimacy involves, as in the threefold structure I have outlined, which provides an exploratory or heuristic framework for identifying the kinds of consideration that are relevant. Such a framework is made possible by the existence of recurrent features of power in all societies, and a common structure of moral argument that is universal however diverse or historically variable its actual content. It is only because of these recurrent features and common structure that it is possible for a person from one culture to understand to any degree what is going on within a very different one.

The above account conforms closely to the anti-behaviouralist programme for social science outlined by Peter Winch in his book *The Idea of a Social Science* (1958), in which he characterises social activity as rule-governed activity, and the task of the social scientist as being to recover the meaning and normative force of rules for the agents involved (cf. Winch, 1964). Such a programme corresponds closely to the analysis I have provided of legitimate power as power that provides grounds for obedience on the part of those subordinate to it, because of the normative force that derives from rules, from justificatory principles, and from actions expressing consent. However, if we were to stop there, with the consequences of legitimacy for behaviour, we should only have completed part of our explanatory task. We also need to explain where legitimacy originates, how the principles and beliefs that comprise it are maintained and reproduced, why consent is continually renewed, and what social forces are responsible for the erosion of legitimacy whenever such erosion takes place. In other words, we need an explanation not only for the behaviour that is affected by legitimacy, but also for legitimacy itself. And to accomplish this we need a level of understanding that is not limited to that of the agents themselves, however much that has to be our starting point. When it comes to the explanation of legitimacy itself, we need a level of understanding that goes beyond that of the agents involved, and therefore transcends the limits of a Winchian programme for social science (cf. MacIntyre, 1970).

One way of approaching this explanatory task is a historical one: to explore the origins of legitimacy in the origins of the particular system of power in which we are interested. Such an approach can only offer very limited returns, however. One reason is that the origins of power relations tend to be so complex that they are difficult to unravel; this is especially true of systems of property or gender relations, stretching into the distant past without any single moment of institution. Even if we consider the political sphere and argue that constitutional rules which are collectively agreed in a founding convention must carry much greater legitimacy than those that are forcibly imposed from above by conquest or coup d'état, this is not decisive for the legitimacy of a political system for all subsequent time; and the less is it so, the longer the time that has elapsed since the moment of institution. Rules of power that are imposed may over time achieve acceptance (compare the history of the two Germanies since the end of the second world war); those instituted by agreement may break down (see the constitutions adopted at independence by the ex-colonial states during the 1950s and 1960s). It is history as a process of evolution rather than as a determinate starting point that is usually important for explaining legitimacy.

To underline this point, let us make the entirely imaginary and fanciful supposition that all social rules – about property, the division of labour, political authority – originated in a deliberate agreement at some historical moment in the past. It could readily be shown that such rules would quickly develop into something quite different from that intended, by well known processes of inequality-formation and power-accretion. Property rules specifying an equal distribution of land between families produce inequality over time, through differences of family size, of health or strength, of soil fertility, and so on, to the point where the only survival strategy for some is to hire out their labour to others. Rules defining a non-hierarchical division of labour between the sexes can readily produce a situation where males come to control a resource that is necessary for subsistence or security, and develop differential capacities and attitudes that have consequences beyond those necessary to the original division of labour. Rules specifying the minimum necessary coordinating and decisional powers for a political authority provide the opportunity for acquiring and accumulating powers unanticipated in the original agreement. None of this requires the assumption of an innate striving for power in human nature; it can be sufficiently explained by the respective strategies of groups differently situated, acting under the pressure of changing circumstances. Where the extremity of force and usurpation tends to moderate over time as power becomes routinised and reproduced within a rule-governed order, so original rules instituted by collective agreement, *if unattended to*, provide the basis for the development of power relationships that are quite unintended. Over time, therefore, an original difference between usurpation and agreement tends to become blurred.

Much more important for the explanation of legitimacy, therefore, than the study of origins, is the study of power relations and their legitimation as an ongoing process, whether in the present or in some historical society with which the social scientist is concerned. To say that the study of origins is less important, however, is not to say that *stories* about origins may not have a crucial part to play in legitimation (Hobsbawm and Ranger, 1983). Consider this famous denunciation by Marx of political economists' accounts of the origins of capitalist class relations:

> 'In times long gone by there were two sorts of people: one, the diligent, intelligent, and above all, frugal élite; the other, lazy rascals, spending their substance, and more, in riotous living . . . Thus it came to pass that the former sort accumulated wealth, and the latter sort had at last nothing to sell except their own skins. And from this original sin dates the poverty of the great majority that, despite all its labour, has up to now nothing to sell but itself, and the wealth of the few that increases constantly although they have long ceased to work. Such insipid childishness is every day preached to us in the defence of property . . . In actual history it is notorious that conquest, enslavement, robbery, murder, briefly force, play the great part. As a matter of fact, the methods of primitive accumulation are anything but idyllic.' (1966, vol.1, pp.667–8)

Whatever combination of force, fortune and effort may actually have contributed to the early development of capitalist class relations, it is certain that stories about such origins are important; and therefore who tells them, or who controls their telling, is of great consequence. This is why the content of history syllabi is so contentious. But historical accounts are significant and contentious precisely because of their relationship to the legitimacy of power *in the present*, and because of their contribution to disputes about it.

Once more, then, we come back to power relations as an ongoing process, and to the central question of how legitimacy is maintained and reproduced within given societies, not how it may have 'originated', if it can ever be said to have done so.

Now the important point to stress about the maintenance and reproduction of legitimacy – the maintenance of rules, the reproduction of beliefs, the continued expression of consent – is that these do not take place independently of the structures of power that they legitimate. There is simply no regular process of belief-formation or consent-giving within historically placed societies that exists independently of their power structures, or that can therefore remain uninfluenced by them, though the degree of this influence, or self-closure, will vary between societies and between different power structures within them. It is because it does not recognise any causal influence at all between power and the process of its legitimation that the so-called 'consensus' model of society falls down, not because it cannot offer any account of power or social conflict in the first place. It is premised on the unsociological assumption that 'consensus' is somehow established and maintained by processes that are completely independent of the existing relations of power within the society. Power exists in one corner, as it were, and legitimacy is conferred, and legitimating ideas developed, in quite another (cf. Giddens, 1968).

By what means, then, do ongoing power structures themselves influence their own legitimacy, or condition their own processes of legitimation? Two quite different accounts of this can be given. The first account concentrates on the *activity of the powerful* in influencing the beliefs of the subordinate, through their preferential access to the means of cultural development and the dissemination of ideas within society. In other words, among the powers any dominant group possesses will be the ability to influence the beliefs of others; and among the most important of such beliefs will be those that relate to the justification of their own power. The origin of such beliefs may be found in the first instance in the need of the powerful for self-justification; but their privileged access to the means of culture and ideological dissemination ensures that their ideas become widespread throughout society, whether as the result of conscious policy or not (Marx and Engels, 1970, pt.1).

The above account is of course the familiar Marxist theory of ideology, which Marxists employ in the context of class relations, but other theorists have also used it in relation to political power and gender. Thus the élite theory of Mosca, Pareto and their followers within political science put considerable emphasis on the 'political formulae' or 'myths' through which political élites justify their rule to the non-élite, and which serve to consolidate their power the more deeply they penetrate the consciousness of the masses (Mosca, 1939, ch.3; Pareto, 1966, pt.1). An important strand of feminist theory, also, argues in relation to gender that the most basic elements in culture, including language itself, are male-constructed, and that it is through their influence that women come to accept a definition of themselves that is supportive of male power and the sexual division of labour on which it is based (e.g. Spender, 1980). In their different spheres these theories embrace the same explanation for legitimacy, and identify the same self-confirming feature of power, that is contained in the Marxist concept of ideology: dominant groups are able to secure their own legitimacy through their influence or control over the processes whereby the beliefs of the subordinate are shaped and reproduced.

Now it must be said that this account of how legitimacy is reproduced is inadequate. In the first place, any explanation for the beliefs held by subordinate groups which confines itself to the processes of influence controlled by the powerful is open to a number of objections. Not only do the powerful not influence, let alone control, all the means of disseminating and reproducing ideas in any society; but even if they did, this could not of itself guarantee the acceptance of their ideas or justifications by others. If we consider the twentieth-century examples of regimes that have come nearest to a total control over the means of information and ideological dissemination within their societies, we do not find that this degree of control necessarily ensures the acceptance of the messages that are disseminated. Indeed just the opposite can occur: such regimes can be debilitated by a general scepticism of official sources of information, which can render them ineffective when they are needed most.

There are a number of related reasons for this effect. One is that the processes of developing and disseminating ideas and information require an independence from the powerful to secure their authenticity. They have their own internal criteria or standards necessary to effective practice, which can best be guaranteed by a degree of autonomy from other social powers; otherwise they are liable to degenerate. Secondly, as much con-

temporary research indicates, people are never merely the passive recipients of ideas or messages to which they are exposed
(e.g. McQuail, 1984). They are more like a sieve than a sponge.
That is to say, they tend to be selective, assessing ideas and
information in the light of their existing assumptions, and against
their lived experience. A third reason, underlying the other two,
is that the power of ideas, unlike other forms of power, cannot
be measured in terms of the *means* of power available to those
who control their dissemination, but rather in terms of their
credibility to the recipient. Any explanation for the ideas or
beliefs that people hold, therefore, must be based upon an
internal analysis of their plausibility or credibility to them in the
context in which they are situated, rather than simply on an
account of the means of their dissemination. If all the power of
the medium cannot ensure the credibility of the message, we
need to understand what makes some messages more credible
than others.

It is at this point that a different kind of explanatory account
becomes necessary, of the sort that I have advanced in the course
of the previous chapters. This is one which shows how a system
of power relations itself indirectly shapes the experiences, the
capacities, the expectations, the interests of subordinate groups,
through a variety of social processes, so that justifications for the
rules of power become credible because they are confirmed by
their own experience. Take, for example, the evidence of differential capacities that justifies assigning individuals to different
positions within a hierarchical division of labour or power structure. Such differences are themselves in part the product of
expectations about future roles that people will occupy, and
are thus constructed indirectly by the power rules, though the
immediate agents of their formation may be found among the
subordinate themselves (mothers, working-class parents, peer
groups and so on).

Or consider the evidence which confirms the claim that the
power of dominant groups serves a general interest, including
the interests of the subordinate. This evidence is provided by
the fact that their interests, for economic sufficiency or physical
security, cannot indeed be satisfied outside the given power
relationship, where necessary resources or capacities are controlled by the powerful. It is also provided by the fact that the

system of power serves to shape some of the desires that it is organised to satisfy, as a gendered division of labour both shapes and satisfies the respective desires of women and men with regard to the private and public spheres, or to caring and non-caring roles; or as the late capitalist system of production generates many of the consumer wants that it proceeds to satisfy, or more generally, defines the satisfaction of consumer wants as the most fundamental need.

In all these different ways the justifications advanced for a given system of power are vindicated by effects generated by the power system itself, but which are not understood as its effects, because they appear autonomous or independent of it. As Marx himself understood well, though not all later Marxists have followed him, or worked out the implications for other dimensions such as gender, it is the appearance of the socially constructed as *natural* that lies at the heart of all ideology. What is socially constructed is not itself imaginary or illusory, and its evidence gives credibility to the justifications advanced for a given system of power. Yet the fact that it is constructed indirectly by that same system of power is obscured by the complexity of the processes involved; and by the fact that these processes, such as those of socialisation, are not necessarily managed by the powerful, but often by the subordinate themselves. It is, for example, within women's historically limited sphere of power, over children in the home, that the differentiation of gender has been primarily reproduced. Both the sphere of power itself, and the evident facts of its limitation, are of course necessary to this process.

One reason, then, why a simple dominant ideology theory cannot provide an adequate explanation for legitimacy is that, on its own, an account of the beliefs of subordinate groups as the product of direct influence by the powerful cannot explain their credibility to them in the context in which they are situated. For that we need a different, albeit complementary account, in terms of the social effects *produced indirectly by the system of power*, which provide evidence necessary for its justification. A further important reason is that power relations maintain and reproduce their legitimacy through their effects on people's actions in expressing consent, not only on the beliefs that are relevant to their justification. Here we can observe a tendency among some neo-Marxists and others who adopt a 'dominant ideology' approach simply to reproduce the Weberian definition of legitimacy as the belief in legitimacy, because it fits so well with their own presuppositions. This Marxisation of Weber, if it can be so termed, by adding the assumption that the powerful directly shape the beliefs of the subordinate to the Weberian definition of legitimacy as belief, produces an appealing, though doubly erroneous, combination.

With regard to consent, it will be sufficient here to recall the account given in the previous chapter of the way in which rules or structures of power themselves set the context and define the terms under which consent to a position of subordination is given, so that the decision to give consent is in practice a highly constrained one. Again, because the constraint is not the result of personal intervention by the powerful, but the impersonal consequence of the rules or structures, it appears as naturally given or determined, and the consent to which it gives rise as therefore entirely voluntary. And because it seems entirely voluntary, it helps to legitimate the rules that condition it in the first place.

Altogether, then, we see a number of processes at work whereby an established structure of power helps maintain and reproduce its own legitimacy, though this self-confirming circle operates in different ways in different types of power relation, and is more closed in some than in others. Alongside the influence of the dominant over the ideas of the subordinate, which cannot be denied, though it is often exaggerated and on its own as an explanation becomes erroneous, there are the indirect effects that a system of power produces: to confirm the differentiation between dominant and subordinate which justifies their respective positions; to structure the common interest so that it can only be met through satisfying the purposes of the powerful; to help shape the desires of the subordinate in directions that the system is capable of meeting; to limit the choices available so that consent to a position of subordination, although constrained, is also at the same time voluntary. Together these processes, relevant to the different dimensions of legitimacy that I have distinguished, serve to maintain and reproduce the legitimacy of an established system of power.

If, therefore, there are these processes at work, confirming the legitimacy of established power relations, how does it come to be eroded? I can offer no more than the merest outline here, since the subject will be taken up in the second part of the book. In the light of the account of legitimacy I have given, we could distinguish two different kinds of erosion. One is when a system of power becomes chronically unable to meet the interests of the subordinate, whether those that it defines itself, or those that the subordinate have come to define independently. This may happen through the impact of external forces, or through blockages that are generated internally within the system of power at a particular stage of its development. A second type of erosion takes place when the system cannot satisfy some basic principle of differentiation or source of authority on which it rests; or else the beliefs that underpin its principle of differentiation or source of authority themselves decay. The latter will happen when social changes taking place within the society, or the evidence available from other societies, reveals that what had previously been assumed to be a 'natural' form of social organisation, or one based upon 'natural' differences, is in fact socially constructed. Finally, both types of legitimacy erosion can occur together, and often do so.

When such an erosion takes place it necessarily has consequences for the attitudes and behaviour of the subordinate. Through their everyday experience as subordinate they are already involved in the negative aspects of power relations – the difference of fates, the transfer of resources and opportunities, the limitations of freedom – though these may have become obscured and redefined by the process of legitimation. Once shorn of their justification, however, these negative aspects are starkly exposed, and experienced for what they are.

On its own this 'negative' awareness may produce a condition of frustration, impotence or resignation on the part of the subordinate, and a general unwillingness in fulfilling the requirements of their position. For it to have a transforming potential, however, something else is needed: the possibility of communication with others and an autonomous space relatively protected from the influence of the powerful within which to do so; and the imagination to conceive of a different set of rules and relations for the fulfilment of basic social needs from the existing ones. In other words, the subordinate have to acquire an institutional facility (formal or informal means of communication, movement, organisation) that is independent of, and a level of consciousness or conceptual position that transcends, the established power relations, if they are to develop the impetus to transform them. What we are talking of is the possibility of a legitimacy, not that is entirely *a*social or *a*historical, but that is constructed independently of existing relations of power. And when such a transformatory consciousness impels the subordinate to action, to the active withdrawal of consent, to the *delegitimation* of power in the sense I have defined it, then the authority system enters a period of crisis, which may be resolved by reform, repression or revolution according to the circumstances and the relative balance of forces.

Let me draw this stage of the enquiry to a conclusion, and pose a final question to be answered. I have said that the purpose of social science is primarily an explanatory one. With regard to the subject of legitimacy I have distinguished two different levels of explanation. The first is the explanation of behaviour within power relations; and I have shown how legitimacy affects this according to its form and degree, its presence or absence, across the different dimensions that I have identified. The second level is the explanation of legitimacy itself; and I have shown how it is maintained and reproduced within established systems of power, and what are the typical conditions for its erosion and/or transformation. These two levels of explanatory question clearly differ from one another, and it is important not to confuse them.

There is a third level of explanatory question that I wish now to confront, of a more epistemological kind: how is the social scientist able to answer these two different kinds of question about legitimacy? What are the conditions necessary for answering them? Whereas answering the first question requires adopting a position internal to the given society or power relationship, so as to make intelligible the norms, conventions and legitimating principles that govern it, and to reconstruct the reasoning of the agents involved; answering the second question necessarily requires adopting a position *outside* it. It is only from a standpoint outside given power relations that it is possible to understand the processes whereby their legitimacy is maintained and reproduced, and what are the forces at work eroding it, where such erosion is taking place.

Is not this standpoint precisely the same as that I have just described subordinate groups adopting, who aspire to an alternative legitimacy, unconstrained by existing power relations, in a situation where the latter have entered a condition of crisis? Is there not a congruence, therefore, between the explanatory purpose of the social scientist and the emancipatory purpose of alternative movements of the subordinate, not in the sense that the social scientist must share the particular ideals of the latter, but that their epistemological position is the same? Do not they both have to be able to conceive of a legitimacy that is unconstrained by established power relations, the one in order to explain the normal processes at work reproducing legitimacy, the other in order to be able to transcend and transform them? Is the social scientist thereby committed, not by individual political choice or ideological predisposition, but by the very conditions necessary for knowledge, to share the standpoint and therefore the emancipatory concerns of the subordinate? Moreover, is this standpoint not also that of the normative philosopher, who imagines (and invites us to imagine) a discussion between equals in a pre-social 'state of nature', in an 'ideal speech situation', or behind a 'veil of ignorance' about our position in any given power structure, because in such a situation alone is it possible to establish philosophically valid principles of legitimacy, or arrive at an agreement about power rules that is truly voluntary because it is unconstrained by them? Have I not begun this work by defining the projects of the social scientist and the normative philosopher as fundamentally different, only to discover that they are, if not precisely the same, then at least congruent or complementary, because their epistemological stance has to be identical?

These are large and fundamental questions, and the reader must wait till the end of the book for a fully considered answer to them. There is, however, one social scientific standpoint that produces the answer 'no' to all these questions, and which I must address here because doing so leads to a conclusion that is necessary for the second stage of my enquiry. This is the standpoint of the knowledgeable sceptic, who, from a position above all power relations, sees how they reproduce the conditions for their own legitimation, and concludes that the subordinate can never break out of this self-confirming cycle of power: either because power structures will always consolidate themselves in ways that escape their control, and will always succeed in justifying themselves through mystificatory processes; or because the conditions of discourse can never be equal, and those who construct or control its terms will always be able to legitimate their position, or conceal that it is a position of power at all. From such a standpoint the activity of an emancipatory movement must be judged Utopian and the project of the normative philosopher as fanciful. They may help to bring about social or political change, to be sure, but not change that is progressive; either because such change in power structures is an empirical impossibility, or because there is no standpoint from which any change could conceivably be judged as progressive at all. For the social scientist to share the standpoint of the emancipatory movement or the normative philosopher, therefore, would be merely to indulge in illusion.

Such a position may sound an extreme one, though it is in effect presupposed by the practice of a 'value-free' social science, which defines its task as being to explore the differences, say, between the legitimating principles of different societies or political systems, but never to make a judgement between them. I want to show that this position is mistaken, and mistaken in a way that has crucial implications for the explanatory task of the social scientist. It is mistaken because the different legitimating principles from different historical societies I exemplified in Chapter 3 are not simply different from one another, but *qualitatively* different, and in a particularly significant way. They differ in the extent to which they in principle encourage or discourage the self-confirming processes analysed whereby power rules maintain the conditions for their own legitimacy by reproducing differential attitudes, characteristics and expectations that confirm existing arrangements of power, and by constructing the circumstances from which consent to a position of subordination is given. In other words, some legitimating principles have to be judged as, not just different from, but more emancipatory than, others.

Of the legitimating principles I have mentioned two possess this qualitative difference. One is the meritocratic principle of differentiation, specifying that positions and means of power should be open to all to acquire, on the basis of an equality of opportunity to attain them. However limited the operation of the principle may be in practice by the social advantages transmitted through the institution of the family, it postulates the ideal that people's qualities, attributes, capacities and opportunities should precisely not be defined or limited in advance because of some determinate role they are bound or expected by birth to occupy. It therefore challenges the mechanisms whereby established rules of power reproduce the differences that serve to justify them; and it provides the means for eroding the processes by which the socially constructed appears as 'natural', because it embodies the recognition of the distinction between the two (natural and socially determined differences) as its central assumption.

The second principle that has the qualitative difference I have mentioned is the principle of popular sovereignty, which locates the ultimate source of authority for political power, and therefore for all power rules, in the people. This principle – again despite all the limitations, qualifications and distortions to which it is in practice subject – postulates an ideal in which all power rules are open to revision by public debate and decision between equal citizens. The institution of the democratic legislative assembly of all citizens is the closest approximation possible in historical practice to the 'ideal speech' situation or pre-social 'state of nature' envisaged by political philosophy, since it embodies the requirement that consent to power rules be given directly at the point of their institution or revision, and from a position of equality, rather than indirectly by consent to a particular power relationship from a condition of inequality. As a principle, therefore, the idea of popular sovereignty embodies within itself the potential for breaking the self-confirming cycle whereby consent to the rules of power is conditioned by circumstances created by the rules themselves, and definitions of the general interest are structured by the interests of the powerful.

Together, then, the principle of equal opportunity to acquire positions or means of power, combined with the equal right to take part in determining the rules that define what the necessary positions and inequalities in the general interest should be, and what should be the limits of power associated with them – these two principles allow the possibility of a legitimacy that is not constructed or reproduced by the established rules of power, through their conditioning effects on the beliefs and consent necessary for legitimation. They could therefore be termed 'transparent' or 'authentic' principles, in that they do not depend for their acceptability upon social processes appearing other than they are: the socially constructed appearing as 'natural'; consensus appearing as spontaneous and consent as voluntary, when both are conditioned by the rules of power.

This 'transparence' or 'authenticity' of the principles mentioned explains two further characteristics about them. The first is that they can act as critical, and not only as apologetic or 'legitimating' principles; that is to say, however inadequately they are realised in practice, they embody within themselves the capacity to generate criticism of these inadequacies. The second characteristic that is explained by their 'transparence', as I have called it, is their irreversibility: once we have attained a form of legitimacy that is not conditioned by power rules, it is inconceivable that we could regress to one that was.

Have I now abandoned my social scientist's concern with explanation for the normative philosopher's interest in an ideal legitimacy? If so, it is only because, unless we do so, certain important features of the contemporary world cannot be adequately *explained*: for example, why ascriptive or non-democratic principles of legitimacy cannot be indefinitely sustained in a world where they are exposed to meritocratic or democratic ones; and why, when the legitimacy of democratic political systems is eroded, it is for very different reasons and with very different consequences than those based on traditional, theocratic or 'scientific' principles of authority, which are vulnerable to an erosion of the central belief system on which they are based, as a source of ultimate authority for power rules, in a way that democratic political systems are not. To work out the implications of this difference will be part of my purpose in the second half of the book.

PART II
LEGITIMACY IN THE CONTEMPORARY STATE

5 Dimensions of State Legitimacy

In view of the argument advanced in the first part of the book about how rules of power come to be socially reproduced in a way that reinforces their legitimacy, it is remarkable how comparatively insecure is the legitimacy of many states in the contemporary world. Legitimacy, it seems, is as much the exception as the rule for contemporary states. Many are subject to military dictatorship, originating in a breach of the constitutional rules whose lawlessness is extended into the subsequent practice of government. In others the political order finds only weak support in popular beliefs and values, or there is widespread disagreement about fundamental aspects of it. In yet others there is only limited legitimation through consent. Those who live in countries whose political legitimacy is secure are likely to take it for granted. On a global scale, however, what is striking is the difficulty that contemporary states experience in achieving such a legitimacy, and their rulers in governing in a manner that maintains it.

Why should this be so? Why should political legitimacy be so difficult to attain in the contemporary world? This is the central question which I shall address and seek to answer in the chapters that follow. As I shall show, the answer is to be found at a number of different levels: in the distinctive character and dilemma of the modern state as a mode of concentrating and organising power; in the impact upon it of a variety of external forces which it is unable to control; finally, in the impossibility of reversing the principle of popular sovereignty as the ultimate source of political authority in the modern world, while at the same time the institutional forms for giving effect to it prove so problematic and difficult to sustain.

117

The interrelationship between these different levels provides a thematic continuity underlying the diversity and detail of the following chapters.

This fifth chapter explores the distinctiveness of the state in comparison with the other power-structures considered in the first half of the book; it identifies the main criteria that have to be met if the contemporary state is to achieve legitimacy; and it outlines in a preliminary way some of the key problems that confront it in doing so. In Chapter 6 I examine the different principles of legitimacy embodied in different types of political system and their respective institutions. I argue that each can be seen as offering different solutions to the common legitimation problems already defined, and each as confronting its own distinctive problems of legitimacy in turn. Chapter 7 distinguishes the different ways in which legitimacy breaks down, and the divergent dynamics of revolution and coup d'état respectively. Its conclusion draws together the different strands for an explanation of why such breakdown is so common in the contemporary state.

Before proceeding with this agenda I should reaffirm my view that the contemporary state is a form of power-structure that requires legitimation, not so much to function, or even to survive over a period of time, but to achieve those purposes that depend upon the support of its population, and to maintain its political system intact in the face of serious policy failure or challenge to it. It is superficially attractive to argue that the only thing the state requires from its subjects, their taxes, are mostly collected via non-state intermediaries, and in the course of transactions that have no overtly political significance; and that, provided the loyalty of the administrative and coercive apparatus is secure, the absence of any normative commitment or sense of obligation on the part of the wider population is irrelevant to the effective functioning of the state. Such a view rests on the mistaken assumption that the state apparatus is entirely self-contained, and can be immunised from the attitudes and actions of the surrounding population, an assumption that will not withstand examination in the light of the political history of the last two decades.

What such a history demonstrates is that the subjection of regimes weak in legitimacy to stress – the failure of some policy they have defined as important, the imposition of some special hardship upon the population, the experience of national humiliation, the death or disability of the ruler, which in more legitimate systems would be resolved by a routine change of government or its personnel – develops into a crisis of the regime itself. This happens because of the low tolerance level of the population, and because manifestations of public opposition to a particular policy rapidly develop into opposition to the system of government as such, and to its authority. Such opposition, whether by key elites or popular masses, is typically replicated in divisions within the military and administrative apparatus itself, and causes serious dislocation in its capacity to rule. The spectacular collapse witnessed over the past two decades of regimes whose control over a powerful military and administrative apparatus looked secure – in Greece (1974), Portugal (1974), Spain (1976), Iran (1979), Argentina (1982), the Philippines (1986) – demonstrates the importance of legitimacy to the effectiveness and continuity of a system of rule. However much the institutions of the state may appear to be independent and self-contained, therefore, their operation, as with all systems of power, involves an interactive process between the dominant and the subordinate, in which the responses of the latter exert their own effects upon the character and effectiveness of rule.

All the examples mentioned above were varieties of personal dictatorship, in which the failure to establish an accepted constitutional basis for rule left open the possibility of a humiliating collapse in the capacity to govern as its eventual termination. A parallel fate overtook the communist regimes of Eastern Europe in 1989, which had only been secured against an autonomous evolution towards a different political order by Soviet intervention or the threat of it, as in Hungary (1956), Czechoslovakia (1968) and Poland (1981). The removal of this threat exposed the regimes to the full consequences of their own lack of legitimacy, and to their ultimate disintegration in the revolutions of 1989.

In other kinds of political system, a weakness of legitimacy will tend to produce a different kind of outcome. In a parliamentary or presidential democracy, the commitment to the rules of electoral competition may be too weak to withstand the loss of office where the stakes are high, and result in a coup d'état.

either on behalf of the losers, or to resolve the resulting social conflict and disorder. In some cases a coup may be preemptive, to prevent an expected loss of power. Examples from recent history are too numerous to list, including most countries in Latin America, many in Africa and Asia, and some in Europe (Greece, 1967, Turkey, 1980). In all types of political system, finally, where there exists basic disagreement about which state a given population or section of it should belong to, or about the nature of the regime type itself, the prospect of civil war looms as a possible outcome, as currently in Ethiopia, Sudan, Angola, Sri Lanka, Northern Ireland, and elsewhere.

The collapse of government, coup d'état, invasion, civil war – these are some of the characteristic outcomes, probable rather than inevitable, of the dynamic processes of interaction between governments and their subjects where legitimacy is in some respect weak or absent. Such outcomes can hardly be judged insignificant for anyone involved, governments and subjects alike. However, we should avoid drawing the conclusion, as some political scientists have done, that because these outcomes are not only significant but usually also unpleasant, involving a threat to human life, that stability must therefore be the supreme virtue of political systems. A period of social conflict and political upheaval may be a necessary, if costly, price to be paid for the transition to a more just or more progressive political order. Although we are likely to disagree about such judgements, we can at least agree that the outcomes described above are significant ones; and it is because of its relation to them that legitimacy is so central an issue for political science.

Any adequate explanation for the erosion of legitimacy in particular countries requires an analysis of the specific dynamic of different political systems, of their respective principles and modes of legitimation, and of their distinctive crisis tendencies. As a preliminary to this comparative study of political systems in Chapter 6, I shall explore here the main legitimation problems confronting the contemporary state as such, and shall do so in terms of the threefold criteria of legitimacy already established: those of legal validity, rule justifiability and expressed consent. An examination of each of these criteria in turn will serve to define where the recurrent legitimation problems of the contemporary state in general are to be found.

The elusiveness of legality

If the first condition of legitimacy is that power should be acquired and exercised according to established rules, then our starting point must be to explain why breaches of the constitutional rules by those who wield state power, or aspire to do so, occur so comparatively frequently, and so often with impunity. Most serious of these breaches are those involving the acquisition of power, since they must call into question the legal validity of a government in all it does. By comparison, infringements of the law in the exercise of power only affect one aspect of a government's performance, not its whole basis. Even these, however, if sufficiently serious or chronic, will erode its legitimacy to the extent that they are publicly known.

Why, then, is it so difficult to ensure that legality is respected in the acquisition and exercise of state power? Any complete explanation will have to explore the diverse circumstances under which constitutional rules come to lack sufficient authority, and the various pressures which lead power-holders or power-seekers to break them. In this section, however, I shall confine the discussion to identifying those problems that derive from the nature of the state itself, and its unique legal position, since these constitute the most immediate source of difficulty.

According to conventional definition, the state comprises those specialised institutions that exercise a monopoly of law-making and adjudication over a given territory, and of the organised physical coercion necessary to enforce it. The state is the supreme law-making and enforcing agency for society. Even this minimalist definition suggests certain legitimation problems that distinguish the political from the other dimensions of power. To begin with, the state is responsible for determining the rules which govern all other power relations in society, and for legitimating these relations by according them legal validity. Whatever the limits in practice to this power, its possession makes the state the site of intense struggle to control it, or to influence those who do. The struggle is all the more intense in that, unlike all other power relations, which are dispersed throughout society in families, units of production, etc., the rule-making power of the state is typically concentrated in a central set of institutions, and attempts to influence or control it are focused on a single point.

On the one hand, then, the state's responsibility for determining and legitimising the rules governing the other power relations in society makes it the site of intense struggle. On the other hand there is no law-making power higher than the state, to which it is subject, and whose authority can validate and guarantee its own rules of power. This is the essence of what is termed sovereignty: that the state determines its own rules, as well as those of all other powers within its territory. In the legal sense it is self-validating. Sovereignty thus represents at once a condition of power and of vulnerability: of power, because the state is independent of any higher authority in the legal control over its own domain; of vulnerability, because there is no superior legal authority to which it can appeal to confirm its own legitimacy, and to enforce its own rules in face of an intense struggle within society to gain control of and exercise that sovereign power.

The above statement about there being no higher authority than the state needs qualifying in two ways. First, the state is part of a system of states, whose mutual recognition of sovereignty confirms the right of each to exercise a monopoly of law-making power within its own territory. Such recognition by the international system of states may be particularly important to a new regime, especially one which is facing internal opposition. Recognition by an established authority itself confers authority. However, such recognition specifically does not involve the legal validation of any particular political arrangements or regime type, since this would constitute an infringement of sovereignty. In so far as there is a recognised body of international law, this is concerned primarily to regulate the relations between states, rather than the conditions within them; and it suffers from the well-known limitation that it possesses no effective means of enforcement. At most, therefore, the international 'system' confirms the legitimacy of each state's sovereignty over its own territory; in doing so, it explicitly acknowledges that there is no higher rule-making authority from which the validity of the state's own rules of power can be derived (Tilly, 1975; Poggi, 1978).

My second qualification is that sovereignty as the exclusive right to law-making and law-enforcement within a given territory is not to be equated with power *tout court*, or the state's ability to achieve its various purposes. States which are economically or militarily weak, or geopolitically vulnerable, may be subject to all kinds of external interference, whether at the hands of other states, of international agencies, or of other non-state powers. Where such interventions are manifest and extensive they must damage the standing of the regime that is compelled to submit to them, even if the formality of sovereignty is preserved, since they infringe the recognised principle that states should be self-determining in their internal affairs. It is partly to compensate for such weakness that states join mutual-security blocs, or regional schemes of economic cooperation, in which they surrender an element of formal sovereignty in return for the prospect of enhanced power in the international environment (Kolinsky, 1981; Held, 1989, ch.8).

With these qualifications, then, about the meaning and limits of sovereignty, we can return to the fundamental problem it poses alike in all states: if there is no higher rule-making power to validate and enforce the state's own rules, what is there to ensure that in the struggle to acquire and exercise its sovereign power, the rules will be observed? The question takes on a particular urgency in the light of the fact that the means all states employ to enforce the law – the institutions of organised physical coercion – are themselves uniquely placed to break the law with impunity, since there is no superior coercive power to which they are subject. What is there, then, to ensure that the state's own rules will be observed; that constitutional legality and the rule of law, the first requirement of legitimacy, will be respected?

Part, but only part, of any answer involves the internal organisation of the state institutions themselves. The maintenance of constitutional legality depends upon two institutional preconditions. The first is the effective independence of the judiciary from the legislative and executive branches of the state, so that the latter can both be rendered subject to the law. In other words, the absence of any higher legal authority than the state, to which state power is subject, can be remedied by a separation of powers whereby one part of the state is made accountable to another for its respect of the law.

However, such a condition is easier to specify in theory than it is to realise in practice. It depends not only upon a formal institutional independence for the judiciary, but upon the development of an ethos of legal impartiality, which takes no account of the status of the individual concerned, and which is capable of withstanding the pressures and blandishments of the powerful, even, on occasion, at personal risk to the judiciary themselves. It also requires an independent press and other media, to ensure that breaches of the law by state personnel, especially its law-enforcement agencies, are brought to public attention. There is a paradox here, however, in that the ability to conceal illegality from the population at large will prevent any damage to a regime's standing, since what is not publicly known cannot have public consequences. Yet where violations of legality are wide-spread, the cumulative experience of them will have a corrosive effect over the longer term.

The second institutional prerequisite for constitutional legality is the effective subordination of the military to civilian control. Again, this is a condition much easier stated than realised. Two different ways have been developed for realising it. One, charac-teristic of single-party, and especially of communist, regimes, is a thoroughly politicised mode, in which the military are system-atically inculcated with the outlook and values of the regime, and have a special role in the attainment, as well as the defence, of its goals. While this model, with its integration of all state personnel into a cohesive elite through the institution of the party, cannot deliver a sufficient separation of powers to guaran-tee the rule of law for its citizens, it has historically secured the effective subordination of the military to civilian leadership (Perlmutter and Leogrande, 1982).

A second mode is a thoroughly de-politicised one, character-istic of liberal systems, in which the army is trained in values specific to the military profession alone, and is expected to give loyal service to the government of the day, whatever its political complexion and whatever policies it happens to pursue, since 'politics is not the soldier's concern'. This model is fine in theory, but it presupposes that the military, however professionalised, can be completely isolated from the pressures and conflicts of the society around them, and from every inadequacy in the government or the constitutional order which they are supposed to defend. It is precisely here that the model tends to break down in practice (Nordlinger, 1977, pp.12–19).

To recognise this practical limitation is to acknowledge the inadequacy of any purely legal or institutional approach to the 'rule of law'. At the end of the day, however thorough the arrangements made to ensure the defence of a constitutional order, it is only as secure as the degree of support it can command from society at large; and that, as with any system of law, is a matter of its substantive content and justifiability, as much as the formal procedures for its implementation. Here lies the inadequacy of accounts of legitimacy in the tradition of legal positivism, such as Weber's idea of 'rational–legal' authority, which assume that legality is not merely a necessary, but also a sufficient, condition of legitimacy; and that it can therefore be guaranteed by bureaucratic norms of rule conformity alone. On this view, if constitutional rules are infringed, the cause must lie in the inadequate socialisation of the relevant state personnel in procedural norms, or in some defect in the legal procedures themselves.

Such a theory takes no account of the content of the constitutional rules, or of the principles and beliefs that underpin them. Major breaches of a constitutional order in the acquisition or transfer of power only take place because that order is itself a subject of disagreement or dispute, or finds only weak support from society or a significant section of it. Institutional procedures to protect legality may deal with minor challenges, and may postpone the point of breakdown in the event of major ones, but cannot by themselves maintain the integrity of a constitutional system when people have lost confidence in it. For this reason, the Weberian concept of 'rational–legal' authority, or procedural correctness in the creation and application of legal rules, may effectively characterise the distinctive mode and temper of modern officialdom in contrast to traditional types of administration, but it cannot provide us with a sufficient criterion or account of political legitimacy in the modern world. For that we need some understanding of the principles and beliefs that give the rules their justification (Habermas, 1984, pp.261–2).

Indeed, it is precisely because of the characteristic dilemma of political sovereignty – with its discrepancy between the power it confers on the one hand, and the absence of a higher authority to validate and enforce its own rules on the other – that the constitutional order needs a firm anchoring within society: through its justifiability in terms of established beliefs and values, and through the evidence of expressed consent on the part of those subordinate to it. It is the very vulnerability of sovereignty that makes these broader dimensions of legitimacy so crucial for the contemporary state.

In conclusion, then, we can say that the first line of defence for state legitimacy is the set of institutional arrangements and practices designed to protect the 'rule of law' in the access to, and exercise of, state power. Without such arrangements, and the commitment of the relevant personnel to uphold them, there is little likelihood that the first criterion of legitimacy – legal validity – will be met. However, these arrangements, although a necessary, are not in themselves a sufficient, condition of legitimacy. For that, the constitutional rules must also conform to principles acknowledged as valid within the society. What these principles must be, will be the subject of the following section.

Constitutional rules and their justification

It follows from what has been said above that, if, in assessing the legitimacy of a particular government, our first consideration must be its legal validity, the second must be the justifiability of the constitutional order from which its power derives. Discussions of this second dimension in the literature of political science have great difficulty in bridging the gap between the underlying principles, or legitimating criteria, of a constitutional system, on the one hand, and the practical, institutional arrangements for their realisation, which may work more or less well, on the other. It is essential to bridge this gap if the theory of legitimacy is not to remain suspended between a wholly abstract discussion of principles and a pragmatic analysis of institutions, which are never able to make contact with one another. My aim is to show how this can be done.

In Chapter 3 I identified a number of criteria that have to be met if a system of power is to be legitimate. Of these, two are crucial for a constitutional order. First is an *authoritative source* for the supreme power or powers. Constitutional arrangements must conform to established beliefs about the proper source from which power should be derived. In doing so they will necessarily embody procedures or rules that reflect those beliefs, such as the principle of heredity in a traditional monarchy, of popular election in a representative democracy, of clerical prerogative in a theocracy, and so on. The link between institutional arrangements and legitimating criteria here is, simply, that institutions embody accepted principles, and their rules reflect established beliefs, about the rightful source of political authority (or, conversely, fail or cease to do so). In the section devoted to the source of political authority that follows, I shall discuss the institutional consequences of the crucial change from belief in heredity to the principle of popular sovereignty marked by the French revolution; consider what other principles are consistent with it; and trace the relation of popular sovereignty to an idea which is central to political legitimacy in the contemporary world – that state institutions should express a national identity and serve distinctively national purposes.

The idea of a 'national' purpose already suggests the second basic requirement that a constitutional order must meet if it is to be legitimate: it must facilitate rather than hinder the pursuit of a *general interest*, particularly in respect of those purposes that the state is expected to fulfil. Although meeting this general-interest criterion might seem to be a matter for individual governments, on the one hand, or depend upon the social structure, on the other, constitutional arrangements form the crucial intermediary between the two. Thus they may serve to intensify or moderate existing social divisions; they may ease or obstruct the replacement of administrations that have failed in some necessary purpose. And, for whatever reason, persistent failure on the part of governments, or the pursuit of a divisive sectional advantage, will bring discredit upon the constitutional arrangements themselves as incapable of guaranteeing the general interest. In the second section, therefore, I shall consider some of the recurrent problems contemporary governments face in satisfying the basic security and welfare purposes of the state, and examine how constitutional arrangements can resolve or exacerbate problems of failure and social division respectively. I shall argue that constitutional rules which satisfactorily embody an accepted source of authority may be less effective at satisfying a general-interest requirement, and vice-versa; in other words, the two main requirements of legitimacy may in practice conflict with each other.

i) an authoritative source of power

The decisive shift in legitimating ideas that marks the modern world was the erosion of belief in the supreme value of birth and historical succession, in the idea that the qualities appropriate to the exercise of power are conferred by the status of one's family and its pedigree. This belief underpinned the rules of property and position throughout so-called 'traditional' societies, as well as the rules of political office; its erosion had correspondingly wide-ranging consequences, extending from the political to the economic and social spheres. As the collapse of the *ancien régime* in France at the end of the eighteenth century demonstrated, the political and social revolutions were inextricably linked, because power and position in all spheres had been based upon a common set of beliefs about the primacy of birth and lineage.

However, in the political domain the basic ideological shift involved more than an affirmation of the new principles of equality before the law, and the career open to talent (at least, to male talent). If that were all, then the leading political roles in the state could simply have been opened up for competition like any other full-time post, and the most 'qualified' be appointed by an appropriate committee, no doubt on submission of suitable character references. For political legitimacy another shift proved even more crucial: from regarding the state as the personal property of the ruler, to seeing it as belonging to its people, and political authority as deriving therefore from the people, and not from the superior status and pedigree of the ruling family. So the French Declaration of the Rights of Man, after enunciating the principles of civil equality and the protection of natural rights, declared that the 'nation is essentially the source of all sovereignty' (1789 version) and 'sovereignty resides in the people' (1793 version) (Stewart, 1951, pp.114, 457). The universality of the idea today was acknowledged in the United Nations Declaration of Human Rights that 'the will of the people shall be the basis of the authority of government' (Article 21). In the contemporary world it is virtually impossible for a political system to attain legitimacy without some acknowledgement of this principle in the accountability of government to a representative assembly, elected on the basis of universal suffrage. (The special conditions that explain the persistence of purely traditional systems in the Gulf states will be discussed in the following chapter).

At the same time, although the principle of popular sovereignty enjoys such universality in the contemporary world, it does not constitute the only legitimating principle, but in many systems coexists more or less uneasily with other beliefs about the rightful source of authority. In constitutional monarchies the belief in traditionalism and heredity lives on, underpinning a range of powers accorded the monarch, from largely ceremonial ones in countries like Holland, Norway or the UK, to a much more executive role in the states of Jordan or Morocco. In communist states the principle of popular sovereignty is qualified by assumptions deriving from Marxist–Leninist doctrine about the leading role of the working-class party in the historical scheme of social development. Most recently of all, in the Islamic republic of Iran, the principle of popular sovereignty coexists with a theocratic principle of political appointment, and the belief in a divine rather than merely human source of law. In each of these examples the legitimacy of the political system is only as secure as the durability of the respective beliefs that complement or qualify the idea of popular sovereignty among the population at large.

It follows from the above that democratic republics, in which the head of the executive is popularly chosen through electoral competition, and which constitute a pure expression of the principle of popular sovereignty, do not comprise the only legitimate political systems in the contemporary world. It is possible for 'mixed' political systems to exist, in which the legitimacy of government is derived from two different, even competing, sources of authority. How is such a mixture possible in practice without contradiction? What sort of constitutional rules or procedures could embrace such differences without incoherence?

One possibility is that the different principles should be embodied in a separation of powers within the constitution, so that the legislature is popularly elected, while the head of the executive is selected according to different rules. This is the position in those forms of constitutional monarchy where the monarch retains the right to select ministers and approve policy, but is subject to the laws passed by a popularly elected Parliament. Such a division was given classic formulation in the French constitution of 1791, and was a typical arrangement in much of nineteenth-century Europe. It could best be regarded as a transitional form, in which the powers of the monarch come to be progressively curtailed as support for the hereditary principle declines in society at large. In revolutionary France the transition lasted a mere two years, since the conflict between the two principles was too acute to be contained within a single constitution.

A different possibility is that the principle of popular sovereignty should be not so much complemented as qualified by another source of authority. In communist systems of the 'classical' type (if those of the pre-Gorbachev era can be so called) popular sovereignty was heavily qualified by the authority the party derived from Marxist–Leninist doctrine, both as unique representative of working-class interests, and as guardian of the evolutionary path towards the future Communist society. It was this authority that justified the one-party state, and the pre-selection of candidates for popular election. In practice the difference between the two principles of authority tended to be expressed in a divergence between formal and informal rules, whereby the constitutional form of elections and a representative assembly resembled that of a liberal democracy, but with actual power over both residing in the ruling party. This difference of levels explains how the system could become so rapidly transformed in the Gorbachev era through a shift in the balance of its legitimating principles, without initially any radical change in the formal constitution.

According to the 1979 constitution of the Islamic Republic of Iran, to take another example, the principle of popular sovereignty was both complemented by the executive powers accorded Khomeini as vice-regent, and qualified by the power vested in the religious Council of Guardians to approve candidates for the presidency, and to scrutinise laws passed by the majlis, or representative assembly. As one commentator put it, the constitution 'left two concepts of sovereignty standing side by side . . . Iranians were still uncertain whether it was the people or God and the clerics who ruled' (Bakhash, 1986, p.88). In the early years of the republic the conjunction of the two legitimating principles produced a situation of dual power, in which the authority of Khomeini was repeatedly used to undermine that of the first elected President, Bani-Sadr. Upon Khomeini's death, however, and with no one of his standing to fill the position of vice-regent, it seemed possible that the two principles might be more effectively integrated in the position of the President, who must be both approved by the Council of Guardians and elected by popular vote; the precise balance of forces, however, remains confused.

So there are mixed types of constitution in the contemporary world, deriving legitimacy from other principles besides that of popular sovereignty. However, even with mixed types the ultimate authority of the people is recognised in the widespread assumption that the constitution itself requires popular approval, even when, or perhaps particularly when, that approval entails the recognition of other sources of legitimacy for political office than the people themselves. In other words, we should distinguish between the legitimacy of a constitutional order which derives from the fact that its rules conform to established beliefs about the rightful source of authority for political office; and the legitimacy that derives from popular consent expressed at the particularly decisive historical moment of its establishment. The issue of expressed consent will be discussed more fully in the final section of this chapter. It is worth noting here, however, that one consequence of the universality of the principle of popular sovereignty in the contemporary world is that consent has to be popular consent, even when the rules of office rest on a non-democratic source of authority.

If that seems paradoxical, or contradictory, we should consider the argument in favour of the French constitution of 1791, to the effect that, since monarchical sentiment was so widespread among the people, they would never approve of a republican constitution; or likewise the possibility, demonstrated in Iran, that religious beliefs be sufficiently strong among a people to sustain a system of clerical power. Yet in each case it was felt necessary that the people should have demonstrated their consent to the principles of heredity and theocracy respectively.

How was such consent to be demonstrated? Most obviously through the election of a constituent assembly, with or without plebiscitary approval of its conclusions. However, besides the electoral mode of expressing consent, there is also what I shall call the mobilisation mode, whereby popular mobilisation demonstrates effective support for a government or constitutional system. The most impressive form of mobilisation is revolution itself, in which the popular masses demonstrate their readiness for sacrifice to overturn a discredited regime and defend a new order in its place. It is just such actions that confer enormous authority on a successor regime, and to which those in power repeatedly return for confirmation of their legitimacy in face of any challenge to it.

It is evident, then, that the principle of popular sovereignty – the idea that the people are the ultimate source of authority for government – has two different implications for the legitimacy of a constitutional order in the modern world. First, that order has to contain some element of popular representation by electoral process, even if this is complemented or qualified by rules embodying a different source of authority, whether hereditary, theocratic or secular–doctrinal (as the Marxist–Leninist scheme might for shorthand be described). Secondly, even the mixed forms of constitution, and indeed especially those, require evidence of popular approval for their legitimacy, whether through a founding convention, plebiscitary confirmation, or the mass mobilisation and suffering of a revolutionary process.

There is a third element, however, that the principle of popular sovereignty contributes to the legitimacy of a constitutional order, and that is the idea of national autonomy, or national self-determination. Once it is accepted that the source of political authority resides in the people, it becomes important to know who exactly constitutes 'the people'. This has consequences in particular for the spatial organisation of the state. Under the *anciens régimes*, in which the state belonged to its ruling dynasty, its boundaries were whatever happened to have been historically determined by conquest, marriage or dynastic alliance; and it was a matter of supreme indifference whether rulers came from the same linguistic or cultural community as their subjects. Once the state no longer belonged to the ruler, however, but to the people, then the issues of national identity and national autonomy came to assume a wholly new political significance.

The importance of the idea of popular sovereignty in this context was that it gave the cultural, ethnic and historical communities with which people could identify, and around which they could be mobilised, a political salience they had not previously enjoyed. To be sure, the features that gave people a distinctive identity separate from others were historically rooted, and developed by the slow accretions of time. Yet to become aware of that distinctiveness, and to demand that it be recognised and protected in a self-governing state, was something that could happen very rapidly, though only as the principle of popular sovereignty itself gained acceptance. Paradoxically, therefore, because of the historical diversity of peoples, the universalistic idea of popular sovereignty produced a highly particularistic outcome in the form of nationalism, with profound consequences for the spatial reorganisation of states. So at the end of the eighteenth century the process of creating sovereign states independent of colonial rule gathered momentum in the Americas. The nineteenth century witnessed a wholesale reorganisation of state boundaries in Europe, whether by secession or amalgamation, or a combination of the two, culminating in the dismemberment of the Hapsburg and Ottoman empires at the end of the first world war. Finally, in the middle of the twentieth century, the ideals of self-determination and national independence were turned against the European powers by the peoples of the Third World, and undermined whatever legitimacy their imperial rule may have had (see e.g. Breuilly, 1982; Anderson, 1983).

What implications does the ideal of national autonomy have for political legitimacy today, now that state boundaries are more or less frozen by international agreement? Where a national identity is securely established, and most people within a given territory associate themselves with it, it provides the state with a powerful source of support, especially in the face of external threat or interference. Where, on the other hand, a sense of nationhood is only weakly developed, and there is no single ethnic or cultural community within the territory with which people identify, its absence will be revealed in the degree of loyalty the state can command when under pressure. Moreover, if a particular community comes to believe that it is being discriminated against or oppressed by another within the same state, and demands political autonomy for itself, or incorporation in another state, then nationalism, from being a unifying factor, will become the most divisive political force, and a powerful agent for the delegitimation of a system of rule.

The continued evidence of the internally divisive effect of the idea of popular self-determination lies all around us, and hardly needs elaboration. In many of the new states of the Third World the boundaries that were inherited at independence were quite artificial creations, bearing little relation to pre-colonial ethnic or political groupings. In the worst examples (the Somalis or the Kurds) historic nationalities were divided between many different states. In Europe itself the post-colonial era has witnessed the resurgence of older definitions of nationhood on the periphery of many states, as regional economic disparities have intensified, and the advantages of connection with the metropolitan centre have declined. The example of Northern Ireland demonstrates in extreme form the historical legacy left by past imperial conquest and colonial settlement for contemporary state legitimacy. In the USSR – last survivor of the great land empires that disintegrated at the end of the first world war – the upsurge of suppressed nationalisms as the first fruits of 'Glasnost' confirms most strikingly the link between popular sovereignty and the self-determination of peoples, and the threat the latter poses to the integrity of the state.

Now it could be argued that the problems posed by these substate nationalisms involve only the geographical periphery of the state, and do not affect the legitimacy of institutions at the political centre. However, if they are severe enough, or intersect with more general problems, they may readily do so. In Third World states, in particular, managing these conflicts imposes an enormous strain on limited resources, and provides a ready occasion for external interference and destabilisation. For this reason, a new constitutional settlement that redistributes power between the centre and the regions, or involves new power-sharing arrangements, may be the only way to reestablish the legitimacy of the central institutions themselves, and prevent demands for secession from bringing about a general weakening of their authority.

In conclusion, then, the decisive shift in legitimating beliefs definitive of the modern era, which locates the source of political authority in the people rather than in the historical pedigree of the ruling dynasty, has had profound consequences for the territorial organisation of states and for the spatial distribution of power within them, as well as for the rules governing access to political office itself. Above all, it means that the ultimate court of approval for constitutional arrangements rests with the people, and that popular mobilisations of protest, whether against the rules of political office or the spatial distribution of power, carry a potent delegitimating force. However much it may be modified by other principles of authority, and whatever complexities it may assume in different contexts, it is with this basic principle of popular sovereignty that we must begin if we are to understand political legitimacy in the contemporary world.

ii) the satisfaction of a general interest

Besides being derived from a source acknowledged as authoritative within the society, state power has also to satisfy a general-interest criterion. As I argued in Chapter 3, all systems of power require justification in terms of meeting the interests of the subordinate, as well as the dominant, and of fulfilling requirements necessary to the society as a whole. The difference between the traditional and the modern state in this regard is not that the former, being the private preserve of the ruler, had no public functions to serve, but that it fulfilled them largely from private resources, and no clear distinction was made between the public and the private in the finances, the domain or even the person of the ruler. The modern state, by contrast, being based upon a sharp distinction between the public and private spheres and their respective concerns, exists to serve public needs by purely public means; and all aspects of law, policy and finance have therefore to satisfy a public interest criterion, and to be justifiable on these grounds.

Now of course all governments will claim that their actions serve the general interest, and their opponents will claim that they fail to do so. Since there is no incontestable criterion of how the general interest can best be realised, such claims would seem to belong to the rhetoric, rather than the substance, of legitimation. However, we should distinguish between the normal, everyday disagreements over policy, and the settled conviction on the part of a substantial section of the population that a government is seriously compromising the public interest. There are two different ways in which it might do so. The first is through a manifest failure of performance, such as presiding over military defeat or rampant inflation, where the government has clearly failed in some essential purpose that the state exists to fulfil. The second is through manifest particularity, or partiality, such as the abuse of public office for private gain, or the pursuit of policies that advantage one section of society at a cost to the vital interests of another: where government, in other words, is seen to be pursuing a particular or sectional interest at the expense of a general one.

Now all these are the presumed failings of governments in the first instance, rather than of constitutional systems; and most constitutions have some means of removing those officeholders who have lost public confidence, whether through parliamentary vote, popular election or some more arcane process of dismissal. Such dismissals ensure that any loss of prestige is confined to the individuals concerned, and does not damage the constitutional rules themselves; indeed, confidence in them can be enhanced by the promptness or effectiveness of dismissal. However, if government failings are chronic, or the prospect of remedy through constitutional process is uncertain or remote, then the legitimacy of the political system will be eroded also. Moreover, it is characteristic of particular types of constitutional arrangement that they may exacerbate government failings in the first place, or hinder their resolution in the second. For this reason the rules of the political system are involved as well as individual governments, and we must pay attention to the interaction between the two.

In view of the complexity of these issues involved in a 'general interest' criterion, I have divided the following discussion into three parts. The first (section a) considers government performance in respect of the basic ends it exists to serve. The second (b) discusses the question of government partiality or sectionalism, and the distinction between particular and general interests. The third (c) distinguishes between the impact of failure or sectionalism on individual governments and on a political system as a whole, and considers the effect of different constitutional rules in exacerbating or resolving problems of government performance.

a) performance and the ends of government
In a much quoted essay, S.M. Lipset drew a distinction between the 'legitimacy' and the 'effectiveness' of regimes. 'Effectiveness,'

he wrote, 'means actual performance, the extent to which the system satisfies the basic functions of government' (1958, p.86). At one level this distinction is valid, since the two concepts are not coterminous. Yet in practice there is a reciprocal connection between the two. I have already drawn attention to the way in which legitimacy makes a difference to the effectiveness of a system of power, through the quality of performance it secures from those subordinate to it. Equally importantly, the performance of government makes a significant contribution to, and forms a necessary component of, its legitimacy (Rothschild, 1977, p.488). After all, how can the enormous powers of the state be at all justified, or people be obliged to obey it, unless it fulfil requirements necessary to the society and their own well being, and that it fulfil them effectively? Lipset's mistake here is to regard performance as something entirely instrumental, and not also as satisfying normative or moral criteria. And that in turn betrays a conception of morality which confines it to an entitlement ethic, based upon origins, to the exclusion of a utilitarian or consequentialist ethic, based upon ends.

This point can be clarified by reference to the distinction drawn by moral philosophers between the 'right' and the 'good', or to the distinction made by political philosophers between justifications based upon rights and those based upon social welfare or utility. 'Rights-based' arguments are typically backward-looking: they make reference to how entitlements are acquired, from whence they derive, or what people have done to merit them. Arguments from social welfare or public interest are typically forward-looking: they seek to show what contribution a given institution or set of political arrangements makes to social utility. The distinction between the two types of argument can be clearly seen, for example, in justifications for private property, and the rules underpinning it (Reeve, 1986, ch.5; Ryan, 1987, pt.2). Any complete justification, however, needs reference to both types of argument. And the same is true of political legitimacy: it requires both a morally authoritative source for government, and an ability to satisfy the ends which justify its enormous concentration of power. While the logic of each needs to be distinguished, not least because they have different institutional implications, both are equally necessary to legitimacy (Schaar, 1969, pp.287–8).

What ends, then, does the state exist to fulfil? Unless we are anarchists, most of us take it for granted that the justification for the state lies in its provision of physical security and of the conditions necessary to material welfare. Marxists may claim that the state fails to make such provision, or in a way that satisfies the general interest, but this claim presupposes that it *ought* to do so. Neo-liberals may claim that material welfare is a matter for individuals and the market, but even they cannot in practice absolve governments from all responsibility for economic performance. Others may claim different purposes for particular states, such as the promotion of international revolution, the defence of the 'free' world, or the salvation of people's souls; yet these are additional rather than alternative to its security and economic purposes.

The definitive statement of the view that the sovereign state exists to guarantee the physical security of its inhabitants, of their persons and property, is to be found in the work of Thomas Hobbes (see *Leviathan*). According to Hobbes, the state's monopoly of the means of organised physical coercion is necessary to protect individuals against other members of society from within, and collectively against the threat of invasion from without. It is from the recognition of this necessity that people's consent to the state is seen by Hobbes to derive, and their corresponding obligation to obey it, whatever its form, provided only that it continues to guarantee their security. Social order and personal security depend upon a coercive framework; the effective organisation of coercion to this end is the basis of the state's rationale and hence of its legitimacy.

Hobbes's argument is an important one, not least in warning against any oversimple antithesis between coercion and legitimacy. In so far as the state's purpose is to ensure the physical protection of its citizens, then the effective application of coercion to this end cannot necessarily be construed as either illegitimate in itself, or as evidence of a deeper-seated weakness in legitimacy. On the contrary, a persistent failure to guarantee physical security will undermine confidence in the system of government, since it will be seen to be failing in its most essential purpose. It is precisely such a failure that provides one of the most typical justifications for the intervention in politics of the military, as the special guardians of 'order and security'; in so intervening, they would seem to be conforming to a characteristically Hobbesian rationale.

However, if the effective threat or use of physical coercion is a necessary condition for social order and hence for the state's legitimacy, it cannot be a sufficient condition, as Hobbes's theory supposes. One of the prime causes of disorder within any society lies in the absence of agreement about some aspect of its power rules (the rules of property, division of labour, political office, citizenship, or whatever), and in the social conflict to which such disagreement gives rise. Disorder and insecurity are as much the *product* of inadequate legitimacy as they are its cause. To the extent that this is so, any attempt to suppress discontent or disagreement by force, rather than resolve it by political means, may only weaken a state's legitimacy rather than enhance it. Hobbes's theory of legitimacy is wrong in supposing that the effective enforcement of rules is a sufficient ground for obligation regardless of their content. And it follows that his explanation of social order is mistaken in imagining that it can be guaranteed in the absence of agreement about these rules.

The relation between coercion and legitimacy is thus a complex rather than a simple one, at least as regards the state's function in ensuring internal security. Here the use of coercion to suppress deep-seated grievances can erode legitimacy in some contexts as surely as the failure to use it to quell disorder can in others; the state can be both too weak and too overbearing. The issue is more straightforward when it comes to defence against external threat, despite disagreements about how such defence is best secured. Nothing is more damaging to a government's authority than military defeat, or the widespread conviction that the country's defence is being compromised through incompetence or insufficient expenditure. At the same time countries vary enormously in their geo-political position, and in the resources they are capable of devoting to defence without crippling their economies. Although inherent military weakness can be offset by alliance policy and collective security arrangements, these can readily infringe national autonomy where much larger powers are involved. In particular, the global contest between the superpowers that has characterised the decades since the second world war has had a decisive impact on the security of many states, whether through the destabilisation of 'opponents', or the compromising of the autonomy of 'allies'. As a consequence, in many regions of the Third World especially, the attainment of security has been only partially under the control of the supposedly sovereign state.

The diminution of autonomy in face of an uncontrollable international environment that affects a country's physical security applies even more to its economic well-being. Nowadays the expectation that the state should guarantee the conditions for the satisfaction of its citizens' material needs is as universal as the demand for physical security. This expectation was given particularly elevated formulation in the US Declaration of Independence, with its claim that the 'pursuit of happiness' was a universal right that states should uphold (Thorpe, 1909, pp.3–4). A similar demand was expressed in more utilitarian terms in Britain by Jeremy Bentham and James Mill, with their criterion of good government as that which secured 'the greatest happiness of the greatest number' (Mill, 1937; Bentham, 1960). At the time they were made, these demands were not interpreted as meaning that the state should itself provide for people's welfare; rather, it should remove the obstacles to people pursuing it for themselves. The demand was thoroughly *laissez-faire* in inspiration. What was radical about it was the claim that everyone's happiness should be given equal consideration.

However, as the political influence of the masses was extended during the course of the nineteenth century, so the responsibility of the state came to be interpreted in a more interventionist manner: in the first place that it should protect people from the most damaging effects of *laissez-faire* capitalism; then that it should provide directly what the market itself could not; finally, that it should take responsibility for the overall performance of the economy. By the middle of the twentieth century the expectation had become general that the state would secure a progressive improvement in the satisfaction of material needs, and that governments should be judged by their capacity to do so.

Although this presumption can be baldly stated, the actual relationship between economic performance and government legitimacy is a complex one, depending upon the pattern of distribution of economic costs and benefits, as well as on the overall level of performance. It also differs systematically according to the type of politico-economic system or production regime in force. As will be more fully explored in the following chapter, governments in a centrally planned economy can much less readily distance themselves from economic failure than in a market economy, since by definition they are directly responsible for it. However, this is a difference that can be easily overstated, and is less important than differences in economic performance itself.

Here the divergence between developed and developing, industrialised and industrialising economies in their ability to satisfy the material needs of their population is most obvious and glaring. Industrialisation in particular is a process that is everywhere accompanied by enormous inequalities and dislocations, which are rendered particularly acute for the developing countries by the manner of their insertion into the international economy. Although generalisation can be misleading, in view of the variety of developing economies, many have been locked into a perpetuation and extension of their colonial role of producing primary commodities for export, a role which has reduced self-sufficiency in food on one side, and made the economies particularly vulnerable to the price fluctuation of a few commodities on the international market on the other. The rise in the oil price in the 1970s, and the collapse in the price of many other primary commodities, as the Western economies went into recession, proved catastrophic for many developing countries. The typical consequence was acute indebtedness and subjection to conditions imposed by the IMF, which bore most heavily on the impoverished majority of the population (George, 1988; Onimode, 1989).

Now, it is a condition of the present world economy that no country is entirely autonomous in economic policy; the state of each is dependent to a greater or lesser extent on what is happening outside it. However, the degree and character of that dependence is what matters. Developed economies are precisely ones that are sufficiently diversified and self-sustaining to be able to protect their citizens from the most damaging effects of the world market, and to adjust to its changes without undermining the conditions for their further development. So-called 'dependency' is a state in which neither of these is possible. Although blaming external forces can provide a convenient scapegoat for the policy failures of governments, there is no escaping the disadvantage of being late-comers to economic development in a world already well-advanced in that process (Wilber, 1984; Szentes, 1983).

In conclusion, the relative success of the sovereign states of the developed world in meeting the security and welfare needs of the majority of their populations has passed on to the peoples of the developing world the expectation that the sovereign state can and should achieve the same for them. Indeed the claim frequently made at the time of independence from the colonial powers was that sovereignty would of itself guarantee these benefits. 'Seek ye first the political kingdom, and all else will be added unto you,' said Nkrumah. In its simple form such a claim overlooked the long history of struggle, even in the oldest states, both to establish a viable state in the first place, and then to extend its benefits from the few to the many. It also overlooked the systematic dependencies on the international system that serve to perpetuate the disadvantage of the economically and militarily weak. There is a marked discrepancy, we might conclude, between the power the contemporary state possesses to control and coerce those subordinate to it, and its ability to meet the social needs that alone can justify its coercive and intrusive power. It is in just this discrepancy that a recurrent problem of governmental legitimacy resides.

b) particular and general interests

Governments may fail to satisfy a general interest requirement because they are unable to fulfil some basic function of government, whether of public security or economic management. They may also fail because they are perceived as partial in the way they carry out their functions: because they use public office to satisfy merely particular or sectional interests. There are connections between these two aspects of performance, since, for example, the condition of underdevelopment that makes the problems of economic management so intractable is also one in which the competition for scarce resources is most acute, and there is thus increased pressure to use state power to favour certain groups at the expense of others, whether legally or illegally. Partiality and corruption exists in all kinds of political system, at all stages of economic development; but they are more acute or chronic in some situations than others.

From a purely legalistic standpoint, a sharp distinction can be drawn between the use of the law to favour certain groups in the population, and the illegal abuse of office for the personal benefit of the office-holder and his or her connections. The former, being a matter of policy, has to be framed in general categories, and to be subject to open justification and defence in terms of the public interest. The latter, being a matter of private and particularistic advantage, is necessarily secretive, since it cannot withstand public scrutiny, and it threatens the basic division between the public and private spheres that is essential to the modern state. The characterisation of the latter as 'corruption' underlines the moral as well as legal distinction between the two types of action.

From more substantive considerations of the general interest, however, the difference is not so clear-cut. On the one hand a government composed of super-tax payers which votes enormous tax reductions for the rich will hardly avoid the charge of partiality, simply because its beneficiaries comprise a general category of the population, rather than the personal acquaintances of those in office. On the other hand political systems that routinely operate on a patronage basis, for instance by channelling government expenditure to areas of electoral support, may have a public opinion that is more tolerant of illegality than those which operate by more universalistic criteria; and this tolerance may be reflected in a different definition of what counts as 'corruption' in the first place. There are many different ways of rewarding one's own in politics; and the moral distinctions between them are less clear-cut than can be captured by a simple contrast between the legal and the illegal, between clean hands and the finger in the till (J.C. Scott, 1969).

To say this is not to underestimate the discredit into which the law can fall if governments are seen to flout it with impunity, nor to overlook the political impact of particularly sensational scandals, even in societies where a certain level of corruption is routinely tolerated. However, what is decisive for crystallising the impression of a government's partiality is not primarily whether its members act legally or illegally. Nor is it even whether its policies are designed to favour its own, since all governments do that to a greater or lesser degree. What matters is whether, and how far, in doing so, it damages the interests of other definable groups in society; and whether these groups are sufficiently organised and powerful to make a significant protest.

These criteria reflect two simple truths. The first is that unequal treatment is more tolerable where it does not take the form of a zero-sum contest. Thus governments can favour their own with impunity if the cost is funded out of general taxation, and so is spread across the population at large, rather than debited to a particular section of it. But secondly, even where the cost is borne by a particular section of society, it will not be politically significant if the section affected is too isolated or disorganised to make any visible protest. It is where the benefit to one group is manifestly gained at the expense of another, *and* that other group is capable of organised protest, that the impact will be politically divisive, and the government will be convicted of partiality, of serving particular, or as the utilitarians termed it, 'sinister' interests.

The point can be illustrated from the example of corruption. Much corruption – for example, taking bribes on government contracts, or favouring acquaintances in official appointments – has the character of a victimless crime, in which the costs are simply passed on to customers at large, or borne by society as a whole in reduced efficiency. This presumably explains why it is tolerated, where it is so. However, where government constitutes a major source of privileged employment, or controls substantial access to business opportunities through its licensing and contracting powers, then the cost to the excluded rises sharply, and resentment at their exclusion is correspondingly intense. And if the excluded comprise a section of the population identifiable on ethnic, regional or religious grounds, then the government's favouritism is bound to be socially and politically divisive. The excluded will protest loudly at corruption and illegality; but what they are really protesting about is their own exclusion, and that the favouritism takes place at their particular expense (Szeftel, 1983).

What applies to corruption applies equally to public policies, legally formulated and implemented, that advantage one section of the population, where they do so at the manifest expense of another. In racially or ethnically divided societies it is almost impossible to favour one group without damaging the other, especially where this involves the modification of existing inequalities. In class-divided societies it is almost impossible to enhance the powers or welfare of subordinate classes without infringing the rights of property owners. The redistribution of powers by political means – the only means available to the subordinate and disadvantaged – is intrinsically more contentious and conflict-laden than the reproduction of inequalities through the persistence of natural-seeming social rules. The latter process may become conflictual; the former is invariably so. Here an appeal to general criteria of justice or welfare, however necessary in matters of public policy, does not resolve the issue, when competing criteria tend to be selected according to social position in the first place. Nor will an appeal to the majoritarian principle avail either. From the standpoint of the minority, if what they define as their vital interests are threatened, it makes little difference by whose agency, or in the name of whom, they are so.

Just such a consideration inspired J.S. Mill's contention that the majority could itself constitute a particular or 'sinister' interest, and that the general interest would be more effectively realised by taking equal account of majority and minority interests, than through the suppression of one by the other. Behind Mill's special pleading on behalf of the propertied there lay the valid insight that, once contentious issues of redistribution, driven by competing interests and theories of justice, are at the forefront of the political agenda, a recognisably *general* interest can only be attained through compromise between them (Mill, 1964, pp.248–56). Whether such a compromise is in practice attainable depends upon the room for manoeuvre available within the economy, upon the ability and willingness of the respective parties to make concessions, and upon the extent to which the constitutional system itself facilitates or discourages it. This latter point in particular brings us to a consideration of the relation between constitutional rules and the general interest.

c) government performance and political legitimacy
In discussing the relation of government performance to political legitimacy it is important to stress once again that the various failures to satisfy a general interest requirement, whether through inability, incompetence or partiality, are failings in the first instance of governments, not of political systems. Too many of those who write about performance as a legitimating criterion omit to observe this distinction. In doing so they overlook the simple point that most constitutions are designed to allow for the replacement of governments or leaders who have lost public

confidence; and that the process of replacement enables alternative policies to be pursued by a different administration enjoying renewed authority. Such replacement can be seen as a means of ensuring that the discredit associated with failure does not attach to the constitutional rules themselves.

What we must ask, therefore, is under what circumstances the political system itself becomes infected with the odium of governmental failure, or the conviction becomes established that the general interest cannot be secured under the existing constitutional arrangements. One situation is where the procedures for dismissal have ceased to be effective, because either they or the personnel responsible for them are under the control of those who need replacing. In extreme cases a society has to wait for its rulers to die before a change of direction becomes possible, however disastrous the policy failures with which they are associated. Single party systems, in which there is no electoral opportunity or incentive to remove a failed leader, who has all the powers of patronage available to consolidate support, have a marked tendency towards immobilism and gerontocracy. In these contexts it is difficult for the political system itself to avoid the odium of governmental failure; and change, when it eventually comes, has all the character of a major convulsion rather than an orderly transfer of power. The advantage of multi-party systems in this respect is that the regularity of the electoral process gives party hierarchies a powerful incentive to remove leaders once they have forfeited public confidence, so as to minimise the prospects of electoral defeat.

If on one side, then, confidence in constitutional rules can be eroded by the inability to replace those who have failed, on the other it can be undermined by the conviction that a change in government will bring no improvement. This may happen because a particular section of society believes that the damage inflicted on it, or in prospect, is irreversible. Or the electoral rules may make it impossible for a given minority ever to achieve a share of political office, so that it is the system rather than just a particular government that is stacked against them. Or the prospect of one sectional group pursuing its own interests in government, only to be followed by another doing the same, destroys confidence in the political system's ability to deliver impartial government at all.

Here the part played by constitutional rules in exacerbating social conflict and government partiality merits attention. A system of electoral competition between parties may be effective at removing those who have forfeited public confidence, but its corresponding disadvantage is that it readily assumes the character of an all-or-nothing contest between different sections of society. To the victors it affords the chance of supreme power, but for a limited term, and with uncertain prospect of being able to control the external circumstances on which performance so much depends; they have a corresponding incentive to maximise the advantages of power in the short term. To the losers it guarantees powerlessness, and with uncertain prospect of recovery in the future. Unlike the competition for position in other areas of social life, where defeat does not necessarily signify exclusion from power, and there are always opportunities to try again elsewhere, the concentration of political power in a central set of institutions makes defeat in electoral competition particularly conclusive. If the damage consequent upon defeat is perceived by the losers as irretrievable, whether on ethnic, religious, economic or personal grounds, then the pressure not to accept the outcome, or to cheat in the process, becomes enormous.

It is worth recalling the advantages of traditional systems in this particular regard. With executive office at the disposal of the ruling monarch or chief, competition for it was necessarily limited by the ruler's own authority, which was itself, except in rare cases of disputed paternity, beyond the scope of competition. The electoral mode of appointment, in contrast, renders that competition in principle unlimited and unrestrained. This is particularly true of winner-take-all political systems like the British, where first-past-the-post electoral rules are combined with a lack of constitutional restraints upon the executive. It is not surprising that the 'Westminster model' has proved largely unworkable outside the special circumstances of mainland Britain. To say that this is because of the absence of a 'democratic culture' or the insufficient integration of key political actors into a common 'establishment' or political elite, as in Britain, is simply to restate the problem, since these essentially cultural conditions cannot be created overnight. Indeed they are themselves the product of an accumulated history of acceptance of electoral outcomes on the part of the losers. And that requires that not too much should be at stake in any one contest: that the costs to the losers in any competition for office should not be so high as to remove all incentive to abide by the outcome.

The weakness of the Westminster model is that meeting this requirement depends on the self-restraint of the victors, and on tacit conventions that can readily be overridden. The requirement can be more securely met by constitutional rules that minimise the costs of defeat to the losers, e.g., by ensuring them some power or influence so that they are not left completely excluded from the political process by their electoral defeat. Federal systems secure this by providing a local power base in the event of defeat at the centre. Systems with a clear separation of powers between a legislature and elected president may produce an outcome in which no one party controls both. Electoral rules based upon proportional representation are more likely to require compromise between political parties, while more formal power-sharing arrangements may be needed in societies characterised by deep ethnic or cultural division (so-called 'consociational democracy') (Nordlinger, 1972; Lijphart, 1977). All these can be seen as devices that limit the damage of electoral defeat in multi-party systems, and therefore encourage a tradition of accepting electoral outcomes on the part of key political actors.

Alternatively, the cost of defeat may be minimised through a limitation in the scope of electoral choice itself. This happens where elections are restricted to the legislature, rather than the executive, or where the choice is limited to candidates of a single party. Single-party systems, whatever their drawbacks in other respects, are much less politically divisive than multi-party ones, because they typically embrace all the major social forces within them, and because they minimise the scope, and therefore the fatefulness, of electoral competition. The other side of the coin, obviously, besides the tendency to immobilism already mentioned, is the reduction of public accountability. And from the standpoint of government legitimacy, the formal restriction of electoral choice necessarily reduces the force of popular legitimation through expressed consent. This, together with the role of political parties in legitimation, will be discussed more fully in the final section of the chapter.

It remains here, by way of recapitulation, to underline the differences between the legitimating criteria discussed in this section, and to draw out some implications that will be developed in later chapters. Legitimacy as the justifiability of constitutional rules comprises two main elements, so I have argued, reflecting the two normative criteria required to justify state power: it must derive from a source that is acknowledged as authoritative within the society; it must serve ends that are recognised as socially necessary, and interests that are general. Constitutional rules in turn will be legitimate to the extent that they conform to established beliefs about the proper source of authority, and that they facilitate rather than obstruct the attainment of a general interest in respect of those purposes which governments exist to fulfil. Their legitimacy will be deficient to the extent that they fail in either of these respects.

Although this summary may seem highly general and abstract, two very specific conclusions can be drawn from it for the contemporary age, in which popular sovereignty is recognised as the main, though as we have seen not the only, source of authority for government. The first concerns the different points of vulnerability of different types of political system. What I have called 'mixed' systems, in which the principle of popular sovereignty is complemented or qualified by another source of authority, are most vulnerable to an erosion in the beliefs that underpin that other authority, and therefore in support for the constitutional rules that qualify or limit the scope of the electoral process. Liberal democracies, on the other hand, which most fully embody the principle of popular sovereignty in the openness and scope of their electoral process, are most vulnerable to the effects of social division, in whatever form, and to an inability to sustain a recognisably general interest. Military regimes, finally, that typically emerge to 'rectify' the failings of democracy, are simply incapable of establishing a credible source of authority for their power, let alone rules of office that might embody it.

A second conclusion concerns the agencies through whom legitimacy deficits and legitimacy crises are characteristically terminated in the contemporary world, whether by a breach of the constitutional order, or some other mode of resolution. Where the legitimacy deficit or weakness occurs because the constitutional rules do not conform sufficiently to accepted beliefs about the proper source of authority – and that typically means that they do not sufficiently embody the principle of popular sovereignty – the main agent of political transformation is the popular masses as chief 'bearers' of this principle. Where the deficit occurs because of the social divisiveness of parties or politicians, the chief agent of political transformation is the military, as claiming to embody a national interest above the sectionalism of party, and representing the permanent interests of the state beyond the transience and particularism of politicians. In brief, in the contemporary world, deficits involving the basic source of authority generate demonstrations of people power and revolutions; deficits in performance alone and in realising a general interest, without erosion of belief in the source of authority, produce demonstrations of military power and coups d'état.

These, necessarily oversimplified, formulations will be elaborated and, where necessary, qualified in the chapters that follow. It is time now to examine the final aspect of legitimacy relevant to the contemporary state, that of expressed consent.

Modes of popular consent

Previous chapters have shown how the consent of the subordinate makes its own distinctive contribution to the legitimacy of power, through the symbolic and normative force of actions which are conventionally recognised as expressing consent to the powerful, and, by implication, to the rules of power or constitutional system also. As I have argued, such actions *confer* legitimacy on the powerful, both through the public acknowledgement that is made of their position, and through the obligations that derive from that acknowledgement. To have this effect, they must be positive actions taking place in public, since inaction or privacy can have no legitimating force. In relation to the legitimacy that governments derive from their appointment according to justifiable rules, that deriving from consent should be seen as complementary, rather than alternative, to it. That is to say, however secure the processes and procedures of their appointment may be, governments also need the confirmation and consolidation of their legitimacy that derives from the explicit consent of the governed.

As I have also argued, it was a characteristic of 'traditional' societies that consent could be given on behalf of others. In the political sphere those who were entitled to give consent in person – who comprised what one might call the political community – were few in number and invariably belonged to the socially and economically powerful. Their actions indicative of consent (swearing an oath of allegiance, participating in a consultative council, negotiating terms of support, etc.) were taken to include their own subordinates and dependants along with them. This was all changed by the idea of popular sovereignty, which not only altered the rules of political appointment as discussed above, but extended the political community – those who were entitled to participate in politics – to the whole adult population, rather than a privileged section of it. Consent in the contemporary era now has to be popular consent if it is to have any legitimating force.

There is, however, more than one form of political participation through which consent to government can be demonstrated in contemporary political systems. We can distinguish between the electoral mode, and what I have termed the mobilisation mode; each has a different logic and different institutional implications. In the electoral mode the act of voting, through which governments are directly or indirectly appointed, is also the means through which the consent of the governed is demonstrated; elections thus perform two quite distinct functions simultaneously. In the mobilisation mode the two processes are separated, since the mass participation in political activity at the grass roots which demonstrates the continuing popular support for the regime is divorced from the process whereby office holders are appointed. As a consequence, political parties serve very different functions in the two modes: in the one, to prepare leaders and policies for electoral choice and approval; in the other (typically single-party regimes), to mobilise the political activity on which the system's legitimacy depends. Although some political systems combine both modes of consent, in what follows I shall treat the two as distinct types for analytical purposes.

As I have demonstrated in Chapter 3, the electoral mode of consent derives from two ideas that are central to the individualism of the liberal tradition: that no one is entitled to give consent on behalf of another unless specifically authorised to do so; and that consent, to be voluntary, requires an effective choice between alternatives. Earlier in the modern era, consent to government was given, not through election of the executive itself, but through the election of a representative assembly which had a limited power of veto over an executive appointed by the monarch. Consent to government, in other words, was transmitted indirectly through representatives authorised to act on their constituents' behalf. In the typical liberal-democratic system of the present day, consent is also given directly through elections for the head of the executive. Effective choice is guaranteed by the freedoms of expression and association that allow parties and policies to be formed and modified in a manner that reflects a range of public opinion. Exercising a choice between them ensures express consent to the government that is so chosen: on the part of the majority, because they have voted for it; on the part of the minority, because by participating in the election they are assumed to have demonstrated their acceptance of the rules by which the government was chosen.

In the previous section I noted an important advantage that traditional systems enjoyed in preserving the supreme office from the impact of public competition. In the context of consent they also derived a significant source of stability from the fact that the political community – those whose cooperation was needed to realise the goals of the ruler, and whose consent was necessary to confirm his or her legitimacy – was largely coterminous with the socially and economically privileged and powerful. The distribution of political power reflected the distribution of power in the economic and social spheres. In the contemporary world, by contrast, this coincidence is no longer guaranteed, since the requirements of popular consent have extended the political community to the economically and socially subordinate, and their right to electoral choice has given them the potential capacity to alter the terms of their subordination through a revision of the rules on which it rests. In terms of the dimensions analysed in the first half of this book, the *formal* distribution of political power no longer reflects the power relations of class or gender, as it did in the traditional order. This disjunction constitutes a potential source of tension and conflict that is ever-present within the electoral mode of consent.

The classical bourgeois era succeeded in protecting itself from this disjunction and its consequences in a period of intensified class and gender inequality by limiting the suffrage to male prop-erty-owners. The limitation was justified by arguments that demonstrated more ingenuity than consistency with the universalist premises of individualism itself. Thus Locke developed the idea of 'tacit consent', arguing that, whereas consent to taxation required explicit authorisation by the propertied through representatives, consent to government as such could be inferred from the mere fact of living under it and enjoying its benefits (Locke, 1967, pp.365–81). In like manner the constitution makers of the first National Assembly in France drew a distinction between 'passive' and 'active' citizenship: between the enjoyment of legal rights, which was universal, and the right to influence public affairs through representatives, which was limited to taxpayers, to those who, in Abbé Sièyes' words, were 'the true shareholders in the great public enterprise' (Stewart, 1951, pp.129ff.). While the exclusion of the working classes was thus justified by appeal to a thoroughly bourgeois image of political society as a shareholders' enterprise, the exclusion of women was confirmed by the persistence of a thoroughly traditionalist conception of consent. Since women had no distinct interests separate from their menfolk, James Mill argued, they could safely be represented by either their fathers or their husbands. Consent, in other words, could continue to be given on someone else's behalf without their explicit authorisation (Mill, 1937, p.45).

Nowadays such arguments seem only too evidently the special pleading of the male and the propertied, and eventually they succumbed to the universalist assumptions inherent in classical liberalism itself, though only when harnessed by mass popular struggles on the part of the working class and women in turn. Today there is no longer any defensible point at which a line can be drawn to limit those eligible to vote, except on grounds of age or criminal conviction. In the Republic of South Africa, for instance, the racial principle of eligibility has provoked a deep-seated crisis of government. The exclusion of non-whites from the political community has led to the active withdrawal of consent, and the delegitimation of the state in respect of its authority over the black and coloured populations. The RSA proves the truth of the proposition that, if any are to have the vote, it has to be given to all; if any are to be excluded, then everyone has to be.

The powerful and privileged can thus no longer protect themselves against the threat from below by means of a discriminatory electoral system. Social and economic inequality has to coexist with a formal political equality in the status of citizenship, and with the potential ability of the subordinate to use their electoral power to alter the terms of their subordination. However, just as there are informal social processes at work, explored in the first part of the book, which serve to reproduce the legitimacy of class and gender power, so also can these power relations reassert themselves within the formally equal sphere of citizenship. This is most apparent in relation to gender. The gendered division of labour reproduces itself in the political domain, as in other areas of life, through the cumulative pressure of role expectations, of time available from domestic responsibilities, and the differential desire or opportunity to develop the qualities deemed appropriate to the exercise of political power (Randall, 1982, ch.3). As a consequence, parties and legislatures – the main instruments of political change – remain dominated by men, who are thus able, if not to block all reform, at least to control its pace and content in a manner that does not prove threatening to themselves. This control, combined with the divisions among women themselves, has ensured that, since the era of the suffrage struggles, the political activity of women as women (rather than as members of other social groups) has not threatened the legitimacy of the political order.

There are some respects in which the history of class reflects that of gender. Most obviously, wealth provides a powerful political resource that can be deployed to influence the outcomes of electoral choice. Moreover, as with gender, the hierarchical relations of production can be readily reproduced within political parties, to consolidate vertical social bonds at the expense of lateral, class-based modes of organisation. This happens particularly in rural areas, where electoral politics can serve to perpetuate traditional clientelist relations. Voting for a social superior is rewarded by particularistic benefits for the locality, which discourage more programmatic demands that might challenge the terms of subordination themselves. However, it is when class-based organisations begin to be formed and win a following that a crisis of electoral politics typically develops. Whether it can be resolved within the framework of the electoral system depends crucially upon the ability and willingness of the dominant classes to effect a compromise that gives enough to the subordinate to sustain their support for the political order (see below, pp.177–8).

If they lack that ability or willingness, the dominant classes will seek instead to secure some restriction on electoral choice. This may be done by outlawing particular movements or parties; or by employing state forces or private armies to repress them; or by general restrictions on the freedoms of expression and association. Any of these may enable the electoral process to continue in a manner that does not threaten the system of class power or the privileges of the powerful. It follows, however, that such elections cannot have the same legitimating force as before, since they infringe the conditions necessary to consent in the liberal mode. Once popular choice is artificially restricted from above, through the operation of the law, or of force, to limit the freedom of association and organisation, then the outcome cannot be said to have the voluntary consent of the governed. At best we could speak of a semi-legitimate, or incompletely legitimated, government, and of a degeneration in the electoral mode of consent, whose logical conclusion is the single-party system or the no-party regime, offering at most a choice of 'yes' or 'no' to the individual leader.

A lack of electoral choice does not of itself, however, indicate the absence of all popular legitimation. Here we need to consider the alternative, mobilisation mode of consent. In the mobilisation mode, consent is expressed through continuous mass participation in political activity supportive of the regime and contributory to the realisation of its political goals (cf. Denitch, 1976, ch.8). Regimes legitimated in this way typically take their origin from a revolution, and the continuing popular mobilisation can be seen as a perpetuation of the revolutionary process into the post-revolutionary era. Although the majority of the population may in fact be politically inactive, the commitment of the substantial minority makes up in degree for what it lacks in universality. Moreover, because the 'vanguard' movement or party is in principle open to all, and those participating in it are distinguished simply by their greater commitment rather than by the privilege of birth or property, they can be seen as representative of the people as a whole, and their activity in the regime's cause as demonstrative of the continuing support of society at large.

In contrast to the electoral mode, here popular participation is divorced from the process whereby office-holders are appointed, and is directed more towards the execution of policy at the grassroots than to its formation at the centre. This divorce explains the frequently cited feature of Soviet-type systems where a much greater proportion of the population than in liberal democracies is politically active, its activity, however, being concerned with 'low' rather than 'high' politics (e.g. Bialer, 1980, pp.185ff.). And the ruling party has a correspondingly different popular function from parties in electoral systems: not to prepare leaders and policies for presentation to the electorate, but to stimulate the mass involvement on which the system depends both for the administration of policy and for its own legitimation. Although in encouraging this involvement the party has material inducements and political privileges to offer, the effectiveness of participation as a legitimating process depends on the commitment of those involved to a cause over and above that of their own personal advancement.

Because of the need for continuous mobilisation, leaders who possess the capacity for arousing mass enthusiasm have a particular place in this mode of legitimation, as exemplified by such figures as Lenin, Hitler, Mao, Khomeini. However, the Weberian concept of 'charismatic authority' is more of a hindrance than a help in analysing this phenomenon, since its assumption that the source of legitimacy resides in the special qualities of the leader assigns far too exclusive an importance to the individual, and leads to fruitless, because unresolvable, disputes about whether particular leaders possess the indefinable quality of 'charisma' or not. Most of the figures named above achieved their authority as the focus of popular resistance to a discredited political order, and as the exponents of a belief system that came to underpin the rules of its successor. They might embody the faith in a particularly exemplary fashion, but the ability of the political order and its legitimacy to survive them indicates that it is the belief system itself, with its distinctive institutions and mobilising power, that is crucial, rather than the particular personality of the individual leader. If Hitler and his Führerstaat constitutes perhaps an exception here, this only demonstrates that leaders play different roles in different circumstances; and that these need careful differentiation rather than inclusion in a general category such as charismatic authority, which has sown more confusion than almost any other in the history of twentieth-century social science.

Since what is central to popular legitimation here is the mobilising power of a belief system or cause, rather than the exercise of choice between different leaders and policies, this mode of legitimation is associated with monopolistic claims on the part of the ruling party: the claim to a monopoly of truth in the realm of doctrine, and a monopoly of organisation in the sphere of political activity. Whereas the electoral mode can tolerate, indeed requires, a plurality of ideas and groupings, in the mobilisation mode the public expression of alternative ideas, or even of opposition to official policy, articulated outside the framework of the ruling party, constitutes a threat to its legitimacy, since it challenges the truth claims on which its authority is based. Such alternatives, while they may be entertained in private, cannot be allowed to emerge into the public arena, and have to be blocked in advance of their public expression. The counterpart to legitimation through mobilisation is thus a system of surveillance and repression, not as an alternative to legitimacy, but as its necessary complement.

The mistake frequently made by liberal commentators is to assume that, because there is no effective electoral choice, and little freedom of expression and association in mobilisation regimes, they can therefore have no legitimacy. This would certainly be true if they depended upon elections for their legitimation; as we have already seen, the restriction of electoral choice constitutes a characteristic form in which popular legitimation is weakened in an electoral regime. Such a restriction does not have the same implications for a mobilisation regime, however. What is critical here, on the other hand, is any general erosion of belief in the doctrine or cause that provides the regime with its justification and its mobilising capacity; without such belief it becomes a system of privilege and repression devoid of any social or moral purpose. Although it is more difficult to chart this process of erosion than that where restrictions are imposed on electoral choice, nevertheless the cumulative indices of degeneration over time are palpable.

What alternatives are possible for a regime whose legitimacy has been eroded in this way? As will be discussed more fully in the next chapter, the recent history of Soviet-type systems shows the clear possibility of a popular relegitimation through a shift from the mobilisation to the electoral mode, with elections offering a real choice between candidates and policies rather than being a mere formality. Such a shift represents nothing short of a fundamental change in the political system, its rules of office and the character of its political parties. On the other hand the reverse process – of the leaders of an electoral system in decline seeking to relegitimate themselves through a shift to a mobilisation regime – is highly unlikely to prove effective, for the simple reason that the continuous mobilisation necessary to legitimation depends upon the vitality of a belief system or cause, and these are typically the product of popular movements of opposition, which cannot simply be called up to order from above.

Conclusion

It is worth at this point summarising what has been a long chapter, so that the wood does not get lost for the trees. With regard to forms of power, I have argued, legitimacy is at once most urgent and most problematic in respect of the contemporary state, in view of its enormous concentration of power on the one side, and the vulnerability of its rules of power on the other, lacking as they do any superior legal authority to validate and enforce them. In considering the different elements necessary to that legitimacy – legality, the justifiability of rules, expressed consent – we need to be able to demonstrate the relationship between underlying principles and the institutions that embody or give effect to them. It is the ability to give a convincing account of this relationship that is lacking in most discussions of political legitimacy, and that this chapter has sought to provide.

At the level of legality it is a relatively commonplace observation that respect for the rule of law on the part of government requires an institutional separation of powers and the effective subordination of the military to civilian control. However, legality itself is ultimately dependent on the acceptability of the constitutional order, and the justifiability of the rules governing appointment to office and the spatial distribution of power. Rules of appointment (access to office, degree of competition, mode of removal, etc.) must conform to a source of authority recognised within the society on the one hand, and facilitate rather than hinder the realisation of a general interest and the acknowledged ends of government, on the other. In the attainment of both, the spatial distribution of power must correspond to people's self-definition of themselves as a distinctive people. Finally, the realisation of popular consent requires a particular kind of party and form of popular participation, according to the system's particular mode of legitimation.

At each point, in other words, it is possible to trace a relationship between a different aspect or principle of legitimacy, and the manner in which it is realised, or fails to be realised, within specific institutions. For legality we look in the first instance (but only in the first instance) to the relationship between the different branches of the state: legislative, executive and judicial. For rule-justifiability we need to examine the extent to which the basic rules of appointment to high office embody an accepted source of authority, and facilitate the attainment of the acknowledged ends of government (the 'right' and the 'good'). For legitimation, or expressed consent, we must consider the form and extent of political participation, and the way in which the party system is arranged to give effect to it. Finally, and most crucially, we need to assess how far these different institutional arrangements are mutually compatible, in the sense that, in realising one aspect or dimension of legitimacy, they are at least consistent with, and do not undermine, another.

Constitutional rules, we could conclude, comprise institutional arrangements designed not only to ensure a sufficient concentration and organisation of power to make the government of a given territory possible, but also to make it legitimate. The different political institutions, from parties through electoral systems to arrangements for the division and distribution of power, can each be evaluated according to the manner and extent to which they embody or give effect to a particular requirement of legitimacy. In doing so in this chapter I have considered them primarily according to the three different dimensions of legitimacy established in the first half of the book, rather than as political systems in the round. The next chapter will consider different types of political system – liberal–democratic, communist, traditional, theocratic – and seek to identify not only how they meet the different requirements of legitimacy already outlined, but what are their distinctive points of vulnerability in turn.

6 Crisis Tendencies of Political Systems

In the light of the previous chapter's discussion, a political system can be defined as a set of constitutional rules whose purpose is not only to effect a particular arrangement of state power, but also to secure legitimacy for that arrangement, and hence for those who exercise power under it, in respect of the different criteria outlined: the maintenance of legality; the derivation from a recognised source of authority; the satisfaction of a general interest in regard to the acknowledged ends of government; the demonstration of consent. Where the previous chapter considered each of these criteria separately, the present chapter will explore their mutual relationship within different types of political system.

The two main types of political system to be discussed – the liberal-democratic and the communist – have manifested considerable variation from one country to the next, and it will be necessary to represent them in their most characteristic form for purposes of analysis: liberal–democracy as typified in the advanced capitalist countries since 1945; the communist system as it evolved in what might be called its classical period from the death of Stalin to the accession of Gorbachev. Each will be presented as an abstract type or model, so as to identify its most essential features, and the internal relationship between them. It will be assumed that each type possesses a certain internal coherence or consistency, which derives from the requirements implicit in its legitimating source of authority.

Besides being definable as a 'pure type' for analytical purposes, the liberal-democratic and communist systems also constitute a 'model' in a different, normative sense: as an ideal for others to copy or emulate. Indeed, it would seem to be a characteristic

161

feature of legitimate political systems in the modern world, that they should claim an exemplary quality that demands imitation by others. Both liberal-democratic and communist systems have sought imitators or followers outside their respective 'heartlands', and the competition thus generated between them has determined much of world politics since 1945. If on the one side the terminal crisis which the communist systems had entered by 1989 demonstrates only too clearly the deficiencies of the 'classical' communist type as a desirable or even a viable model, on the other side the inability of the liberal-democratic type to survive outside the capitalist heartlands, without deformation or a recurrent slide into military dictatorship, suggests that it represents no unproblematic model either. The aim of the following analysis will be to identify the chief source of legitimacy weakness or deficit in each type: to show its crisis tendencies, as they might be called, not as contingent or unconnected, but as systematically generated.

The final section of the chapter will consider political systems in the Islamic world. One reason for including them is that the attempt to derive political legitimacy from a religious source of authority not only constitutes a conscious rejection of the exemplary claims of both liberal-democratic and communist models; it also challenges a basic premise of Western social science which links 'modernisation' firmly with the process of secularisation. As I shall argue, the idea of the 'Islamic state' is both inherently ambiguous and politically contested, and has been used to give a façade of legitimacy to many regimes that inherently lack it. However, there are two political systems in the Islamic world that are of particular interest for any theory of legitimacy, by virtue of their distinctiveness. One, Saudi Arabia, represents an almost pure form of traditional legitimacy. The other, Iran, constitutes a novel version of the theocratic state, combining a religious principle of authority with consent through mass mobilisation. Both claim an exemplary significance, if only within the region or within Islam, rather than universally; and the competition between them has constituted a potent additional source of tension within the Middle East, at least until it became submerged by Iraq's invasion of Kuwait. Both systems require a special effort of the imagination, particularly on the part of Westerners, if their legitimating principles are to be made intelligible, and their inherent points of weakness to be accurately identified (cf. Said, 1981).

In considering the distinctive character of the different political systems mentioned, and the points at which their legitimacy is typically most vulnerable to erosion, it will be necessary to take into account the form of economy with which they are associated, since economy and polity are so closely intertwined and mutually determining in the contemporary world. It is not by chance, for example, that liberal-democratic systems have been typically associated with a capitalist economy, or communist ones with a system of extensive public ownership and state planning. Furthermore, when it comes to the actual erosion of a political order's legitimacy, it is usually changes or problems in the economy that provide the catalyst, since these often lie beyond the control of particular governments. On a historical plane, it was the twin processes of urbanisation and industrialisation that gave the subordinate classes the mobilising potential which made the restriction of the political community to the ranks of the propertied ultimately untenable. In the contemporary world, it is the pressures generated by economic change, or the failure to change, that expose the weak points in a political order, whether it be in its source of authority or its ability to resolve distributional conflicts. If we are to talk of the systemic character of legitimacy crises, therefore, then it is the politico-economic system, rather than the political system on its own, that should properly be the subject of our analysis. This will be the procedure adopted in what follows.

Liberal democracy

In its evolved contemporary form, as exemplified in the advanced capitalist countries of Western Europe, North America, Australia, New Zealand and Japan, this type of politico-economic system is characterised by the following legitimating features:

1. The principle of popular sovereignty is carried through consistently in electoral terms, in that not only the legislature but the head of the executive also is chosen directly or indirectly by ballot, on the basis of universal suffrage. The

formal guarantee of the freedoms of belief, expression and association, exercised within an autonomous sphere of civil society, ensures that, in principle, electoral outcomes reflect the 'popular will', and that public opinion can be brought to bear on government in a continuous manner. Since all beliefs are possible that do not challenge the idea of popular sovereignty itself, the ultimate test of correct policy can only be its popular acceptability, electorally determined, not its conformity to some established body of doctrine. Elections provide not only the method of appointment to political office, but also the avenue through which consent to government is expressed, though the operation of the majority principle means that the minority only consents to government indirectly, through its participation in the electoral process, not by virtue of having chosen it in preference to the alternatives. The role of political parties in such a system is to prepare candidates and policies for approval, to focus electoral choice, and to provide the discipline needed to secure effective government in the event of being elected.

2. Economic activity is based upon the private ownership of property and upon private decisions about investment, employment and consumption within a formally free market, on the principle that the market constitutes both an arena for individual choice and an effective mechanism for coordinating the manifold decisions of individuals and firms in the general interest. However, since the state is itself the ultimate guardian of the public interest, it is necessarily involved in guaranteeing the conditions for profitable investment and the public acceptability of economic processes, where the market on its own cannot. This requirement involves the state in wide-ranging market interventions and supplementations: in providing the material and immaterial infrastructure for production; in ensuring a sufficient workforce with the requisite skills; in remedying the damaging consequences of production for individuals and the environment; in tempering the distributional inequalities of the market and moderating its cyclical disturbances. In effect, the contemporary state underwrites the legitimacy of capitalism by ensuring its social acceptability as well as its legal validity. Moreover, since any radical challenge to the rights of property, although

in theory compatible with democratic principle, would provoke a crisis in the political system itself, in underwriting
the legitimacy of capitalism the state is indirectly securing a
condition of its own legitimacy also.

This politico-economic system of capitalist democracy is one
that has evolved over a long period of time. In particular, the
relationship between state and economy has developed from the
nineteenth to the late twentieth century under the impact of two
separate processes. One, economically determined, under the
pressure of market competition, has been the shift from what
might be called liberal to oligopolistic capitalism: from small-
scale, low-technology, labour-intensive production to large-scale,
high-technology, capital-intensive industries. Although a new
shift may be occurring with so-called 'post-Fordism', its general
direction has required increasing state intervention through
market-regulating and market-supplementing activities, to ensure
the overall conditions for capitalist profitability. The other, more
politically determined, process has been the development from
limited suffrage to welfare democracy under the pressure of
popular struggles, which has involved the state in modifying the
unequal distributional outcomes of the market, both indirectly,
through providing the legal rights necessary to trade-union
activity, and directly, through taxation policy, transfer payments
and welfare provision. While both the above types of state intervention are necessary to secure the legitimacy of capitalism, the
second, distributional kind, requires a capitalist class able and
willing to concede a sufficient share of the surplus to the working
class to reconcile it to the inequalities of property ownership and
to its own subordinate position at the workplace. Provided this
condition is satisfied, which it has been in the situation of class
compromise and economic growth that has prevailed in the
advanced capitalist countries since 1945, the legitimacy of capitalist democracy seems secure.

Not everyone, however, would subscribe to this conclusion.
Most persuasive among the sceptics have been the theorists of
so-called 'legitimation crisis', Jürgen Habermas and Claus Offe,
who have argued that the contemporary state is unable to fulfil
its required tasks in relation to the capitalist economy, without
encountering severe legitimation problems of its own, problems

which became particularly evident during the course of the 1970s. An examination of their arguments will enable us to explore more fully the basis of legitimacy of capitalist democracy (Habermas, 1973, 1976b; Offe, 1984, 1985).

The argument takes its starting point from the fundamental 'contradiction' of the capitalist system, between the social process of production and the private appropriation and use of the product – simply put, the essentially public activity of production is dependent upon private ownership and private initiative, so that, for example, decisions about the balance between investment and consumption take the form of a conflict between classes, and so on. This contradiction is not *resolved* by state intervention to deal with its consequences, but is simply *displaced* onto the state itself, where it manifests itself as incompatible steering objectives, fiscal crisis and legitimacy deficit.

The idea of 'displacement' here can be elucidated by contrasting the political economy of advanced capitalism with liberal capitalism on one side, and a planned economy on the other. In the period of liberal capitalism, when governments undertook the minimal functions of guaranteeing the security of property and contract, state legitimacy was protected from crises in the economy, since these took the form of natural disturbances of the market, beyond human control. Under a centrally planned economy, on the other hand, the state cannot avoid responsibility for any inadequacies or interruptions in production, and economic crises are experienced directly and transparently as a problem of government, with unavoidable consequences for the legitimacy of the state. The system of advanced capitalism conforms to neither of these relatively simple, if also oversimplified, models. Here the state's intervention to complement the market, so that its privately determined activities produce socially acceptable outcomes, creates problems for the state which appear as autonomous problems of the political domain, quite separated from the underlying contradiction which is their cause. It is this complex process, whereby solving one set of problems systematically produces other problems of a quite different kind at a different level, that the idea of 'displacement' suggests.

What are these problems for the state? One generic problem, so it is argued, is a problem of performance: the range and complexity of tasks the state is required to undertake far outrun its capacity to fulfil them. Symptoms of this are the ability of powerful economic groups to veto or nullify interventions made in the public interest, or the fiscal crisis that regularly afflicts state finances, as its labour-intensive services prove unable to match the productivity levels of manufacturing industry. Persistent increases in taxation erode the economic profitability on which the state itself depends, while the scope for cutting services is limited by electoral considerations. Underlying these conflicting requirements is a more fundamental contradiction, according to Offe. The state has to secure and protect the integrity of the market, while simultaneously intervening in it in the social interest. It must uphold the logic of market valuation and the production of commodities for profit, while its own activity follows the antithetical and subversive principle of provision according to social need, so, for example, undermining the labour discipline and achievement orientation on which capitalist production depends. The problem of the state's performance, in other words, is not simply a lack of capacity, but a systematically generated incoherence in its goals. The basic contradiction of the capitalist system is reproduced as incompatible steering objectives at the level of the state itself (see Keane, 1984).

Performance problems affect the legitimacy of the state by undermining its authority, and hence the support on which it can rely. However, its legitimacy is more directly impaired, according to Habermas, by the absence of any normative agreement which might serve to validate the expanded intervention of the state, and make it acceptable to those it adversely affects. A purely technocratic definition of the public sphere, Habermas argues, is impossible when its necessary counter-part of civic privatism – the definition of citizenship as a purely private status – is itself disrupted by the intervention of the state in the family, in education, and in the value autonomy of the private sphere. On the other hand, the evolution of capitalism has destroyed the traditional moral legacy on which it depended to moderate the unrestrained pursuit of self-interest, and which might validate state involvement in the economy (e.g. 1976b, pp.75–9). One area where this erosion is widely acknowledged to be significant is the sphere of distribution. Now that distribution of the social product is to such an extent politically determined, any perceived unfairness cannot be attributed to the impersonal chances of the

market, but demands correction according to a publicly defensible standard of justice; yet there is simply no agreement on
what such a standard might be. The lack of agreement results in
a potentially endless succession of demands on the state from
one sectional group after another. At this point the insufficient
legitimacy exacerbates the steering problems in a mutually reinforcing cycle (see Plant, 1982).

The above is an all too brief summary of the main claims of
the 'legitimation crisis' literature. How valid are they? In my
view the idea that the basic contradiction of capitalism is displaced onto the political plane, and constitutes the source of the
latter's recurrent problems, is a highly plausible one. But do
these problems amount to a legitimation crisis, or even to crisis
tendencies (as Habermas is careful to call them), rather than a
set of tensions to be managed, of competing demands between
which a compromise has repeatedly to be struck? Before we can
decide whether recurrent problems have *crisis* potential, we need
a precise account of what a crisis of legitimacy would actually
amount to. In particular, since it is claimed that the contradictions of capitalism have been displaced onto the state, we need an
account of what would constitute a crisis of the liberal-democratic
political system. It is here that the literature on legitimation crisis
seems to me to be least adequate, because insufficiently specific
about the political domain.

According to the concept of legitimacy I have been arguing
for throughout this book, a legitimacy crisis could be said to
occur when there is a serious threat or challenge to the rules of
power, or a substantial erosion in the beliefs which provide their
justification. In the case of a liberal-democratic order, that means
a threat to the electoral rules and their associated freedoms, or
an erosion of commitment to the idea of popular sovereignty
underpinning them. Agreement about these rules is, in principle,
the only normative consensus that a liberal democracy requires
for its legitimacy. The problems of state performance and incompatible steering objectives, on the other hand, which the literature of legitimation crisis is preoccupied with, may serve to
weaken or undermine the authority of particular governments,
but do not thereby erode support for the rules themselves.
Indeed, as I have argued in the previous chapter, it is one of
the strengths of the electoral process that it enables ineffective

administrations in due course to be dismissed, alternative solutions to be canvassed and tried out, and the authority of government to be regularly renewed. Theorems of legitimation crisis, in other words, do not adequately distinguish between the authority of governments and the legitimacy of the system; between the normative agreement necessary to sustain particular policies and that needed to support the rules of the political order; between agreement on a substantive criterion of distributive justice, and agreement on procedures whereby competing definitions of justice might be resolved through compromise.

The ability of the electoral process to produce changes in state policy and personnel, and to renew the authority of governments, is demonstrated by the history of liberal democracies in the 1980s. The decade saw the election of right-wing governments in many countries, committed to a neo-liberal programme and ideology that directly addressed the problems of state capacity identified in the 'legitimation crisis' literature, but who treated the source of these problems as primarily political rather than economic or structural, and thus as amenable to political solution. According to their analysis, the problem of 'government overload' was not attributable to capitalism *per se*; it was the result of a combination of misguided Keynesian theory and irresponsible electioneering drawing governments into areas of economic intervention which they were incapable of handling, that had aroused exaggerated expectations and eroded monetary discipline. The solution was to reestablish the autonomy of the market and the authority of the state together by means of a thoroughgoing withdrawal of government from the economy, through cuts in taxation, the privatisation of public services, and the reduction in state support to the losers in market competition. This strategy would leave governments strengthened to concentrate on those limited market-supporting activities that only they could perform: providing security for property and contract, guaranteeing sound money, setting and policing the rules of competition itself (Hayek, 1976; see King, 1987).

What was surprising about such a programme, involving reductions in welfare provision and increased levels of unemployment, was that it proved at all electorally viable. However, its emphasis on the virtues of individual consumer choice in contrast to the least attractive aspects of collective action and collective provision found considerable popular resonance. And the chief losers from the neo-liberal agenda of rolling back the state were unorganised groups of the population who were least capable of mounting any political challenge to it: part-time workers, the unemployed, the homeless, women forced to care for dependent relatives at home. Here, right-wing governments took advantage of a characteristic feature of liberal democracy, whereby interests that are not organised and articulated in the political domain can be ignored with impunity. Although injured minorities can prove the Achilles' heel of democracy, where they are powerful or well organised, minorities that lack collective voice or presence can be the object of considerable injustice, without any consequence for the legitimacy of the state.

Now it cannot be claimed that the neo-liberal strategy, where it was put into effect, has conclusively solved the underlying contradictions of advanced capitalism, rather than reducing their political salience through a reassertion of market forces at the expense of society's weakest groups. Yet there is nothing to suggest that liberal democracies cannot zig-zag indefinitely between a market-oriented solution to the problems of the state, and a governmental solution to the problems of the market, with a shifting point of balance struck between the two. Indeed, the electoral process facilitates such a fluctuating course in the alternation of parties between left and right, with in-built self-correction when the movement in one direction tends to get out of hand. The rules of the democratic system, in other words, serve to blunt the contradictory tendencies of the capitalist political economy by extending their effects over time.

The evidence of the whole period since 1945, in fact, suggests that the rules of the democratic process provide considerable resilience in problem-solving in the advanced capitalist states, once the basic conditions of class compromise have been secured; and that claims about legitimation crisis constitute an exaggerated extrapolation from particular difficulties experienced during the 1970s. It does not follow, however, that the possibility can be ruled out of crisis tendencies developing, or crises occurring, that are specific to particular states within the liberal-democratic universe. In Western Europe these have typically occurred when the management of post-imperial political decline and resurgent sub-state nationalism has exposed particular weaknesses in the constitutional arrangements. In the USA, by contrast, it has been the tensions generated by its neo-imperial role that have most frequently subjected the political system to stress. In almost every case, however, the liberal democratic order has shown itself capable of an internal resolution of the crisis, without any break threatened in the legality of the constitutional arrangements. It is the sharp contrast between this experience of liberal democracy in the advanced capitalist countries, and that of the less developed world, where legitimation crises can more properly be described as systemic, that I turn to next.

Liberal democracy in developing countries

The success of the liberal-democratic system in the capitalist heartlands, at least since 1945, and its active self-promotion of its own virtues have made it a prestigious model for others to copy. Yet its record of achieving or sustaining political legitimacy outside these heartlands is derisory. There are very few countries in the less developed world which have been able to sustain a system of open party competition allied to freedoms of expression and association for any length of time. Such a system has usually been brought to an end by military coup, or by transformation into a one-party state that breaks with the principle of free association central to liberal democracy.

Purely cultural explanations for this sorry record, to the effect that the peoples of these societies lack a commitment to democratic procedures and the ability to work them, apart from being patronising, tend to circularity, as I have already argued, since one of the conditions for a settled commitment to the rules of party competition is a past history of successful alternation of parties in power; and it is precisely this that remains elusive. A more plausible explanation is a situational or structural one: there are certain politico-economic conditions, typical of most developing countries, in which the different requirements of legitimacy come into conflict with one another, because effective electoral choice can only be realised at the cost of an intensification of social and political division. In other words, the ability of liberal democracies to satisfy the legitimating criteria of an accepted source of authority and expressed popular consent, is incompatible with the attainment of a recognisable general interest in the circumstances of most developing countries.

What are these circumstances? At the cost of grossly over-simplifying the enormous diversity within the so-called Third World, I would single out two characteristics of underdevelopment which make the attainment of legitimacy particularly diffi-cult within a liberal-democratic system. The first is an overdevel-oped state in relation to society, which is in part a consequence of the leading role the state has come to play in the process of economic development. The most obvious indication of this is the size of the state apparatus, and the fact that the public sector constitutes a, if not the, major site of privileged employment opportunities and means of social advancement. This, in turn, has a number of consequences. One is that the competition to win control of government assumes a special intensity, in view of the command over appointments and the means of patronage that it provides, including the denial of such resources to political opponents. The electoral system has to carry the strain of compe-tition for scarce economic resources as well as the contest for political power (Clapham, 1985, ch.3).

A further consequence is that the state's monopolisation of talent and social initiative hinders the development of an inde-pendent 'civil society', with autonomous associations that have an accepted place in the political process. The relation between state and society assumes a correspondingly paternalist form, which has great difficulty in accommodating political demands and initiatives that are not prompted or controlled from above (Thomas, 1984; Mouzelis, 1986). It is not so much the character of the state as such, it should be emphasised, as its relation to society that is important here. The relative overdevelopment of the state renders exceedingly difficult the autonomous organis-ation of civil society and its acceptance as a normal part of the political process, which is a necessary concomitant of consent expressed through electoral choice.

The second relevant feature of underdevelopment is to be found in the sharp economic inequalities and dislocations that characterise the process of capitalist penetration of traditional economic relationships, and the early stages of industrialisation. Although these are conditions that the older capitalist economies themselves underwent, they are intensified and prolonged by the subordinate position in which the late-developers stand to the capitalist 'centre'. The form of their industrialisation is one in which the most advanced sectors of production, typically foreign-owned, are detached from the other sectors, and make no positive contribution to their development. In short, developing economies tend to be ones which experience the sharp inequalities and dislocations of the industrialisation process on a capitalist basis, without generating the self-sustaining economic expansion that might enable its benefits in due course to be spread more widely (Cardoso and Faletto, 1978; Szentes, 1983; Szeftel, 1987).

From the standpoint of political legitimacy, the most significant contrast with the early industrialisers is that the latter experienced the process of industrialisation, when capitalist legitimacy is at its weakest, under a political system based upon a restricted suffrage. In other words, the legitimacy of the state did not depend upon securing the consent of those most adversely affected by the economic transformations taking place. The suffrage was only extended to the propertyless at the point when they were no longer considered a threat to the rights of property, and when the strains of the early period of industrialisation had been overcome. The late industrialisers, on the other hand, have no such restriction available to them, if they are to meet the requirements of consent through electoral choice; and they are thus fully exposed to the potential contradiction between the costs that economic transformation inflicts upon the subordinate classes, and the electoral power that the political system formally assigns to them.

Whether a competitive electoral system can survive at all in such circumstances depends very largely on the character of political parties, and on the extent to which they cut across rather than coincide with potential divisions within society. A common form of party is the hierarchically structured patronage party, in which subordinate classes are organised by their social superiors, and which is directed more towards particularistic benefits than to programmatic demands that might pose a challenge to the interests of property or the powers of the state. In rural areas such parties may be organised as the political extension of traditional 'clientelist' networks, whereby casting one's vote becomes another form of service to the local patron, landowner or tribal chief (Weingrod, 1968; Schmidt, 1977, pt.2). Although such networks can be recreated in urban contexts, patronage parties there will be organised around more modern institutions such as trade unions, which, however, tend to enjoy much less autonomy than their counterparts in the West, being initiated and controlled from above along paternalist lines (Mouzelis, 1986). Wherever such parties exist, we could speak of a system of managed consent, or guided democracy, in which the organisation of patronage within established vertical relationships ensures that the exercise of electoral choice by subordinate classes poses no threat to the dominant powers within society or state.

However, a system of competition between hierarchically structured patronage parties is vulnerable to two different forms of evolution, according to the context. Where class formation is well developed, as in much of Asia and Latin America, the formal recognition of freedoms of expression and association periodically allows new types of party organisation or electoral programme to develop, which escape beyond the limits tolerable to dominant classes or political élites. It is often said by commentators on clientelism, for example, that clientelist relations are not incompatible with the existence of a potentially conflictual class structure. What they hinder is the emergence of forms of consciousness and organisation on the part of subordinate classes which would bring that conflict into the open (Flynn, 1974; Scott and Kerkvliet, 1977). (In Marxist terms, they hinder a class 'in itself' from becoming a class 'for itself'.) However, when economic changes weaken the hold of traditional relationships, or severely limit the benefits available for local distribution by ruling parties, then more class-based organisations can emerge with programmes that directly challenge the powers or prerogatives of property. At this point the latter can only be preserved intact by the use of legal or extra-legal repression to limit the freedom of association and electoral choice, or else to abolish it altogether. The better organised the movement or the demands of the subordinate classes, the more extensive the repression will have to be to achieve its purpose (O'Donnell, 1973; J.C. Scott, 1976, ch.7).

In many African countries, on the other hand, it is not so much the erosion of a hierarchically organised party system under the pressure of class conflict that has undermined electoral democracy, as the intensification of regional or ethnic divisions through the competition for control over state patronage. While vertically integrated parties are able to moderate the political salience of vertical or class-based divisions, they only serve to intensify those divisions that are laterally or geographically based. The process of competition for access to economic opportunities, through control of the state, itself heightens the significance of the ethnic or regional connections through which opportunities for business or upward mobility can be organised (Szeftel, 1983; Joseph, 1987). As I argued in the previous chapter, where the cost to those excluded from the benefits of state patronage is high, and the excluded comprise identifiable sections of the population, corruption ceases to be something reluctantly tolerated, and threatens to discredit the political process altogether. In such circumstances, military intervention to abolish the rule of corrupt politicians can claim the merit of 'clean hands' as well as salvation of the general interest; and it is typically accompanied by much less repression than where a mass movement of the subordinate classes has to be suppressed.

In view of the social divisiveness of party competition that forms the typical counterpart to freedoms of association and popular consent in liberal democracies in the Third World, it is not surprising that those systems are most durable in which there exists a dominant party enjoying a marked electoral ascendancy and long continuity in office, such as those of India or Mexico (Randall, 1988). Such parties have successfully incorporated the major social forces within them, i.e. they are truly national parties, while their continuity in office ensures the effective subordination of state officials, and in particular the military, to political control. Such features are of course more securely guaranteed in a formal one-party state, such as those in East Africa, which may also provide the opportunity for limited electoral choice between candidates, if not between parties or policies. In the absence of any competition from other parties, however, these ruling parties tend to become simply an extension of the state administration, and lose their mobilising capacity (Tordoff, 1984, ch.5). Although the stability of these systems may look impressive in comparison with their competitive counterparts, the absence of legally recognised freedoms of association and political organisation constitutes a substantial departure from the liberal-democratic model, and from the requirements of popular consent through electoral choice.

It must be concluded, then, that the evidence from the Third World casts doubt on the claim of the liberal-democratic model to provide an effective solution to the problems of political legitimacy in the circumstances of underdevelopment. In particular, its inherent tension between the requirements of popular authority and popular consent on the one hand, and the attainment of a general interest on the other, proves unresolvable in these circumstances. The evidence also confirms doubts about the existence of any generally positive connection between a capitalist economy and liberal democracy, such as has most recently been reasserted in the context of the changes in Eastern Europe. I have argued that we should consider the political and economic systems together, since the legitimacy of each is bound up with the conditions of the other. By way of conclusion, therefore, it will be useful to consider more systematically the interrelationship between the two elements in the portmanteau concept of 'capitalist democracy'.

Proponents of a positive connection between capitalism and liberal democracy have usually argued that there are principles common to both, such as the freedoms of association, movement, ideas and so on, which have a mutually reinforcing effect on the legitimacy of each domain (e.g. Friedman, 1962). Thus the free market in commodities is paralleled by the electoral market in programmes and policies, and success in each is measured by the number of people who can be attracted to support a given product or programme. There is a democratic test of validity, in other words, which applies equally to goods as to policies, to firms as to parties, and which in turn requires open competition in the development and promotion of new products or policies. At its strongest it is argued that a free market in commodities is a necessary condition for the political freedoms intrinsic to a democratic order. A weaker version points to a congruence between the two that is conducive to the maintenance of both.

Now although there is undoubted validity in the idea of mutually supporting principles in different domains, the above argument only tells part of the story. In particular, it treats economy and state simply as parallel and coexisting spheres, rather than as systematically interacting on the basis of different logics. As a consequence, it overlooks the problems that a capitalist economy poses for liberal democracy. Among these problems two stand out from the experience of developing countries.

First, the driving force of a capitalist economy is the pursuit and maximisation of economic self-interest, from which a general interest emerges only as unintended consequence, via the 'hidden hand' of the market. The state, in contrast, must act as the conscious agent of a public interest, and is required to intervene both to provide the basic regulatory framework for the market, and to apply corrective action where the market fails to satisfy the public interest on its own. In the context of a contemporary developing economy, in particular, these interventions have to be substantial, to ensure that the market power of international capital does not undermine national priorities and interests, and that limited indigenous resources are utilised in the most effective way. Yet the greater the intervention, the greater the potential scope for the state to be colonised by the self-interest of the market place, to be penetrated by the forces it seeks to direct and regulate, and to become simply an extension of the particular interests and dominant motivations of the economic sphere. Party competition, as I suggested earlier, is more likely to intensify than moderate this process; indeed, parties can become one of the main instruments whereby the competition of the market place is systematically transposed into the political domain. In such conditions, therefore, far from the common principles of economy and polity mutually supporting one another, the logic of the market can undermine the distinctiveness and integrity of the public sphere, which are essential to its legitimacy as guardian of the public interest.

Secondly, the market, far from being a uniformly democratic device, tends if left on its own to intensify economic inequalities in a manner that frustrates the principle of political equality central to a democratic order. This inegalitarian process can only be moderated by political intervention, which may take broadly one of two forms. Redistribution can be effected from above, through a paternalist or authoritarian state dispensing benefits in a way designed to pre-empt or frustrate the autonomous action of the disadvantaged themselves. However, where the political system acknowledges at least the formal freedom of association, such action cannot be prevented indefinitely. The other mode of economic redistribution is through the operation of autonomous institutions of a subordinate class (trade union, political party), and on the basis of a conscious class compromise with the economically privileged. This mode, however, requires a dominant class with sufficient economic room to make such a compromise, and also willing to coexist with autonomous institutions that involve some diminution of its own power. Neither condition is easy to achieve in the circumstances of developing countries. As a result, attempts to make the difficult transition from one mode to the other, which is essential to the long term viability of a liberal-democratic system, become blocked or frustrated.

What we have here, in fact, is precisely those features which theorists of 'legitimation crisis' have pointed to – the capitalist erosion of traditional values that might inhibit or restrain the pursuit of self-interest; the absence of any agreed conception of distributive justice, or of compromise between competing conceptions, that might validate the state's intervention in the market – only proving much more critical to political legitimacy in developing countries than in the advanced capitalist states. The reasons for this, as I have suggested, are more situational or structural than cultural, and lie in the contradictoriness of the tasks the development state is required to perform: to satisfy the requirements of a developing indigenous entrepreneurial class and the expectations of subordinate classes simultaneously, in the context of a world market that is systematically tilted against both. Such contradictions are much more acute than anything confronting the state in the advanced capitalist economies. For the principles of the market and liberal democracy to be mutually supportive, in other words, rather than mutually destructive, requires specially favourable politico-economic conditions to secure. And if it could be shown that the economic development of the advanced capitalist societies was systematically connected to the underdevelopment of the colonial and post-colonial societies of the Third World, then we should have to conclude, further, that the security of liberal democracy in the former was dependent upon the conditions making for its insecurity in the latter. In other words, it would be doubtful whether the successful legitimacy of capitalist democracy could ever be other than a localised, not a universal, one.

The communist model

Anyone who writes about the communist or Soviet system today has to begin from the obvious fact that it entered a phase of deep crisis during the 1980s; that the programme of radical change initiated in the Soviet Union by Gorbachev to resolve the crisis prepared the ground for the spectacular collapse of the communist regimes across Eastern Europe in 1989; and that the brutal suppression of the Tiananmen Square demonstrations in China radically altered the basis of communist rule in that country even as it sought to immunise the political system from the pressures of change. In other words, the communist system in the form we have known it since the end of the second world war must now be regarded as a historical phenomenon, in the sense that, although it has not been entirely superseded, it no longer provides a viable alternative model to liberal democracy, owing to its loss of legitimacy in its own heartlands.

How are we to explain the process of change that reached such a dramatic dénoument in 1989? Was it the product of a classic legitimation crisis, in which the limits of system development had been reached, and no further evolution was possible without a transformation in its rules of organisation and underlying principles of legitimacy? Or did it reveal, as some would argue, that the communist regimes had never enjoyed any legitimacy at all, and had simply run out of stratagems for managing recalcitrant populations by a mixture of inducement and coercion? Was it a crisis of legitimacy, or one borne of chronic illegitimacy? How we answer this question depends upon our analysis of the communist system in what could be called its 'classical' form prior to Gorbachev. This, far from uncontentious, task must form the starting point of any discussion.

To begin with, it will be important to draw a distinction between those communist systems that were established as the result of an indigenous revolution, such as the USSR, Yugoslavia, China, Vietnam or Cuba, and those that were imposed by conquest or kept in place by the threat of military intervention, as in most of Eastern Europe (Denitch, 1976; Rigby and Feher, 1982). The former, as the product of popular struggles against a discredited regime, which were also national struggles against an external enemy, have always derived part of their legitimacy from the sufferings and exploits of the revolutionary period. The communist systems of Eastern Europe, in contrast, were associated with the infringement of national autonomy, and the externally dictated suppression of any spontaneous evolution in their political process – most dramatically in Hungary in 1956, Czechoslovakia in 1968, and Poland in 1981. A system associated with national subordination is *prima facie* an unlikely candidate to enjoy widespread moral authority (Lewis, 1982). Even with the Eastern European regimes, however, the form that their recurrent crises took is only intelligible in terms of the generic features common to communist systems, and the principles from which they have sought to derive their legitimacy. The communist model as it developed in its classical form in the Soviet Union must therefore provide the reference point for understanding these regimes as well.

At this point a further source of difficulty lies in the persistent disagreement that exists among those who have written on the legitimacy of the Soviet model, as to what its basis might be. Those who have started from a Weberian typology have been unable to agree whether its source of legitimacy was primarily charismatic, focused upon an exceptional leader such as Stalin, Mao, Tito or Castro (Gill, 1982); or traditional, deriving from the revolutionary inheritance or the persistence of longer-standing national traditions (Lane, 1984); or goal-rational, based upon progress towards an ideal communist society (Rigby, 1980, 1982); or some combination of all three (Heller, 1982). Even those who have not been constrained by the Weberian straight-jacket have disagreed as to whether the legitimating basis was doctrinal and scientific, located in the official doctrine of Marxism–Leninism (Brunner, 1982); or unofficial and paternalistic, conforming to the authoritarian family and personality type characteristic of an enduring social culture (Feher, 1982); or again whether legitimacy was something that concerned élites alone (Bialer, 1980; Rigby, 1982), or had a mass dimension (Lane, 1984; Lomax, 1984). Such confusion is less an index of fundamental disagreement about the nature of the Soviet system in its classical period than a demonstration of the disarray attending the concept of legitimacy in political science, and the absence of any agreed theoretical foundation that might enable us to distinguish legitimating elements from other more derivative features of a political system (Ludz, 1979; Pakulski, 1986).

My own analysis will start from the premise that the legitimacy of any political system is intimately linked with its basic organising principles and rules of power, which it serves to validate in the different ways already distinguished; and that, as with the system of capitalist democracy, we should treat the polity and economy as two parts of an interrelated whole. Starting from this premise I shall identify the legitimating elements of the Soviet model as it existed prior to Gorbachev, and consider possible explanations for the legitimation crisis of the 1980s. The fact that at the present time of writing the precise shape of the future evolution in the USSR remains unclear is immaterial, since we can at least be certain that a return to the old system as a *legitimate* politico-economic order is no longer possible. Although we can therefore no longer talk of it in the present tense as a contemporary system, the advantage of hindsight which the close of an epoch affords should help us to identify its legitimating features with greater clarity. I take these to be as follows:

1. The communist system of rule in its classical form derived its authority from a dual source. First was from the people; here it stood in the mainstream of legitimacy from the French revolution onwards. However, it was the people only as defined in a certain way – as the working class or classes – and as represented uniquely by the Communist party in its role as 'vanguard'. This definition of the people and limitation on their representation was justified in turn by reference to a second source of authority, which qualified if not actually displaced the first: the doctrine of Marxism–Leninism, and its claims to exclusive knowledge of the conditions of evolution towards a communist future. It was this doctrine that privileged the working class as the most progressive social class, with its interests identical to those of society as a whole, and the Communist party as the exclusive interpreter and representative of those interests. Popular consent in this system was not expressed primarily through elections, which lacked the alternatives necessary for effective choice, and were largely propagandistic in purpose. It

was expressed rather through the extent of mass activism at the grass roots, which provided a continuous demonstration of popular commitment to the party's cause, and served to validate its claim to the leading role in society. As explained in the previous chapter, in this 'mobilisation' model the expression of popular consent is divorced from the process of appointment to office and choice of policy alternatives, which remain an élite prerogative in accordance with the superior knowledge or capacities to which they lay claim.

From these legitimating elements of the polity a number of features can be seen to follow, which are relevant to the disputes in the literature mentioned above. First, whereas under liberal democracy the source of authority is identified by reference to a simple *principle* – that of popular sovereignty – and a straight-forward electoral device for ascertaining the people's will; in the communist system, authority was primarily located in an elaborated body of *doctrine*, Marxism–Leninism. Hence the reproduction of that doctrine, the protection of its orthodoxy, the identification of authentic interpreters, etc. assumed a central place in the organisation of power. Moreover, since the test of 'correct' policies lay ultimately not in what the people, freely organised, would accept, but in what the party hierarchy, informed by scientific doctrine, would determine, the relation between rulers and ruled necessarily assumed a paternalist character, as it does wherever it rests on the claim to superior knowledge. The doctrinal source of authority determined the paternalist character of rule, rather than being in conflict with it.

Secondly, the process of legitimation operated at both élite and mass levels, albeit in different ways; and the party was the instrument of both. At the élite level, a life-time's socialisation into the party's norms, and the careful filtering out of non-conformists, guaranteed loyalty to the system and ensured the necessary élite cohesion in face of struggles for succession and position, as well as guaranteeing the subordination of the state and military apparatus to the party. At the mass level, the party mobilised the grass-roots activity which provided the continuous evidence of popular commitment to its rule, and which served as the surrogate consent of the population as a whole.

Thirdly, while the expression of consent which confirmed the party's claim to rule depended, on the one side, upon continuous popular activity in its cause, it also required, on the other, that any divergent opinions which might challenge the party's monopoly of representation should not reach the public domain. Unlike in liberal democracies, where public opposition to government policy is validated by the basic rules of free association, in a communist system any public dissent expressed outside the party, especially by the working class, had a delegitimating consequence for the system as a whole, since it challenged the principle of the party's leading role and its monopolistic claim on representation. The systematic obstruction of an alternative or independent public opinion and the means to its organisation, therefore, through the state's monopoly of communication and its apparatus of surveillance, constituted a necessary feature of the system's legitimacy, rather than an alternative to it. The state's demobilisation of dissent, if need be by illegal or extra-legal means, formed the necessary counter-part to the party's mobilisation of consent.

If, then, legitimacy and suppression went hand-in-hand in this manner, it helps explain why commentators have had such difficulty in deciding whether communist systems had any legitimacy at all. In determining this question, we need to draw a distinction between the everyday processes geared to preventing the emergence of dissent, which themselves operated in secret, and the highly visible and dramatic repression of a mass protest that had somehow managed to escape the constraining effects of demobilisation, and had emerged into the public domain. The former could be regarded as systemically normal, and was a necessary counterpart to its legitimation. The latter was abnormal – the response to a process of public delegitimation, which only further compounded it. It was one of the system's weaknesses, however, that the first, everyday, mode of repression constituted a recurrent source of grievance; and that, in stifling any expression of dissent outside accepted party channels, it ensured its emergence with all the more force when it did eventually break out.

2. The economy in the classical form of communist system was organised on the basis of public ownership and centralised planning, on the grounds that only in this way could the systematic exploitation and unemployment that the working

class suffers under capitalism be overcome; and that, since
determining investment priorities and the distribution of the
social product are matters of essential public interest, they
should be consciously decided by political authority rather
than left to the sway of private interests and the uncertain
outcomes of the market. These organising principles, which
derived their credibility from capitalism's most vulnerable
features, especially as exemplified during the 1930s, comprised a part of what was understood by 'socialism'. The
other part was conceived of dynamically: as a process of
economic development towards a future society in which
material needs would be met for all, and the 'all-round development of human powers' would become possible. Progress
towards this goal provided a necessary confirmation of the
validity of socialism's organising principles, and of the historical schema that lay at the core of Marxist–Leninist doctrine.

The system of central planning through administrative control
proved itself capable of developing an industrial base and the
public services necessary to support it, such as transport, education, health, scientific research, and so on. It laid the foundation for impressive industrial and economic development. But
it also showed itself chronically incapable of producing food and
consumer goods in sufficient amounts, variety or quality to satisfy
the basic needs of the population. The reasons for this are intrinsic to a system of centralised planning itself, and are located in
its inability to ensure effective lateral coordination between firms
and economic sectors on the basis of vertical command. A 'command' economy stifles initiative and self-determination at the
level of the enterprise, without, however, being able to secure
the information or control the responses necessary to make the
plan work, much less provide corrections when it fails to do so.
This basic defect proves increasingly evident as the command
economy moves from an 'extensive' phase of development,
characterised by the production of heavy goods and expanded
utilisation of labour, to an 'intensive' phase, where the provision
of more sophisticated consumer goods and improvements in productivity are the key (Brus, 1972; Nove, 1983).

This chronic problem of the command economy in the communist systems gave rise, on the one hand, to a parallel unofficial

economy, and, on the other, to an expansion of the apparatus of administrative supervision, as it sought in vain to control the uncontrollable. The bureaucratic apparatus itself constituted the main obstacle to reform in a more market-oriented or decentralised direction, since such a reform would deprive it of its chief *raison d'être*. Here lay a systemic contradiction more acute than anything under capitalism – between the goals of the system and its basic principles of organisation – which was experienced as an increasingly acute conflict between the economic needs of society and the interests of the administrative apparatus employed to realise them (Bahro, 1978; Feher *et al.*, 1983).

The problem at issue here was not just a matter of economic performance, but of its consequences for the belief system of socialism, which played such a central part in both economy and polity. The communist model was publicly dependent upon a uniformity of belief system to a degree that capitalist democracies are not. In the latter, a belief in individual liberty, popular sovereignty, etc., is needed to underpin the rules of political and economic organisation. But these beliefs constitute a background condition, as it were, against which a pluralism of particular and competing beliefs occupy the foreground. Nor are they threatened by a retreat of the population into a privatised existence of purely personal motivations, which indeed they serve to justify.

In the communist model, in contrast, beliefs played a continuously public role. This was not just a question of the status of Marxism–Leninism as the official doctrine, with its exclusive claim to truth. It was also that society was organised for the pursuit of a collective purpose – the realisation of socialism – and belief in the validity of that purpose was necessary not only to the legitimacy of its rules of power, but to key motivations also, at a number of levels. In the absence of procedures of public accountability, this belief was necessary to ensure a minimum of integrity in the holders of power. In the absence of electoral consent, it was necessary to the mobilisation of a mass base for the party, with any degree of commitment. Because of the deficiency of material incentives for economic production (or the disincentive of bankruptcy or unemployment) it was necessary to the work motivations of the population at large.

Without the belief in the validity of a collective purpose, in short, the communist model lost its vital stimulus; it became reduced to a pursuit of private interests destined to frustration, and a structure of élite prerogatives and civil restrictions and harassments devoid of any public justification. Yet it was precisely the system's own evolution that undermined this belief, as the contradiction became more apparent between the societal goal, of expanded human powers and fulfilment of needs, and the framework of bureaucratic planning fashioned to realise it; between the socialist end and the socialist means, as these had come to be defined within Marxist–Leninist doctrine. What we have here is the classic pattern of a 'legitimation crisis', in which the evolution of the system brings it up against the limits of its own organising principles, and in so doing erodes the beliefs that are necessary to sustain them.

At the same time the course of economic development also produced the agents of a new politico-economic order in increasing strata of educated personnel, for whom acting upon commands from above proved less and less tolerable. Most visible of these were the dissident intelligentsia, to whom the decay of communism was not a failure of economic system merely, but a moral bankruptcy exposed in the party's distortion of truth, and in the gulf between official rhetoric and the reality of everyday experience (e.g. Havel, 1987). Yet it was only when the expression of dissent extended to the working classes, and to a public delegitimation by those whose interests the regime claimed to represent, that the underlying contradictions and legitimacy weakness of the system could develop into a full scale crisis of political authority.

The process of disenchantment described above ran its course much more rapidly in the Eastern European countries, where the communist system was associated with national subordination rather than with the prestige of leadership of a world movement, and the achievement of great power status, as in the Soviet Union. That much is evident from the history of repeated uprisings against communist rule, which could only be maintained in being by military intervention, from Hungary in 1956 through to Poland in 1981. Although the Czech situation in 1968 was different, in that the reforms initiated by the party enabled it to stem its own crisis of legitimacy, the invasion which cut them short demonstrated the gulf that existed between the archetypal Soviet model that was reimposed, and the direction that the system would have taken under the impetus of an autonomous, nationally determined, evolution. The fact that a general recognition of the limits of Soviet tolerance became thereafter a self-imposed limitation on demands for political change in Eastern Europe cannot be taken as evidence of legitimacy, i.e. of an acceptance of the rules of power as *justifiable*; only of a prudent recognition of the conditions for survival in the face of superior force. Any doubt on this score was resolved by the dramatic collapse of the communist regimes during 1989, once Gorbachev's renunciation of the Brezhnev doctrine of intervention was proved to be serious. The rapidity of the collapse provided a copybook demonstration of the fate of political systems lacking moral authority, once they are unable or unwilling to suppress their populations by force.

The policy of renunciation which set this process in train was prompted by the internal impasse that the communist model had reached in the Soviet Union itself, compounded by the costs of sustaining a great power role in competition with the USA. At the heart of the impasse was the impossibility of improving economic performance within a centralised planning regime, and the necessity of a radical shift to a system of market coordination and a more consumer-oriented economy. However such a shift in turn could not be carried through, as Gorbachev clearly recognised, without a fundamental change in the rules of the political system and its underlying principles of legitimacy.

The reasons for the necessary linkage between the economic and the political dimensions of reform in the Soviet Union can be judged from the past history of economic reform programmes in Eastern Europe (McFarlane, 1984). Without a clear mandate from society, such as competitive elections would provide, the economic reform process of the communist system has proved liable to obstruction at the hands of the party and state apparatus, whose rationale as well as privileges depend upon its own administrative control over the economy. And without a more secure legitimacy, the government has been unable to sustain the short-run costs involved in a market-oriented reform, since, to paraphrase Jaruzelski, only a government that enjoys public confidence can demand sacrifices. The result has been that, as soon as reforms have run into difficulties, the conservatives within the party have been able to play on popular discontent to secure their reversal. On this evidence, economic reform could only become irreversible if the reformers could secure a basis of legitimacy that rendered them immune from manoeuvrings within the party hierarchy, and a popular mandate that would enable the reform process to withstand the short-term costs and dislocations it would impose upon the working class. And that necessitated a shift from a mobilisation to an electoral mode of legitimation.

At the institutional level such a shift in the basis of political legitimacy has been relatively simple to effect, since the communist states already had an apparatus of elections, parliamentary assemblies and so on, ready to take on a quite new significance once they were released from the processes of pre-selection and coordination by the party hierarchy. But the significance of the shift has been profound, since the guarantee of effective choice necessary to electoral legitimation has opened up the sphere of high politics to popular influence, and signalled the abandonment of doctrinal orthodoxy as the basic principle of political cohesion. The very rapidity with which the old political order has unravelled as a consequence has brought serious problems in its train.

Of these problems, the most obvious is that the process of democratisation initiated by Gorbachev from above has called forth responses from below that reach far beyond his own programmatic aims. The national conflicts in the republics, and the demands for secession, threaten the spatial integrity of the Soviet state. And the dramatic eclipse of the Communist Party, not merely as the ruling party but as a serious electoral force, in the popular revolutions of Eastern Europe poses a serious question mark over its future in the Soviet Union as well. However much the party may be needed there to provide a basis of cohesion and continuity in the difficult process of 'perestroika', the logic of electoral legitimacy, with freedom of association and a choice between policies as well as candidates, leads powerfully in the direction of a multi-party system. Whether the evolving political order can combine the open articulation of social conflicts at the highest level of the state, with the unity of direction needed to implement the tough decisions involved in the marketisation of the economy, must remain an open question.

A second major problem concerns the very different time scales of political and economic reform; of 'glasnost' and 'perestroika' respectively. Removing controls on the flow of information, on the expression of ideas and on political organisation produces immediate and dramatic effects, whereas economic reorganisation is a slow and painful process that takes time to produce the results that provide its justification. The danger is that the strains and dislocations of the economic process will undermine the support necessary to sustain the new political order, and give its opponents powerful ammunition to discredit it. Although the cost of reversing the process of democratisation in the Soviet Union would be enormous, yet the possibility that social and economic dislocation may become so deep as to provide the occasion and justification for a military or 'Bonapartist' solution to the political situation cannot be discounted. No society in history has been called on to manage the end of empire, the marketisation of its economy and the democratisation of its political system simultaneously.

Whatever the precise outcome of the process of change initiated in the Soviet Union by Gorbachev, the disintegration of the communist model as a legitimate politico-economic order marks the close of an epoch in contemporary state systems. Does it follow, therefore, as Francis Fukuyama has argued, that capitalist democracy is left holding the field, not merely as the only legitimate form of contemporary system, but as the ultimate embodiment of human aspirations, as the 'end of history'? (Fukuyama, 1989).

Let me try to answer this question by recalling two potent images from the revolutions of 1989, both involving mass action in the streets. The first image is that of the popular demonstrations in Leipzig, Prague and elsewhere: of people collectively calling their rulers to account, and demanding a form of government in which they had a say in the choice of leaders and the determination of policy. These actions demonstrate the power of the principle of popular sovereignty to disrupt those institutional arrangements that limit or frustrate its realisation, once the beliefs that support them have become eroded in the population at large. The communist model in its indigenous revolutionary form may be seen initially to have been politically progressive in comparison with the dictatorships and traditional systems it replaced, in that it established the principle of equal opportunity and extended the political community to include the whole population. Yet its doctrinal base in Marxism–Leninism perpetuated a paternalist relationship between rulers and society, which became vulnerable once the credibility of its belief system was eroded, and the people claimed the right to decide their interests for themselves. Here my own analysis of the irreversibility of the principle of popular sovereignty in its unqualified form gives some support to Fukuyama's claim.

The other image that stays in the memory is of a different form of mass action: the East German population pouring through the Berlin wall with their shopping bags to share in the consumer abundance of the West. This reminds us that the communist model was not undermined by internal processes alone, but by the competition with Western capitalism that it had itself endorsed, and which it had been able to withstand in the industrialising phase of its development, but was hopelessly mismatched for in the mass consumption phase of advanced capitalism (Bauman, 1990). At first sight the image of the East German consumer invasion endorses the idea of a positive link between the democracy of the market and the democratisation of the political order. However, we have also subsequently witnessed the effects of exposure to the international market on the productive base of the East European economies: the other face of capitalism as a disruptive force, as harbinger of unemployment and intensifier of inequality, both within and between countries. This other side of capitalism, which I discussed earlier, exposes the limitations of Fukuyama's perspective. Liberal democracy could only achieve a universal significance, not to mention a final one, if the *conditions for its realisation* could be universalised; and that would require a different kind of international economic order from any that capitalism has so far produced.

The dual character of capitalism as an attractive and disruptive force could stand as a paradigm for the impact of external factors in general upon the internal legitimacy of states: for the attraction (and repulsion) of normative models on the one side, and the intrusiveness of empirical powers on the other. Both are evident in the examples from the Islamic world to be considered in the final section.

Types of Islamic state

One reason for including a discussion of Islam at this point, however cursory it must be, is that the revival in the political significance of Islam over the past two decades has provided the most direct challenge to a longstanding presupposition of Western social science, to the effect that political legitimacy in the contemporary world can only be securely grounded on a secular basis. Central to this presupposition is the belief that secularisation is an essential feature of modernisation, and that modernisation itself is a multi-faceted process whose elements each provide a necessary complement or support to one another. These assumptions are directly challenged by the recent Islamic revival, which emerged as the unexpected product of modernisation, and has proved strongest precisely in those countries whose economic development, fuelled by oil revenues, has been most rapid (Keddie, 1988).

Now it is of course possible to preserve the original assumptions by arguing that the Islamic revival is not only the product of modernisation, but also a *reaction* to it, and one that finds strongest support among those social groups which have benefited least from the process of economic expansion; in other words, that it constitutes an essentially reactionary phenomenon, which can only hinder further social and economic development because it stands in opposition to some of its essential requirements. Such a judgement, however, only achieves plausibility by ignoring the point on which the Islamic revival challenges Western assumptions most strongly: its rejection of any universal validity inhering in Western development models, whether capitalist or communist, and its search for a development path that is more in tune with its own history and traditions. The Islamic revival as a political phenomenon, in other words, has attained its momentum from the discrediting of the capitalist and communist models, both for their intrinsic defects – pursuit of profit without social responsibility on one side, hostility to private property on the other – and above all because they have involved subordination to foreign influences and interests, whether those of the USA or the USSR.

Like nationalism, then, to which it is closely related, the Islamic revival draws its appeal from an explicit rejection of external models and external interference in an anti-imperialist age. It also has more specific political determinants, deriving from the Arab – Israeli conflict, and in particular from the Egyptian defeat in 1967, which discredited the Nasserite socialist version of development, and from which many concluded that a secular ideology was no match for an enemy inspired by religious conviction, and whose state had a primarily religious purpose. The strength of the more fundamentalist movements, such as the Muslim brothers, can be systematically related to the different phases of the Palestinian crisis, and the reactions of the Western powers to it (Enayat, 1982, ch.3).

Despite these common features making for a revival of Islam as a politically significant force, the form of that revival has varied considerably according to differences of local situations and tradition. Islam is no more monolithic an entity than Christianity. The political ideal of an 'Islamic state', in particular, has been subject to an enormous range of interpretations. At a minimum it can mean a state which gives protection to the institutions and practice of the Islamic faith. More substantially, it can mean a state whose policies are themselves conducive to Muslims living a life in accordance with the requirements of their religion. A more stringent demand is that the state should embody the *shari'a*, or Islamic law, in its own legislation and judicial procedures; though, here again, what this amounts to in practice will depend on how narrowly the *shari'a* itself is to be interpreted. Finally the idea of an 'Islamic state' can mean the subordination of the state to the religious project of creating a spiritually transformed community, inspired by 'the true Islamic mentality and moral attitudes'. Each of these conceptions has very different implications for the relationship between religion and politics, and for the kind of critique that is made of the established order (Enayat, 1982; Ahmed, 1987).

From the standpoint of political legitimacy, however, it is important to note that, apart from the idea of a full-blown theocracy, subject to the rule of the *ulama*, or jurists, none of the conceptions mentioned above carries any implications for the particular *form* of political system. The ideal of an Islamic state or Islamic order is compatible with, and can be realised within, any constitutional form: monarchical, representative, or whatever. This is because its primary concern is to specify the purposes or goals which the state should serve, rather than the source from which its political authority is to be derived. By the same token, however, the project of establishing an Islamic order has proved insufficient to secure the legitimacy of regimes whose source of authority is itself in doubt. Many rulers have sought to bolster a failing legitimacy by appeal to their Islamic credentials, and by instituting an Islamic revival from above; but without notable success. President Sadat's grandiose mosque-building programme in Egypt revealed a religion based more on outward show than authentic conviction (Gilsenan, 1988). President Zia's introduction of an Islamic code in Pakistan aroused widespread opposition, particularly among women, and demonstrated the gulf that existed between the idea of a state for Muslims and his more robust conception of an Islamic state (Alavri, 1988). President Numeiri's introduction of a similar code in the Sudan antagonised the Christian south, and intensified the divisions in that country (Niblock, 1987, epilogue).

These attempts suggest that the manipulation of religion from above to secure political legitimacy is ineffectual if not counterproductive. Islam began as a revivalist movement from below against a corrupt society, and its most dynamic political manifestations in the modern period have all contained elements of such revivalism (Mortimer, 1982, ch.2). In particular, it has only provided a secure basis for political legitimacy in the twentieth century when a movement from below has been successfully harnessed to a political project at the level of the state. The two distinctive types of political system in the contemporary Islamic world – the conservative monarchy of Saudi Arabia and the revolutionary theocracy of Iran – both had their origins in such a conjunction. In the former, the revivalist movement was harnessed to the expansionist ambitions of a hereditary dynasty, and served to reinforce a purely traditional type of legitimacy. In the latter, the revivalist current took a politically revolutionary form, and created a unique mass-mobilisation regime organised on theocratic lines. Both reveal the limitations as well as the strengths of Islam as a support for state legitimacy. As I shall also explore, both demonstrate the complex interrelation between politics, religion and an economic development based on oil.

The distinctive feature of the Saudi Arabian political system is that it is an absolute monarchy whose legitimacy is based entirely on the hereditary principle, and yields no place to ideas of popular sovereignty. Power resides with the Al Saud family, who approve the succession, advise the monarch and staff a number of the leading ministries of state. Proposals to create a constitution to limit the king's powers, and provide a means of popular representation have never been accepted. Consent to rule is expressed in traditional manner by meetings of tribal leaders and other figures of influence, acting on behalf of society as a whole (Niblock, 1982, ch.5).

The obvious question to ask is how such a purely traditionalist system has been able to survive, not only in Saudi Arabia, but in most of the other Gulf states as well. One reason has to do with their small size. In other parts of the world the process of colonisation created states whose territory either cut across traditional political units, or incorporated a number of them. The alteration of the spatial range of government necessarily prevented the traditional structures from forming the basis for the post-colonial state, and the hereditary principle from providing its source of legitimacy, even had it survived erosion from other forces. In the area of the Gulf, in contrast, British influence served to consolidate rather than disrupt the traditional political units and system of rule, through the principle of 'non-interference' in the internal affairs of the sheikdoms.

Such an explanation, however, will not suffice for Saudi Arabia itself. Although the house of Al Saud traces its ancestry back for 500 years or more, the kingdom of Saudi Arabia is the product of relatively recent conquest, dating from the 1920s and 1930s. What requires explanation, therefore, is not only the survival of a traditionalist system of rule, but its ability to maintain its hold over a substantial territorial state. It is here that both religion and oil have had a crucial part to play.

The significance of religion in the Saudi state derives from the fact that the process of conquest of the Arabian peninsular was simultaneously a religious crusade to spread Wahabism – a movement of Islamic revival associated with the Al Saud family since its origins in the eighteenth century – among the Bedouin tribes of the interior (Hopwood, 1982). The converts provided a militant force, both religious and military, for use in the further conquest of the region, and in driving the unpopular Hashemite monarchy out of the area bordering the Red Sea (the Hijaz) which contained the holy cities of Mecca and Medina. Although the crusading force thus created, the Ikhwan, had in due course to be suppressed by King Abdul-Aziz when it threatened British control of Iraq, the prestige that the royal house has enjoyed in the peninsular has been intimately bound up with its religious credentials and mission: as principled upholder of Islamic law and as protector of Islam's holy places (Habib, 1978). This mission has necessarily given the *ulama* a substantial influence over legislation in the kingdom, especially in areas of public morality; in return they have underwritten the legitimacy of the monarchical order (Mortimer, 1982, ch.6). Indeed, the traditionalisms of religion and of dynastic succession have proved as mutually supportive in Saudi Arabia as in Christian Europe of the past. Moreover, it is a connection which the recent revivalist tendencies in the Islamic world have served to strengthen, even when Saudi rule has been criticised for its conservatism and support for US interests.

However, if the historic family link with a revivalist strain of Islam has given the Al Saud their claim to moral influence, their hold over the peninsula has also depended on the material resources provided by the thoroughly modern phenomenon of oil extraction (Niblock, 1982). Holding together a predominantly tribal system requires substantial economic resources, since the allegiance of local leaders has to be continually confirmed by grants, personal gifts, hospitality and other favours. During the early years of the state the revenue derived from customs and pilgrimage dues was quite insufficient to meet these requirements, and it was only the exploitation of oil in the 1940s that enabled the state finances to be put on a sound footing. From that time on, the central control exercised from Riyadh over ever-increasing oil revenues has provided an effective deterrent against secessionist tendencies, and a potent means for consolidating the traditionalist system of rule. Indeed, an oil-based 'rentier state' can be particularly well-suited to the preservation of a traditional legitimacy in the modern world, since it maximises the largesse available for distribution by rulers, while allowing change in established patterns of economic production to be kept to a minimum. It is only since the 1970s, in fact, that substantial industrialisation has taken place in the country through downstream development from petrochemicals.

In conclusion, it is only a unique combination of religious authority and enormous oil revenues that has enabled the traditional system of rule to survive in Saudi Arabia, and to resist the threat from the secular movements of Arab nationalism that brought down the monarchies in Egypt, Syria and Iraq in the 1950s, as well as to withstand the repeated shocks of the Arab – Israeli conflict, and most recently of the Iranian revolution. However, it must be doubtful whether a purely traditional legitimacy can survive indefinitely without some concession to popular representation, now that the state has embarked on a substantial programme of industrialisation. All the evidence of industrialisation elsewhere indicates that its characteristic by-products are an intensification of social divisions, and pressures for working-class self-organisation that translate in time into a demand for political rights. Thus, although the Al Saud have so far successfully resisted demands for a constitution, it is unlikely that they can control the consequences of economic development sufficiently to prevent their recurrence in a more insistent form. In other words, while the survival of a purely traditional system is impressive, it has been dependent not only upon a unique conjunction of factors, but also on a particular phase in the country's economic development which is unlikely to last. The shock waves created by Iraq's invasion of Kuwait have only emphasised the vulnerability of traditionalist rule to future expressions of mass discontent in a world where the principle of popular sovereignty is a legitimating norm, and have underlined the dilemmas of a regime so manifestly dependent upon US protection.

When compared with Saudi Arabia, Iran presents a marked contrast with respect to both the political systems it has had over the past decades. The Pahlavi monarchy demonstrated the weakness of a system of supposedly traditional rule which actively sought to divorce itself from all other elements of traditionalism within the society, Islam included. And the Islamic republic which replaced it by revolutionary overthrow is as different as anything could be from the traditional monarchy of Saudi Arabia, not least in the way religion has been used for the purpose of radical mass-mobilisation. The change from one regime type to the other is instructive for any analysis of political legitimacy in the contemporary Islamic world (see Keddie, 1981; Abrahamian, 1982).

Although Iran had had a monarchical system of rule for centuries, the Pahlavi dynasty enjoyed only limited legitimacy, for a number of reasons. First, the dynasty was only created in the present century, and rested on nothing more solid than the military exploits of Reza Khan, not on the prestige of a royal lineage stretching unbroken into the past, or on the support of an extended family network, as in Saudi Arabia. Secondly, both Reza Khan and his son Muhammed resisted all attempts to limit their powers by making them accountable to a representative assembly, as required by the 1905 constitution. Their autocratic form of rule was of doubtful legality, since the 1905 constitution was never formally replaced. Muhammed Reza Shah's powers in particular were consolidated by a CIA-financed coup which brought down the government of premier Mossadeq in 1953, in order to prevent his proposed nationalisation of Iran's oil assets. The Shah's later attempt to demonstrate the continuity of his rule with Iran's pre-Islamic past in the grandiose celebrations for 2500 years of the monarchy in 1971 served more to expose the weakness of his authority than to consolidate it. Lacking any credible claim to traditional right, his regime was also hostile to any genuinely popular source of legitimacy that cooperation with a freely elected assembly might have provided.

However, the absence of any legitimating basis in a recognised source of authority is not itself sufficient to explain the collapse of a regime, especially one sustained by such a powerful army and extensive means of repression. It was the actively delegitimating force of the huge mass demonstrations during 1978 that undermined the will and the capacity of the Shah to maintain his repressive system in being. These demonstrations marked the culmination of two interrelated processes that had been at work during the 1970s: on the one side the intensification of popular grievances brought about by the Shah's programme of economic development; on the other, the increasingly dominant role played by religious leaders in the opposition to the Shah, and the increasingly Islamic terms in which that opposition came to be expressed. Both processes merit examination.

That a state-sponsored development programme based on enormous oil revenues should come to undermine the authority of the state, rather than reinforce it as it did in Saudi Arabia, is to be explained by the particular interrelationship between the pattern of economic development and the character of state institutions, rather than by any general category such as that of the 'rentier state' (Mahdavy, 1970). In Saudi Arabia the oil revenues were deployed in a way which strengthened the traditional order based upon patronage, and confirmed the loyalty of local chieftains and political leaders to the ruling family, which controlled resources at the centre. In Iran, by contrast, the Shah's more ambitious programme of 'modernisation' simply intensified the gulf between a privileged Westernised élite and the vast majority of society. This gulf was most evident in the economic disparities of the cities, between those who could afford to sustain a Western consumer lifestyle, based largely on imported goods, and the impoverished masses who had been driven off the land by agrarian reforms into the insecure employment, slum housing, and inadequate infrastructure of urban life. The austerity measures introduced by a new premier in 1977 to deal with the overheated economy intensified discontent, and underlined the contrast between the resources lavished on the military and bureaucratic apparatus of the state and the impoverished condition of the majority (Halliday, 1979; Keddie, 1981, ch.7).

The gulf between regime and society was further widened by the emphasis given to Western, and particularly US, interests in the Shah's policy. Ever since the coup that brought down premier Mossadeq, the regime had been associated with subordination to the USA. The diplomatic immunity granted to US military personnel and 'advisers' in 1964 had caused particular offence. The pace of economic development, which accelerated with the increase in oil prices in the early 1970s, brought a huge influx of foreign staff to the multinational companies established around Tehran, and a sharp rise in rents in the capital. And with the import of Western consumer goods for the Iranian élite came also Western lifestyles and culture, films and TV programmes and the pervasiveness of consumer values. The Shah's policies, besides intensifying economic inequalities, thus came also to be associated with the undermining of any distinctive Iranian identity and its submergence in an alien culture (so called 'Westoxication').

In such a context, although there was a strong tradition of

secular opposition in twentieth-century Iran, the link between royal dictatorship, economic inequality and cultural alienation proved to be much more effectively exposed in Islamic terms (Keddie, 1982). The categories of the secular opposition, whether those of a democratic republic or a socialised economy, had the disadvantage of themselves being of Western origin, and were incapable of addressing the cultural dimensions of the society's malaise. An Islamic analysis, in contrast, which linked the Shah's lack of legitimacy with his policies of secularisation and his disregard for the country's religious heritage, offered a much more persuasive socio-political critique, and one that spoke much more powerfully to the sense of national humiliation. A return to Islam offered a solution to moral decline, an assertion of national independence and a restoration of political legitimacy simultaneously. In delivering this message, the Shah's religious critics had the advantage over the secular opposition of much closer links with the deprived masses, both urban and rural, and an institutional autonomy that enabled them to survive the extremes of repression, for all that the Pahlavis had systematically sought to limit the role and influence of the mullahs over many decades. They were thus able to link their own particular and longstanding grievances with the general discontent towards the regime, and so give their critique of the Shah's policies a universal significance for the society.

Once a religious definition of the country's discontents had become prevalent, it was not surprising that the symbolic leadership of the opposition should focus around the person of the Shah's most consistent and unyielding religious critic, Ayatollah Khomeini, who had been exiled as far back as 1964, and whom the Shah singled out for special condemnation in January 1978. What took everyone by surprise, however, was the mobilising power of Khomeini's message, evidenced in the enormous mass demonstrations of 1978 and the exemplary readiness of demonstrators to sacrifice their lives in public opposition to the regime. Although the role of armed mujehaddin units in the final stages of the revolution in February 1979 should not be overlooked, Iran was distinctive among Third World revolutions in that the regime did not succumb to guerrilla warfare in the countryside, but to the urban masses demonstrating peacefully on the streets; it was not defeated primarily through armed struggle, but through a process of popular delegitimation which undermined its authority from within. Here Iran set an example of 'people power' that was to be repeated throughout the 1980s (Ahmad, 1982; Halliday, 1988).

However, the difference between Iran and the later examples of 'people power' is that none of the others resulted in a mobilisation regime, i.e. one legitimated primarily through mass-mobilisation rather than electoral competition. For that to take place, other preconditions were required besides the revolutionary process itself, in particular the establishment of a monopolistic doctrine laying exclusive claim to the truth, and an organisation capable of mobilising the masses in its service on a continuing basis. Of crucial importance in this context was Khomeini's distinctive innovation in Shi'ite political thought. Traditionally, Shi'ism has always been pluralistic, acknowledging no single authority or source of religious interpretation; and it has defined only a limited political role for the *ulama*, as critics of rulers who threatened the practice of the faith or affronted the beliefs of the faithful, as the Shah had done. All shades of religious opinion had been agreed on a negative critique of the Shah. What Khomeini proposed, however, went much further: it was that the *ulama* should themselves wield political power, with the aim of transforming society according to Islamic law, of creating 'conditions conducive to the production of morally upright and virtuous human beings'. If the only legitimate government, as he argued, was government which actively sought to implement the *shari'a* in all spheres of life, then only those trained to interpret Islamic law were competent to oversee legislation, and any opposition to them must by definition be illegitimate (Rose, 1983; cf. Zubaida, 1982).

The symbolic leadership that Khomeini came to exercise over the revolution enabled him to appropriate its energies for his own political project; to treat it, as he subsequently claimed, as a referendum for an Islamic constitution. Yet the political system he advocated was not established all at once, or without a struggle (Bakhash, 1986; Hiro, 1987, pt.2). The early years after the revolution were marked by a condition of dual power, between the President and Khomeini as Vice-Regent, between the formal institutions of the state and the revolutionary institutions of law enforcement, and between two incompatible principles of legitimacy: appointment to high office through electoral choice in open competition; and appointment by virtue of qualifications in religious law, confirmed by mass acclaim and the power of mass-mobilisation. That the second came to prevail over the first was due not only to the prestige of Khomeini himself, but to the forces of a militant revivalism pushing him from below, and to the impact on society of external events such as the Iraqi invasion and the running sore of the Arab – Israeli conflict. To be sure, elements of electoral legitimation remained, but they were significantly weakened by the requirement that candidates for the presidency be approved by the Council of Guardians, and by the effective suppression of alternatives to the Islamic Republic Party. And that party, in turn, with its links to the mosques and local prayer leaders, operated more as an organisation for mass-mobilisation than electoral competition.

Expectations that the regime would quickly collapse under-estimated the potency of the Islamic revival when harnessed to an anti-imperialist crusade. They also overlooked the distinctive strength of a mobilisation regime, which Iran shared with both the fascist and the communist exemplars. This is that the mass mobilisation of the ideologically committed serves at the same time to provide a public legitimation for the leadership, to over-awe the uncommitted and to generate support for the repression of opponents. From the standpoint of its victims Khomeini's repression was no different from that of the Shah. From the standpoint of the character of the regime, however, it was less a sign of weakness or lack of support than a necessity for preserving the doctrinal exclusivity around which its support was mobilised. In a mobilisation regime the legitimation of the leadership and its policies and the radical delegitimation of opponents are systematically connected; and repression serves as part of a political crusade as much as the interests of 'state security'. Although a more pragmatic temper may have come to inform state policy since the end of the Iran – Iraq war and the death of Khomeini, the potential for the reawakening of revolutionary fervour remains present within Iranian society. Nor is there to date any evidence of the political system itself evolving in a more pluralist direction, as the shift to a more genuinely electoral mode of legitimation would require.

Anyone comparing Iran and Saudi Arabia, in conclusion, must

be struck by the difference in the forms of Islamic revival with which their regimes have been associated, and the difference in the types of political system that Islam has served to validate. In Saudi Arabia, Islam has underwritten a conservative monarchy, whose family and tribal networks, nourished by oil revenues, have given it sufficient authority to keep the masses at arm's length from the political process, and to sustain collaboration with US interests in the region. In Iran, Islam has provided the ideological focus for a revolutionary movement, radically anti-monarchical and anti-imperialist, which has brought the deprived masses onto the centre of the political stage, first in undermining the Shah's regime, then in legitimating the rule of the *ulama*.

What is common to both states, however – and this is the key to their political legitimacy – is the organic connection forged between the definition of a religious purpose and the acknowledged *source of authority* from which the rules of the political system are derived. In the one, a traditionalist religious purpose, which seeks to maintain the precepts of the *shari'a* intact in a changing world, has made common cause with a hereditary dynasty that also derives its authority from the distant past, and seeks to preserve its essential principles of rule unchanged under modern conditions. In the other a radical, transformative purpose, whose goal is to transform individual character and with it social relations also, has given a leading role in the state to the *ulama*, and has required a politically mobilised society rather than one that is merely quietist or apolitical. In each case there is a congruence between the religious purpose and the basic principles of political authority.

As with all legitimate political systems, both Saudi Arabia and Iran have seen themselves as models for others, if not universally, then at least within the Islamic world. Saudi Arabia is the leading representative of conservative forces within the Middle East. And Iran has actively sought to export its revolution to neighbouring states. Yet there are considerable obstacles to either providing a replicable model for others to copy, not least because of the particular historical trajectory that produced each type of system. It has required specially favourable circumstances for monarchies to survive in the Middle East; once a ruling family has been overthrown, it is difficult to see how it could be restored to anything other than a decorative function, since the whole rationale for traditional legitimacy rests on the proof of superiority that comes from unbroken continuity with the past. Iran for its part may seek, or at least may have sought, the exemplary role played by previous revolutions, whether the US, French or Bolshevik; but it is handicapped by its minority position, as Shi'ite and non-Arab, among the populations it seeks to influence. At most it has the disruptive power to cause problems for other states, rather than to provide a compelling model for them to emulate.

If neither political system offers a generalisable model to others, what alternative legitimate order is available to set against the general run of personal dictatorships in the Islamic world? The communist model has lost its attraction, and in any case its militant secularism was always an affront to religious believers. Liberal democracy, on the other hand, besides facing the difficulties that are general in Third World countries, confronts a further handicap where fundamentalist movements have established themselves in any strength. If by 'fundamentalism' we mean the demand for strict adherence to a literalist interpretation of sacred texts, then this typically threatens the political equality between the sexes that is entailed in universal suffrage, and the equal right to hold public office. If we include further the claim to possess a monopoly of truth, then this entails opposition to the freedoms of expression and association necessary to electoral legitimacy.

Islam is no more inherently fundamentalist than any other belief system. Its history embraces pluralism of interpretation and coexistence with other religions. The modern period has witnessed many attempts to develop a creative synthesis from Western and Islamic elements in the social and political spheres. For these to be effective in helping establish a more generalisable form of legitimate political order depends upon a decline in fundamentalism; and among the necessary conditions for that must be a resolution of the Palestinian issue, and a reduction in neo-imperialist tendencies on the part of Western powers, neither of which looks particularly likely at present.

Throughout this chapter, in fact, what has become apparent is the importance of external influences for the legitimacy of the supposedly sovereign state. Sovereignty, as I have argued, is a condition of vulnerability as well as of legal supremacy and self-sufficiency, in that there is no superior authority to guarantee the rules of political power, which have to be legitimised internally. Yet that legitimacy is itself conditioned in form and degree by the impact of external forces, both ideological and material, and will increasingly be so conditioned in future, with the growing interdependence of states. At the ideological level, the success of capitalist democracy in its heartlands continues to prove a potent source of attraction to other societies, as the communist model does no longer. At the same time, the power associated with that success has worked to undermine alternative bases of political legitimacy, as well as to provoke significant movements of reaction appealing to indigenous sources of authority. If we cannot always predict the consequences that the impact of such external forces will have, their continued significance for political legitimacy is beyond doubt.

7 Modes of Non-legitimate Power

The previous two chapters have discussed the legitimation problems of the contemporary state in general, and of particular types of political system. The final topic to consider is the actual process of breakdown of political order, and the way in which legitimacy deficits develop into delegitimation and then illegality. In the first section of this chapter I shall distinguish the different modes of non-legitimate power at a conceptual level, and show how they are systematically related to one another as a dynamic or sequential process. The second and third sections will then analyse two different types of such a process: those leading to revolution and coup d'état respectively; and will consider the prospects for the successful relegitimation of revolutionary and military regimes in turn. In a concluding section I shall draw together the different elements in an explanation for the repeated breakdown of legitimacy experienced by states in the contemporary world.

A recurrent theme throughout the book has been that the legitimacy of power must be understood as multi-dimensional, comprising legality or rule-conformity, the justifiability of rules, and confirmation through expressed consent. One consequence of clarifying this threefold structure is that it becomes possible to distinguish different ways in which power may fail to achieve legitimacy. It may be acquired in contravention of the rules, in which case it is *illegitimate*. The rules may find only weak justification in terms of accepted beliefs about the proper source of authority or ends of government; here we should speak more correctly of a *legitimacy deficit*, or weakness. Finally, those whose consent is necessary to the confirmation of legitimacy may act in ways which demonstrate the withdrawal of their consent; this is called *delegitimation*. I shall consider each of these in turn, before showing how they are related to one another as a sequential process.

Illegitimate power is, simply, power that is acquired through a breach of the constitutional rules. The typical forms of breach are coup d'état, revolution, conquest, secession. The first two involve an illegal assumption of power – in the one case by the military, in the other as the culmination of mass struggle – which leaves state sovereignty over an existing territory in principle intact. The latter two involve an infringement of territorial sovereignty, in the one through subjection to an external power, in the other through its rejection in favour of a new self-governing state. Most of these breaches of legality will involve the use of force; where not, they usually require the use of force to defend and consolidate the power that has been illegally acquired.

The point of using the strong negative term 'illegitimate' for these acquisitions of power is that they constitute a clear and indisputable negation of the first condition of legitimacy, which is legality. As such they confront particular problems of legitimation which many of them are unable to overcome. First, as with any infringement of the law, they require special justification by reference to extra-legal norms that are widely acknowledged, and an exigency sufficiently compelling to warrant such action. In particular, since those who have breached the law will themselves require that legality be subsequently observed, they have to provide convincing reasons why others should not copy their behaviour. Then secondly, in creating a definitive break with an established constitutional order, they have to find a new basis of legitimacy for the system of rule they inaugurate in its place. The term 'illegitimacy' thus conveys at once the idea of manifest illegality, the definitiveness of the break with an established constitutional order, and a task or programme of relegitimation that may or may not be successfully carried out.

All the above examples of the illegal acquisition of power are relatively clear-cut. However, there are others that are much less so. As with any system of law, there are areas of uncertainty that give rise to constitutional dispute. Did the Head of State have the power to invite this party leader to form a government, or to dismiss that one, in the given circumstances? Was the province legally entitled to secede from the federation by a decision of its own parliament? The constitutional position may be unclear, or the validity of the constitutional system as a whole may be disputed, e.g. on the grounds that its own establishment was of doubtful legality. Or again, as with any other system of law, the factual basis of any infringement may be uncertain. The most common example is electoral fraud. It is not always easy to detect, to assign precise responsibility for, or to assess what effect it has upon the outcome, especially where it extends back to the process of electoral registration, or even to the compilation of the census returns. Is the victor legitimate or illegitimate? In all these examples it is best to talk of 'disputed legality' or 'contested legitimacy'. As with the most clear-cut cases, any of them may provide both occasion and justification for further violations of legality.

The term 'illegitimacy', then, denotes a breach of the constitutional order; and it is with the clear cut instances of revolution and coup d'état that the present chapter will primarily be concerned. Illegitimacy is to be distinguished from a condition of 'legitimacy deficit' or 'weakness', where the constitutional order diverges from accepted beliefs about the proper source of political authority; or where it either magnifies, or is incapable of resolving, chronic problems of government performance; or where judgement about these questions is a matter of fundamental disagreement within the society.

As the previous chapters will have made clear, there are many forms of legitimacy deficit or weakness, with widely differing significance. However, the basic distinction drawn earlier between the source of political authority and the ends or purposes of government, between the 'right' and the 'good', is of equal importance here. A legitimacy deficit involving the former can best be described as a *divergence* or *discrepancy* between the constitutional rules and the beliefs that should provide their justification, whether the divergence exists because the rules have been established or altered in a manner that is incompatible with established beliefs about the rightful source of authority, or because the beliefs of a society have themselves evolved over time in a way that weakens support for the constitutional order. A legitimacy deficit involving the ends or purposes of government, on the other hand, can be described as an *inadequacy* or *incapacity* of the constitutional rules to facilitate successful

government performance, or to provide resolution in the event
of failure, whether the failure is one of ineffectiveness or of
partiality in respect of the ends that government exists to attain.

This distinction can be further clarified by relating it to two
very different metaphors or analogies that have historically been
used by political theorists to describe constitutional systems: the
organic and the mechanical respectively (e.g. J.S. Mill, 1964,
pp.175–7). The organic analogy sees political systems as a kind
of natural growth, evolving over time, and dependent upon a
particular soil or environment for their flourishing. This seems
an appropriate analogy to use to describe the conformity or lack
of conformity of a constitutional order to the 'culture' of a given
society, and in particular to its beliefs about the valid source of
political authority. The mechanical analogy, on the other hand,
sees constitutional systems as deliberate constructions, designed
more or less effectively to fulfil the ends or purposes of government. This seems a more appropriate analogy to use to describe
the ability of a political system to facilitate government performance or resolve government failure. My argument, of course, is
that legitimacy embraces both; and that a legitimacy deficit can
occur either because of a divergence between constitutional rules
and given beliefs about the source of political authority, or
because of their inadequacy to resolve problems of government
performance; or indeed both simultaneously.

If we are to look for an analogy that combines both elements,
then perhaps it is to be found in civil engineering, where a given
structure has to be both appropriate to its particular site and
environment, and effective for the function it has to serve. The
advantage of this analogy is that it enables us to make a further
distinction, between the inherent strength or weakness of a structure, in its context and for its purpose, and the stresses to which
it may be subject. If we translate this into political terms, then
the strength or weakness of the structure represents the degree
of legitimacy of a constitutional system, and the stress to which
it is subject represents the impact of government failure upon it.
By 'failure' here is meant some evident inability of government
to fulfil the purposes expected of it, or to do so without intensifying social divisions. It is government failures, in this sense, that
constitute the pressure or load with which a political system has
to cope. The more secure its legitimacy, the greater the stress it

will be able to withstand. On the other hand, where legitimacy is weak, government failure will deliver the decisive pressure that will set in train a crisis of political authority.

Analogies should not be pushed too hard. Those drawn from the natural sciences convey an illusion of exactness that is out of place in the analysis of societies. Those drawn from construction tend to be static, and cannot adequately capture the dynamic process of interaction and 'feedback' between different elements of a social or political system. Even 'systems' analogies run the danger of treating societies as if they were composed of impersonal elements rather than living people. Thus the 'level of tolerance' of a political system is actually the tolerance level of the human agents involved in it; and legitimacy as a system characteristic is actually a relationship between rules and the beliefs that underpin them. However, provided due caution is observed, the ideas of 'stress' and 'critical load' can help illuminate the relation between the pressures imposed by government failure, and the inherent strength or weakness of the political order on which they bear.

A legitimacy deficit or weakness, then, is a condition of inappropriateness or inadequacy in the constitutional rules, which limits the degree of support that they, and those deriving power from them, can command when subjected to the stress of government failure. 'Delegitimation', finally, denotes a process whereby those whose consent is necessary to the legitimation of government act in a manner that indicates their withdrawal of consent. Mass demonstrations, strikes, acts of civil disobedience: such actions can have damaging consequences for the moral standing of a government and also its capacity to rule; the more so, the larger the numbers involved or the more crucial their cooperation is to the attainment of the government's purposes.

However, the precise significance of such actions must depend upon the context and the nature of the political system. In a liberal democracy, the expression and organisation of opposition to particular policies is an accepted feature of politics, and has no delegitimating significance for government. It is only when it is designed to make the policies of government unworkable, or actively to bring it down, or to demonstrate allegiance to a different political order, that it crosses the threshold from normal opposition to delegitimation, or attempted delegitimation. The difference here is in the declared intentions of the actors involved. On the other hand, in a political system where there is little freedom of expression and association allowed, the organisation of opposition to particular policies itself constitutes a challenge to government authority, whatever the intentions of the actors. In a communist system for example, the expression of opposition outside the ranks of the party, especially by the working class, challenges the party's claim to a monopoly of representation, and therefore the terms on which its own legitimacy is defined. And under authoritarian regimes of whatever hue, the banning of a demonstration or protest against a particular policy turns it into an action of very different significance, and one which, if it takes place, thereby becomes a challenge to the authority of government as a whole.

What makes these actions all examples of delegitimation, whether through the declared intentions of the actors, the nature of the political system, or the response of government itself, is that they challenge the claims of government to govern with the consent of the population. As such they serve to weaken or undermine whatever moral authority a government possesses. The more so, where the action involves an explicit refusal of people to 'do as they are told', since the humiliation of impotence intensifies the loss of moral authority. It is of the essence of such actions, however, if they are to have any delegitimating effect, that they should take place in public, and be publicly known. It is for this reason that governments will do all they can to prevent such manifestations from taking place at all; to suppress them if they do take place, so as to discourage repetition; and to stop news about what is happening from spreading to the rest of society. Just as consent has no legitimating force unless it is expressed, so the withdrawal of consent has no delegitimating impact if it is not generally known. Recent history shows many examples of the crucial role that journalists play in amplifying the delegitimating effects of civil disobedience, from the townships of South Africa through the 'intafada' in occupied Palestine, to Tiananmen Square and the mass demonstrations throughout Eastern Europe in the autumn of 1989. Governments have good reason to try and curtail or suppress news coverage, since they understand only too well that the dissemination of information in such a context can have profound political consequences.

The distinctions drawn above between the different ways in which political power may lose or lack legitimacy – through a breach of legality in the acquisition of power, through normative inadequacy of the constitutional order, through the active delegitimation of government – follow logically from the three-dimensional conception of legitimacy developed earlier. To set them out in this analytical way may appear somewhat schematic or formalistic. In practice, however, there is an integral connection between them. Thus a major breach of legality typically follows the loss of authority produced by acts of delegitimation, and these in turn typically take place, with most damaging consequences, where the legitimacy of the constitutional order is itself weak. In other words, we can posit a developmental sequence whereby some failure of government performance, compounding a normative inadequacy of the constitutional rules, sets in train a process of delegitimation and loss of authority, which culminates in a seizure of power in contravention of the legal order. Such a sequence accords with the reasoning of the political agents involved, since a normative inadequacy of the constitutional order, when accentuated by government failure, provides a sufficient ground for disobedience or withdrawal of consent, and the consequent loss of authority provides both reason and occasion for a breach of constitutional legality.

The main part of this chapter will focus on two such sequential processes that are typical of the contemporary world: one leading through revolution to a democratic or mobilisation regime; the other through coup d'état to a military dictatorship. The first, revolutionary, process typically takes place under an authoritarian system, whose source of authority is problematic because it is insufficiently anchored in the principle of popular sovereignty, and which lacks popular legitimation because the masses are partially or completely excluded from the political process. Although the regime is further weakened by its inability to overcome problems of government performance, the key element in its legitimacy deficit lies in an inadequate source of authority. In this context some damaging measure of government policy provokes widespread protest, which breaches the authorised limits of political expression, and involves a direct challenge to the government's authority. Responding with characteristic repression, the government only succeeds in widening the scale of the protest beyond its particular policies to include the rules of power themselves, and their exclusion of the people from the political process. The terminal point for the regime is only reached when its loss of authority over society penetrates the armed forces themselves, and substantial sections refuse to obey orders, or defect to the popular movement. At this point power can be seized in the name of the people, and a new order be constituted, deriving from a valid source of authority and legitimated through elections or continued popular mobilisation.

The second sequential process typically takes place under a democratic regime, whose authority is grounded in the acknowledged principle of popular sovereignty, but which is beset by problems of performance, and where the rules of the political system come to be perceived as themselves part of the problem, rather than a means to its solution. The electoral process offers only an intensification of competition, and the continued vulnerability of the losers. At the same time the freedoms of speech and association, which are necessary to electoral legitimacy and to the continuous expression of public opinion, are pushed to the limit by sectional interests determined to frustrate government policy and so to undermine its authority. Here it is not so much the exclusion of society from the political process, as the consequences of its inclusion, that is the problem. Here delegitimation – acts of disobedience, withdrawal of consent – takes the form, less of an assertion by the populace of its right to intervene, than of the use of that right by particular interests to undermine government policy. And the force of delegitimation is to expose, not so much the government's lack of a valid source of authority, as its inability to secure the general interest. It is in such a context that a section of the military defects and seizes power in the name of a general societal interest that has been compromised, and the reassertion of order and authority that have been undermined.

The two processes of revolution and coup d'état sketched out above should be seen as ideal-typical ones only, which do not exhaust the full range of historic possibilities. There is, for example, a third such typical process, which begins with a basic disagreement within society, particularly over the spatial organisation of the state, and which moves through various forms of delegitimation towards secession and/or civil war, depending on

how the respective populations are distributed over a given territory. There is not the space to deal with this process in any detail
here. Even with revolution and coup d'état, not all instances fit
neatly into the typical aetiology outlined above. Not all coups
have their origin in democratic systems: military regimes themselves, lacking legitimacy, are particularly vulnerable to repeated
coup attempts; and the examples of junior officer revolts in the
Middle East in the 1950s show that they can also take the form
of substitute revolutions where a traditional legitimacy has been
exhausted, and the source of political authority is itself in question. Equally, as the example of Nazism shows, it is possible for
a revolutionary or quasi-revolutionary mobilisation to take place
in a democratic system, and to lead to a mobilisation regime
based upon an exclusive claim to truth. However, the two processes as I have outlined them are sufficiently typical in the
contemporary world to provide at least a framework for the
more detailed analysis that follows.

Revolutions and legitimacy

Revolutions are forced changes of political system which take
place under the pressure of extra-legal mass action, and lead to
an extension of popular involvement in a new political order.
Revolutions share with rebellions or revolts the feature of mass
insubordination to government; they differ from them in that
they result in a change of political *system* rather than merely of
policy or personnel. They share with coups d'état the characteristic of system change through extra-legal action or overthrow;
they differ, as I have already argued, in that the prime agency
of change is the subordinate masses rather than the military
apparatus, and that they result in an extension of popular participation in the political process, rather than its curtailment.
Against those who hold that the defining characteristic of revolution is violence, I would urge that it is rather that of extra-
legal mass action, which may or may not be violent. Against
those who maintain that the only 'true' revolutions are social
revolutions, I would insist that revolutions are by definition political events, though they may or may not be accompanied by
profound social transformation. Against those who argue that

the only 'true' revolutions are those which seek to establish a quite new order, or realise a completely new ideal, I would contend that revolutions may be restorative as well as innovative, as when they reestablish a democratic constitution that had previously been corrupted or violated. In other words, there can be different types of revolution. But what distinguishes them all as revolutions is the combination of a particular form of agency – extra-legal mass action – with a particular type of outcome: a forced change of political system involving expanded popular participation.

The literature on revolution is enormous, and the range of explanatory theorising about it is very wide, not to say contradictory, reflecting the sheer complexity and variability of the phenomenon. No attempt will be made here to survey these theories, or to adjudicate between them. (For comparative studies see Dunn, 1972, Skocpol, 1979, Krejci, 1983; for surveys of theory see Stone, 1965, Freeman, 1972, Kramnick, 1972, Zagorin, 1973, Cohan, 1975, Kimmel, 1990). My purpose is more modest: it is to identify the contribution that an understanding of legitimacy can make to the analysis of revolution, as one element in a complex whole. This contribution is twofold: first, in explicating the loss of moral authority by the old regime, its character and different phases. The second part lies in identifying what is involved in the relegitimation of a new political order. In discussing each of these in turn, I shall make reference to the most recent decade of revolutions, from Iran and Nicaragua in 1979 to the revolutionary year of 1989, as well as the classic revolutions of the modern period that have been much analysed (France, Russia, China).

At the heart of every process which leads to the overthrow of a political system lies a legitimacy deficit: a conviction that the existing regime cannot satisfy the general interests of society, whether through persistent incapacity or chronic divisiveness and partiality. What makes the process a revolutionary one is not only that this conviction becomes widespread, but that the regime's inadequacy comes to be linked to the absence of any valid source of its authority. In particular, those who wield power are seen to lack effective authorisation 'from the people'. It is the failure to acknowledge the people as the ultimate source of authority in the system's rules of power that is not only seen as unjustifiable in itself, but comes to be defined as the root cause of the regime's failings. In other words, the process of revolution is inextricably linked with the emergence of the principle of popular sovereignty in the modern age. Revolutions result not only from the exclusion of the masses from political influence, but from their assertion of the right to be included. Before the emergence of popular sovereignty as a principle, there could only be rebellions or civil wars, not revolutions.

What form the demand for a political order deriving its authority 'from the people' comes to take, itself depends upon the nature of the old order, and the point where the latter's source of authority has become eroded. Where it is the principle of traditional or dynastic legitimacy that has suffered erosion, at the forefront will be the assertion of popular sovereignty as such, in any form. Where it is foreign domination that is under challenge, it will be the principle of national autonomy and the authority of indigenous political forces that will be asserted. Where it is the limitation of popular sovereignty by a more hierarchical principle of appointment that is at issue, the demand will be for free elections for the chief offices of state. Where it is the restriction of the suffrage to a minority of the population, it will be for a fully representative test of the people's will. At the heart of revolution lies the erosion of some principle of power which has served to exclude the masses, partially or completely, from the political process; to the particular form of exclusion or limitation there stands a corresponding demand for their inclusion. Revolutions are the eruption of this demand with the force of a quasi-natural event.

To trace an integral link between the erosion of a hierarchical principle of authority, the mobilisation of the masses and the form of the demand for their political inclusion, is not to commit the error of seeing revolutions as consciously intended, or their outcomes as predictable. Revolutions are paradoxical phenomena: intelligible but also unintended, explicable at the same time as they are unpredictable. Thus the erosion of a regime's source of authority can take place over a long time before there is any widespread recognition of it, much less any readiness to act on that recognition. Dissident intellectuals may labour for years at considerable risk to expose the moral bankruptcy of a regime, without any apparent effect. It usually requires a serious assault on people's interests by a government to make them aware of the lack of justification for its rules of power. And the link between problems of government performance and the inadequate basis of its authority is often only consciously made under the impact of political struggle itself.

Thus a popular mobilisation to protest at some damaging policy, which is answered by repression, will turn people's attention from the specific grievance to the rules of power themselves, and lead them to connect the damage to their interests with their systematic exclusion from the political process. It is this that explains the typical 'agenda shift' that takes place in a revolution: what starts out as a protest against a particular policy escalates rapidly into a challenge to the political order as a whole, without this consciously being intended. Yet it is only possible where the potential for such an outcome is already present in an exclusivist principle of authority whose intellectual basis has been eroded over time.

One essential element, then, in a regime's loss of moral authority is the process whereby people come to make the link between the policy failures from which they suffer, and the invalidity of a principle of authority which excludes them from political influence: to make the link, so to say, between the 'bad' and the 'wrong'. Such a connection occurs over different timescales for different people; what is characteristic of revolution is that it is sparked simultaneously for large numbers by some notable event. This is the 'shift of consciousness' that contributes to a regime's loss of moral authority. However, there is another essential contributory factor, and that is provided by the acts of mass disobedience and insubordination – the demonstrations, strikes, etc., undertaken in explicit defiance of authority – which very publicly delegitimate the regime. Although the shift of consciousness and the acts of delegitimation may in practice occur simultaneously, it is helpful to distinguish them analytically.

Delegitimation is the dramatic loss of prestige incurred by a regime when large numbers of its subjects refuse to do as they are told in a public and collective way. Those who have always claimed to 'represent' the nation are now exposed as unrepresentative; their pretensions to serve the public interest are declared fraudulent by the public in person. Above all, those who wield enormous power are suddenly glimpsed as impotent. It is not so much that the emperor is revealed to have no clothes; the act itself divests him. And the memory of this public stripping will persist even where the 'emperor' reasserts his authority through force. Moreover, the suffering endured by an actively mobilised population under fire only increases its moral authority in face of the regime. Where the 'martyrs' in the consciousness-raising, pre-revolutionary stage are typically drawn from the intelligentsia and established leaders of moral opinion, here in the phase of public delegitimation it is typically the young who are the most determined, most self-sacrificing agents of defiance and popular mobilisation.

Acts of public delegitimation, bringing a massive loss of authority, constitute the crisis point for a regime. Facing a revolutionary situation, it is confronted with the unpalatable choice between concession or repression. Any concession short of a radical and negotiated change of political system – *de facto* surrender of power – will prove insufficient. So often in a revolutionary situation governments are caught out by the rapidity of the 'agenda shift', and find themselves lagging behind the point of popular demand; they offer concessions on policy or personnel, when it is the system itself that has become the target. Insufficient concessions both increase resentment and signal the regime's weakness and vulnerability. At the same time the strategy of making far-reaching concessions to demobilise people and prepare the ground for later repression is a highly risky one, since the reform process may become irreversible under its own momentum.

Repression, on the other hand, has to be massive and ruthless to succeed. The outcome of the repressive choice depends crucially on the unity of the armed forces, and on their willingness to carry out orders to fire on a defenceless population, the defence of whom is their chief rationale. The regime's loss of moral authority through its public delegitimation produces an acute conflict of loyalty among the military command. Are they with the people or against them? The outcome will always be a matter of local circumstance, as the revolutions of 1989 demonstrated. In Bulgaria, Czechoslovakia and East Germany the high command signalled its unwillingness or inability to undertake wholesale repression, and the regimes simply crumbled without a fight. In Romania the security forces initiated the massacre for which they had been recruited and trained, but the regular army, with its own grievances against Ceausescu, sided with the people in a bitterly fought struggle. In China, the loyalty of the army, or at least strategically deployed units of it, held sufficiently to carry through the massacre of Tiananmen Square – an act from which its prestige, and the legitimacy of the party that ordered it, can hardly recover.

Where the repressive strategy succeeds, the population is in for a long haul; the remnants of opposition are forced underground, or take to the countryside to prosecute the armed struggle. This is the prolonged rural route to revolution via guerrilla warfare and liberated zones. Where the regime is overthrown, however, the process of its delegitimation has one further stage to run. This is the retrospective exposure of its past crimes, as final justification for the breach of legality. The contrast between the private opulence of the regime and the extent of popular extortion and repression is now made fully available to public view. There is the simultaneous opening up of the contents of torture chambers and luxury villas; of security files and secret bank accounts; of empty public coffers and burgeoning private wardrobes. The ability to cover up acts of illegality, which served to prolong the regime, now adds retrospectively to its discredit.

The importance of the loss of moral authority to regime collapse, such as I have outlined above, may seem self-evident. Yet it has to be asserted against those who would claim that legitimacy has no part to play, or at most a trivial or subsidiary one, in any account of revolution. Among the most distinguished of these sceptics is Theda Skocpol, who in her book *States and Social Revolutions* advances what she calls an 'organisational' or 'realist' perspective on revolutions. According to her account it is the loss of organisational capacity on the part of the state, particularly under the pressure of external competition, working to diminish the self-confidence of key élites, and with it the repressive power of the state apparatus, that is the central explanatory factor in revolution. This account she seeks to sustain, on the one side, against traditional Marxist explanations of revolution in terms of class conflict; and, on the other, against those who 'treat the *legitimacy* of political authorities as an important explanatory concept.' The relevant passage is worth quoting at length:

'If state organisations cope with whatever tasks they already claim smoothly and efficiently, legitimacy – either in the sense of moral approval or in the probably much more usual sense of sheer acceptance of the status quo – will probably be accorded to the state's form and rulers by most groups in society. In any event, what matters most is always the support or acquiescence not of the popular majority of society but of the politically powerful and mobilized groups, invariably including the regime's own cadres. Loss of legitimacy, especially among these crucial groups, tends to ensue with a vengeance if and when . . . the state fails consistently to cope with existing tasks, or proves unable to cope with new tasks suddenly thrust upon it by crisis circumstances. Even after great loss of legitimacy has occurred, a state can remain quite stable – and certainly invulnerable to internal mass-based revolts – especially if its coercive organisations remain coherent and effective.' (1979, pp.31–2).

The above passage illustrates the erroneous conclusions that follow from an inadequate conception of legitimacy. Two points can be made in response to Skocpol's basic line of argument. Firstly, insufficient organisational capacity on the part of the state is certainly one possible cause of a loss of political legitimacy. Yet it only leads to a revolutionary situation, as opposed to some other outcome, if it is associated with an erosion of belief in the source of authority that underpins the system's rules of appoint-ment. It is the link between the two, as I have argued – between the failure to realise some basic purpose of government, and the erosion in its source of authority, between the 'bad' and the 'wrong' – that makes a regime crisis a potentially revolutionary one. Secondly, division within the state apparatus and its leading cadres is certainly critical to a revolutionary outcome, and may be engendered by a recognition of the regime's own failures. But nothing brings such divisions to a head, or makes them so fateful, as the delegitimating force of mass-mobilisation in defiance of authority. In short, loss of moral authority induces organisational incapacity every bit as much as incapacity contributes to a decline in legitimacy.

Both these points are clearly illustrated from the example of the Iranian revolution of 1979. It was manifestly no lack of organisational or extractive capacity on the part of the Iranian state, or of repressive capacity on the part of its military apparatus, that led to the Shah's downfall. The latter was the product of socially damaging policies prosecuted by a regime whose source of authority was insecure, and highly vulnerable to a radical critique by intellectual leaders. And the division within the military apparatus that precipitated the Shah's downfall was manifestly not self-induced, but resulted from the delegitimating effects of mass demonstrations. No doubt a certain relaxation of repression may have given confidence to the popular forces to seize the initiative, but the relaxation did not have its origin in any organisational imperative. Indeed, it would be difficult to find a clearer example of a loss of moral authority inducing organisational incapacity, even paralysis, rather than vice-versa. To be more pointed, the chasm between the enormous power of the Shah and the justifiability of that power was what ultimately rendered that power itself impotent. Skocpol's 'realism' is simply not realistic enough at this point, since it does not take people seriously as moral agents.

Revolutions are complex events, subject to multiple causation, both long and short term, systemic and contingent, predisposing and precipitating, etc. I have no wish to underestimate the role that governmental failure, whether it be the product of internal and external pressures, organisational incapacity, personal incompetence, or whatever combination, plays in the creation of a revolutionary situation; nor to discount the importance of intra-élite division, especially among the military, to the final outcome. Yet none of these are sufficient to make a governmental crisis a revolutionary one, without the loss of moral authority that has its origin in some weakness in the regime's source of authority, and that is intensified by the impact of mass delegitimation. In other words, Skocpol is correct in what she asserts, mistaken in what she denies. And although her later analysis of the Iranian revolution goes some way towards correcting her original disparagement of the role of intellectual and cultural forces in the revolutionary process, these are not integrated into a more general account of legitimacy (Skocpol, 1982). The reason for this is not far to seek. Skocpol associates the whole 'problematic' of legitimacy with the Parsonian theory of the value-integrated society, with its emphasis on social uniformity rather than diversity, consensus over conflict, and its assumption that revolution results from a self-conscious attempt to remove a 'dis-synchronis-ation' between values and their environment (Skocpol, 1979, pp.11–12). None of this follows if the starting point of legitimacy-theory is located, not in some exaggerated conception of social harmony, but in a theory of power, where it properly belongs; or if we recognise that revolutions can be intellectually and morally intelligible, without their outcomes being necessarily intended. Both these points will become clearer through an analysis of the process of relegitimation.

Revolutionary regimes and relegitimation

One aspect of relegitimation has already been discussed, and that is the retrospective justification of the breach of legality involved in the overthrow of the old regime. This primarily negative task is relatively straightforward in comparison with the positive task of establishing the legitimacy of the new order that replaces it. Here the process of overthrow carries an ambivalent legacy for the successor regime. On the one hand it derives enormous legitimating force from the mass-mobilisations and sac-rifices of the revolutionary period. As beneficiary of the popular struggles it inherits all the moral prestige associated with their achievements. On the other hand, the 'failures' of the old regime, compounded by the dislocations of the revolutionary process, make it exceedingly difficult for the new government to meet the expectations of the population; the economy may be dis-rupted, and the institutions of the state themselves may be in disarray. There is a potentially serious discrepancy, in other words, between the moral prestige of the new regime and its capacity to accomplish the tasks with which it is confronted. The prospects for its relegitimation will depend in part upon the relationship between these divergent aspects of its inheritance.

The central issue in relegitimation, however, is the establish-ment of a new principle of legitimacy, or source of authority, that has sufficient popular basis to sustain the new rules of power. Some writers argue that a new principle of legitimacy has to be widely acknowledged in the pre-revolutionary society as a con-dition for the delegitimation of the old regime; and that the process of delegitimation itself therefore presupposes the alternative principle that will come to replace it. However, this is not always so, or at least not in any straightforward way. People may have a much clearer sense of the injustice of their exclusion from the political process than of the precise form which their inclusion ought to take. This will depend upon the context. In many revolutions the collapse of the old regime only signals the beginning of a fierce struggle between competing groups, each striving to appropriate the revolution for their own alternative project. This struggle may involve a conflict between different principles of authority; or over how far a particular principle should be extended; or between political and social definitions of the revolution. It is precisely such struggles that make the outcome of many revolutions unpredictable, since no single alternative is inscribed in the loss of legitimacy of the old regime. Particular groups or individual leaders may have a clear idea of the new order they envision; but the outcome may well be the unintended result of a struggle between them under the unpredictable conditions of spontaneous mass action on one side and counter-revolution on the other.

The complexity of such processes defies any easy generalisation. Even developing a typology of revolutions is problematic, since each one will produce something different from its predecessors. From the standpoint of relegitimation, however, a distinction can usefully be drawn between revolutions that are politically restorative, and those that are socially transformative. The former, as the term implies, involve the *return* to a previously established constitutional order, after a period of authoritarian government or 'corrupted' democratic politics. Since the ideas underpinning a representative system are already present within the society's tradition, and what is involved in the demand for a 'return to democracy' is widely understood, the need for intellectual innovation and constitutional experimentation after the overthrow of the old regime will be limited. Moreover, insofar as the revolution is confined to a primarily political agenda, party competition will be possible without threatening to tear society apart, and free elections without the danger of handing power back to the forces of counter-revolution. In restorative revolutions, in other words, the task of relegitimation is a limited one: the principle of authority underpinning the new rules of power is already widely acknowledged, and the evolution of 'people power' from the mass-mobilisations of the revolution to the electoral mode of legitimation is relatively straightforward. Such an evolution also conforms to a desire to return to a less politicised way of life after the excitement and intensity of the revolutionary period.

Now there is a view that such revolutions do not count as 'real' revolutions at all (e.g. Kramnick, 1972). The point is often made that, whereas until the middle of the eighteenth century, the term revolution meant a turning full circle, a return to constitutional order, the restoration of a relationship of trust between rulers and ruled, etc., the distinctive feature of modern revolutions, in contrast, has been precisely their radically innovative character; and that this conception of revolution developed alongside the Enlightenment view of history as unilinear, open-ended, and above all progressive, rather than cyclical. There is no doubting that many revolutions since 1789 have indeed conformed to such a conception. At the same time there is no reason to abandon the older idea as characterising one type of revolution that continues to the present day. The overthrow of President Marcos in the Philippines exemplified this type, as did the popular mobilisations in Burma in 1988, had they proved successful. And the Eastern European revolutions of 1989, although not properly restorative, in that only Czechoslovakia had a convincingly democratic past, nevertheless shared some of the characteristics of such a type, in that they represented the adoption of an established norm, even if the norm was a Western European one rather than deriving from each country's own past. Indeed, the revolutions of 1989 signalled precisely the desire to end innovation, and the readiness to adopt a common European politico-economic model 'off the shelf' as it were. To say this is not to underestimate the strains that the marketisation of the economy will impose on the new democratic polities, nor the difficulty of purging the apparatus of the state of the personnel and habits of the past. It is simply to make a judgement about the character of the revolutions themselves.

The point about politically restorative revolutions, then, is that with an established principle of authority ready to hand, and a straightforward transition possible to an electoral mode of legitimation, the task of relegitimating the political order is a relatively limited one. The matter is very different with those that I have termed socially transformative, not least because the trajectory of the revolutions themselves is so different. To understand this trajectory we need to make a distinction between two quite different ways in which revolutions can be socially transformative. They can be so, first, because with the collapse of authority of the old regime, and with the rights of exclusion necessary to private property no longer enforceable, the people may simply take possession for themselves of the estates and factories in which they had previously worked. This could be called the spontaneous social transformation 'from below'; and it will happen where the principles underpinning the rules of property as well as political power have become widely discredited under the old regime. It should be distinguished from the form of social transformation that takes place when a revolutionary party or leadership equipped with a socially transformative project wins state power, and succeeds in mobilising society towards its own consciously chosen goals. This could be called the organised social transformation 'from above'. Of these two forms of revolutionary social transformation, the first can take place without the establishment of the second (France) and the second without the first (Iran); or they can take place successively (Russia), or simultaneously, as in the piecemeal extension of liberated zones through guerrilla warfare (China).

If we keep this distinction in view, two points can then be made about the process of relegitimation of state power. The first is a negative one. Wherever a socially transformative revolution takes place it is very difficult if not impossible to establish a settled parliamentary regime with electoral legitimation as its outcome, even supposing the main political actors initially favour it, and the popular basis of the revolution would seem to point towards it. This is because of the degree of political resistance that the social transformation provokes, and the consequences that follow from its suppression. This is most evident where a transfer of property rights has taken place. Any revolution involving the dispossession of the propertied will provoke an organised counter-revolution by the dispossessed, which will be the more intense the larger their numbers. And counter-revolution brings civil war, suspensions of legality, and terror, which are hardly compatible with a settled parliamentary regime. Its conclusion in turn produces widespread exhaustion, economic hardship and disillusion that the fruits of revolution do not match either its promise or the sacrifices that have been made. These are hardly the circumstances in which an established revolutionary leadership will submit itself to electoral competition, with the possibility, however remote, of losing power or seeing a reversal of the changes brought by the revolution. Rather than commit electoral suicide, it is more likely to consolidate the authoritarian rule of the civil-war period.

The authoritarian tendencies provoked by counter-revolution will be intensified where the successful party or leadership has its own project of social transformation to effect. At the same time, however – and this is the second point to be made – such a project provides the necessary basis for the new regime's legitimation. On the one hand its particular ideology of social transformation will embody a principle of legitimacy to justify its authoritarian structure of power. As we have already seen, Marxism–Leninism assigned the leading role to the party hierarchy in identifying the historically determined route to the socialist or communist goal. In similar vein, the forms of Islamic fundamentalism associated with Khomeini in Iran gave pride of place to the *ulama* in overseeing the moral transformation of society. What was required in addition was the dissemination and consolidation of this belief system through the institutions of formal and informal education, so that it achieved popular implantation among at least a new revolutionary generation.

If one way in which the project of social transformation from above serves also to legitimate the revolutionary regime is through the source of authority it provides for a hierarchical political order, a second is through the continued mass-mobilisation that it requires. The transition from revolutionary mobilisation to mobilisation for social transformation or reconstruction, whether or not via military mobilisation for revolutionary defence, forms an almost unbroken continuum. The agencies and modes of mass activism that helped to bring down the old regime – street committees, communes, factory councils, soviets, religious assemblies, or whatever – can be readily adapted to the work of civil defence and social transformation, albeit in a more top-down and 'coordinated' manner. And the habit of political activism will have been developed widely enough to survive the inevitable exhaustion and desire for a return to normalcy. From the standpoint of legitimation, continued mobilisation confirms the popular and 'democratic' character of the new regime. The electoral mode, by comparison, can be criticised for demobilising the people, for stifling the process of social change, and 'freezing' public opinion at a particular and arbitrary moment of electoral choice.

If we compare a number of different socially transformative revolutions in the light of the above discussion, then France after 1789 can be seen to have experienced the vulnerability of parliamentary rule in the face of counter-revolution and civil war; but no group with an ongoing project of social transformation was subsequently able to establish itself in power. It was thus left to military dictatorship – to authoritarianism without any legitimating principle of authority – to consolidate state power, but leave the problem of its legitimacy essentially unresolved, as the history of the French state in the nineteenth century amply demonstrated (cf. Richter, 1982). In Russia the second form of social revolution – the Bolsheviks' project of a heavy-industry-led economic transformation under Marxist auspices – provided the ideological thrust for legitimising the reconstructed state order. But the project proved antithetical to the first, spontaneous social revolution – the peasants' redistribution of land – and narrowed the party's base of mobilisation to the urban working class, with fateful consequences for the character of Stalin's subsequent regime. In China, the revolution's form and timescale themselves ensured a much greater consistency between the party's project for economic development and the pattern of property redistribution in the countryside, since both evolved together. The result was a much wider social base for continued mobilisation, and a much more coherent model for other peasant revolutions in the Third World than that provided by the Soviet Union, for all the latter's prestige as the first communist regime. In the Iranian revolution there was no change of property rights, since the social transformation was primarily cultural and spiritual in purpose, though its internal and external crusades had significant material consequences, as well as an identifiable social base among those who had benefited least from the Shah's modernisation programme. Here it was the leadership position that Khomeini came to hold over the opposition in the year preceding the revolution that turned the movement against the Shah from one of constitutional restoration to one of social transformation, thereby excluding a subsequent liberal-democratic development with free electoral competition. This was a revolution whose outcome was determined very largely at the ideological level, rather than by the exigencies of counter-revolution and civil war, and whose legitimacy was more solidly grounded in traditional beliefs and institutions than the others mentioned.

The contrast I have drawn between politically restorative and socially transformative revolutions, then, is a contrast between typical political outcomes, and their respective agendas for the relegitimation of state power. The former result in competitive multi-party systems, with electoral legitimation and limited ideological innovation. The latter produce systems of authoritarian rule that require for their legitimacy the commitment to an on-going project of social transformation, carrying with it both extensive ideological activism and continued mass-mobilisation, typically under the hegemony of a single party.

Not every example of revolution fits neatly into one or other of the above categories. The Nicaraguan revolution, for instance, was a bold attempt to embrace the two. On the one hand it embodied a determined project of social transformation, not so much in that there was widespread redistribution of property, except of Somoza's extensive estates, but in terms of continued mass-mobilisation around grass-roots health and welfare programmes, popular defence and education for a new civic ideal (Coraggio, 1986). On the other hand the ruling front, in explicit repudiation of the orthodox communist model, proved scrupulous in preserving parliamentary legality and electoral competition in face of a ruthless counter-revolution and economic blockade, both orchestrated by the US government (Harris and Vilas, 1985, chs.8–10). Indeed the outcome of the 1990 election in Nicaragua seemed to provide retrospective justification for all those earlier revolutionary leaderships who had refused to submit themselves to electoral competition on the grounds that it would jeopardise the social gains of the revolution as well as their own position; and that parliamentary democracy and progressive social transformation in a developing country are indeed mutually exclusive.

What the Nicaraguan experience most clearly demonstrates, in fact, is the role of external forces, of crude intervention as well as ideological attraction, in the outcome of modern revolutions. In particular, Nicaragua's transition in 1990 under US pressure from a socially transformative revolution to a purely restorative one ('making the country safe for democracy', as even Daniel Ortega described the achievement) indicates the lengths to which the USA will go, even in defiance of international law, to stifle any revolutionary process that does not conform to the model of its own Lockean revolution, or that attempts to alter the balance of economic inequality in favour of the poor and the dispossessed. It will do so even in favour of right-wing dictatorships if necessary, though to be sure it will also later prod such dictatorships in the direction of democratisation, once any prospect of a progressive social transformation is safely over (Borosage and Marks, 1976). Given the importance of the USA as the world's sole remaining superpower, the consistency of its record in this regard has obvious significance for the fate of any future revolutions.

Coups d'état and military regimes

In this section I shall examine the place of legitimacy in an understanding of coups and military governments, and their difference from revolutions and revolutionary regimes. At the beginning of Chapter 5 I pointed to one of the central dilemmas inherent in state sovereignty: the absence of any superior or external coercive power which might deter the armed forces of the state from breaching legality and usurping power themselves. The factors restraining them must therefore be internal ones. They are found in the organisation of state institutions, in the relations established between the civil and military powers, above all in the degree of legitimacy of the political order. Of these the last is the most crucial. As I noted in Chapter 5, the procedures and traditions that encourage the subordination of the military to the civilian power may delay, but cannot ultimately prevent, a military intervention when the civilian power has lost its authority, and the constitutional rules prove inadequate to resolve the crisis. If the legitimacy of government is important to securing the cooperation of society at large, therefore, it is above all so in ensuring the subordination of the military to the civilian authority. From this it follows that, where the military do seize power, it does not happen 'out of the blue', but only as the culmination of a process of erosion in the legitimacy of the civilian order, whose warning signs are evident well in advance.

Such an erosion provides both a prime reason for military intervention, and the means of justifying the breach of legality after it has taken place. Here it is not only the erosion of legitimacy itself that is important, but the contrast that can be drawn between the deficiencies of the civilian regime on the one side and the distinctive self-image and operating style of the armed forces on the other. As I have already suggested, the context in which coups take place is primarily one in which the civilian regime has lost public confidence in its ability to sustain some basic purpose of government; the crisis, in other words, is one of government performance, and usually government performance alone. It is also one where the military believe that their distinctive qualities and mode of organisation are such as to provide a resolution of the crisis. The contribution that the theory of legitimacy can make to the study of coups, therefore, lies in the connection to be drawn between the form of legitimacy deficit and the distinctive character of the military in its particular context.

In his book *Political Order in Changing Societies*, Samuel Huntington coined the term 'breakthrough coup', which many others have adopted, to identify a particular type of coup occurring in terminally weakened monarchical or aristocratic political systems. Here the military, equipped with a secular education and trained in the use of sophisticated technology, constituted the chief bearers of the ideology of modernisation in opposition to the traditionalist values of the regime, and the chief advocates of the career open to talent against the privileges of birth and heredity. When the civilian regime faltered, they put themselves forward as the representatives of progressive social forces, and as agents of an urgent programme of economic modernisation. Such, Huntington argues, were many of the coups in Latin America in the 1920s and 1930s, and in the Middle East in the 1950s (1968, ch.4).

However adequate Huntington's view of the military as a 'modernising' force may have been at the time, such coups must now be regarded as a feature of the past, if only because there are so few monarchical or aristocratic regimes left to overthrow. Most coups nowadays take place in democratic political systems, and need to be understood in the light of the problems typical to those systems. Although the circumstances vary enormously, what is primarily at issue here is not the source of authority of the regime, or the belief in the principle of popular sovereignty itself, which underpins the rules of the democratic order; it is rather problems of government performance, of weakness, corruption or divisiveness, as these are exacerbated by typical democratic procedures, or appear unresolvable by them. In other words, it is the very institutional arrangements that contribute to the legitimation of government in a liberal democracy – the freedoms of expression and association, electoral competition, majoritarian procedure – which themselves become the obstacle to resolving the crisis of government performance, and thereby lose public confidence. (For general accounts of democratic breakdown see Linz and Stepan, 1978, Nordlinger, 1977; for Latin America, Collier, 1979, Philip, 1985; for Africa, First, 1970).

Of the different problems mentioned above, that of government weakness, or inability to fulfil the basic economic or security purposes of the state, is most damaging where a government is confronted by powerful groups taking advantage of the freedoms of expression and association to press their claims. Where, for example, chronic inflation is exacerbated by a government's inability to resist the demands and sanctions of organised economic interests; or where social conflict is intensified by press agitation and popular mobilisation; the origins of economic and social disorder will be attributed, less to deep-seated socioeconomic causes, than to government weakness on one side and the opportunities for disruption afforded by political freedoms on the other. At such a juncture, the imposition of military 'discipline' and the suppression of civil liberties may come to seem, if not a positive virtue, then at least a regrettable necessity.

The phenomenon of corruption, as I suggested earlier, can occur under any type of regime. However, it is likely to be much more visible in a democratic system, where publicity is not controlled by government. And in a society where the state provides a major means of access to economic opportunities or resources, the process of electoral competition will generate manifold obligations to be honoured from the spoils of victory, as well as powerful incentives to fraud on the route to office. Instead of elections providing the means of resolving government failure and restoring the authority of government, therefore, they become identified as themselves the prime cause of the problem. At this point the military offers the image of 'clean hands', and the military coup seems to provide what the electoral process should but cannot – the removal of a discredited government. Here is the coup, less as eliminator of civil liberties than as a form of substitute election.

A different source of military intervention from that of either government weakness or corruption is where the policies of a democratically elected government come to threaten the interests of powerful minorities, especially the propertied, who can enlist the sympathy of the military in their cause. Here it is not initially government weakness that is a problem, but rather its determination to promote the interests of disadvantaged and expectant supporters. Seeking to rectify injustices is always politically more divisive than perpetuating them. However, it is rare for the military openly to intervene on behalf of a privileged minority as such, however threatened, and so risk appearing divisive itself. The propertied will have to prepare the ground first for the destabilisation of the regime by means of the economic resources and external contacts available to them. Runs on the currency, investment strikes, the withdrawal of funds, disruptions of trade: any of these may serve to undermine confidence and precipitate an economic downturn, which will adversely affect the government's own supporters and bring them into conflict with its policies. In an atmosphere of general crisis, where the regime is assailed from many directions simultaneously, the military will more readily be able to present themselves as an instrument of national salvation, and their intervention as serving a general interest that the elected government has jeopardised through its divisive policies.

The above are only some of the typical scenarios for a coup d'état. At the root of their justification lies not only an inability of democratic processes to resolve a crisis of government performance, but a corresponding rationale for military rule. Two elements in this rationale can be distinguished. One is the establishment of a mode of government which 'solves' the problematic features of democratic politics at a stroke, by simply abolishing them. Military rule reasserts the authority of government over society by removing the freedom of organised groups to pursue their interests independently of the state; it imposes unity on a divided nation by removing the political avenues for competition and conflict; it 'abolishes' fraud and corruption by eliminating every occasion for electoral pressure and manipulation; it restores confidence in the ability and integrity of government by removing every independent means for discovering and publicising what it is up to. In short, the military resolve the problems of democratic politics by abolishing politics altogether; they immunise the state from the problems of society by elevating the state above society.

Along with a depoliticised mode of government the military offer, secondly, a public image of themselves that is the opposite in every key particular to that of politicians. The armed forces traditionally pride themselves on being a national institution, drawn from all sectors of society, and embodying a national interest above the sectionalism of political parties. They are trained to action rather than debate, for getting things done rather than making speeches, for taking decisions on technocratic grounds rather than through the wheeling and dealing of politicians. Above all, they embody discipline and order, in contrast to the untidiness and disorder of politics. Such virtues become all the more attractive, the more incapable politicians appear of resolving chronic problems of society through political means.

It is one thing, however, to justify a coup d'état retrospectively; quite another to secure the legitimacy of military rule on an ongoing basis. The dilemma of the military is that the rationale they offer for breaching constitutional legality and dispensing with the rule of politicians, not to mention the human rights abuses they may commit in the process, make it impossible for them simply to return power to a civilian government after a brief interlude, even should they wish to do so. The task of making society once more 'safe for politics' almost always turns out to be a protracted one, which requires the establishment of military rule as an ongoing system of government. Such a government may come to enjoy a certain internal stability, in the sense that, where there is sufficient cohesion among the armed forces, it may be immune from further coups. It may over time achieve a certain social basis of support, for example among the propertied. It may acquire a civilian façade, through the incorporation of carefully vetted politicians. But what it can never acquire is legitimacy.

The reasons for this are twofold, and can be deduced from the analysis of legitimacy so far developed. First, the rationale for military rule is to be found in a crisis of performance of the democratic regime it displaced; and its own justification rests on the promise of resolving that crisis. In contrast with revolutions, the basic source or principle of authority – that of the people, or popular sovereignty – has not itself been discredited. A loss of public confidence in certain institutions and procedures of liberal democracy there may have been, but not an erosion of belief in the principle of popular sovereignty itself. Moreover, the military regime has no alternative source of authority to offer in its place, that might underpin its own rules of appointment. Indeed, it acknowledges the principle of popular sovereignty by claiming to 'represent the people', to 'embody the national interest' more effectively than the politicians themselves have done.

In assessing such claims we should recall the important distinction between the 'good' and the 'right': between promoting national ends and deriving authority from the nation; between serving the people and representing them. The military may do the former, but cannot do the latter. To do the latter requires just those institutions of representation and election that the military have seized power to dismantle. As a result they are compelled to equate the good with the right: to make serving the ends of government equivalent to an entitlement to office, and promoting the nation's interests the same as deriving authority *from* the people. Justifications for military rule, in short, rest upon a conceptual and normative elision, which may serve to confuse people for a while, but cannot make good a basic deficiency in a crucial dimension of legitimacy.

The first weakness of a military regime, then, is that its rules of office, if it has any, cannot be justified in terms of a recognisably valid source of authority. The second is that it is not subject to any public legitimation in terms of expressed consent. Its origins are not to be found in mass-mobilisation, as with a revolutionary regime. On the contrary, power has been seized precisely to exclude the people from politics, and to stifle the mass-participation that is necessary to political legitimation in the era of popular sovereignty. The military regime, therefore, in both origin and purpose, is a non-legitimated one.

Now it does not follow from this that the military can have no social basis of support, especially among the privileged or the propertied. Here again, however, we need to observe another important distinction: between enjoying support, and possessing the institutional means for the regular expression of consent. The military may construct a form of oligarchical order, with privileged access for its supporters to influencing policy. But there is no publicly justifiable rule that can limit political participation to one section of the population only, however it is defined. In abolishing formal political rights for one, they have to be abolished for all. In so doing, the military regime necessarily deprives itself of the means of any public legitimation.

The distinctions drawn above are essential if we are to understand the lack of legitimacy of military regimes. Nowhere in fact is it more important to analyse the internal structure of legitimacy, if we are not to be taken in by the 'legitimations' of the powerful. If we operate with a purely subjective conception of legitimacy as whatever people believe to be legitimate under the propaganda influence of government; or if we define legitimacy, with Lipset, as the ability of a regime to convince people that its institutions are the most appropriate ones for the society; then there is no reason to suppose that military rule might not become as legitimate as any democratic system. After all, society needs strong government to maintain order, eradicate corruption, preserve national unity, promote economic development, and so forth, does it not? Strong government a military regime can supply in good measure. If people acknowledge this need, does this not by definition guarantee the military's legitimacy?

The simple answer is 'no'. The legitimacy of any political system rests, like a tripod, on three legs. The first is the acknowledged source of authority underpinning the rules of appointment to the leading offices of state. The second is the capacity of its institutions to facilitate achievement of the ends or purposes of government. The third lies in the mechanisms for the regular expression of consent. A military regime rests on the second of these alone; it is a tripod supported on one leg. To achieve this balancing feat at all, the leg has to become grossly enlarged. Performance is everything, and the achievements and capacities of the regime have to be disproportionately magnified. Lacking any title to rule, the regime has to affirm its unique qualifications to fulfil the country's historic destiny. Lacking any authorisation from the nation, it has to stimulate every nationalist sentiment in its favour. Lacking any manifestation of popular consent, the leader's charismatic qualities have to be repeatedly proclaimed.

The basic problem of regimes whose legitimacy rests 'on one leg', however, and depends on performance alone, is that they are highly vulnerable in the event of policy failure. Military regimes may be better able than civilian ones to suppress dissatisfaction with their policies. Yet failure of performance removes the only justification for their rule, since they lack any valid source of authority. Moreover, since there is no way of distinguishing between the particular government and the system of military rule as such, in the absence of any legalised mode of succession, any failure will discredit the regime as a whole (see Clapham and Philip, 1985; O'Brien and Cammack, 1985).

This fundamental weakness drives military regimes in one of two directions. One is the search for ever new policy initiatives where they can secure some easy and preferably dramatic success, to cover up failure in other areas together with any internal opposition it may have provoked. Since they are military regimes, this typically involves military exploits and external adventurism, such as recovering disputed territory on their borders. So the Greek Junta tried to bring down President Makarios in 1974 to further the unification of Cyprus with Greece; Idi Amin's troops made incursions into Tanzanian territory in 1978; the Argentinian generals invaded the Falkland Islands in 1982; Saddam Hussein attacked Iran in 1980, and annexed Kuwait in 1990; and so on. In the first three examples the adventurism provoked military retaliation that brought the regimes tumbling down. The outcome of Iraq's invasion of Kuwait is at this moment in doubt (1990), but may well follow a similar pattern.

The other course for a military regime to take is to seek a more substantial legitimacy through a return to electoral politics.

Pressures also work in this direction from external 'sponsors', responding to adverse publicity about human rights abuses. In many cases there is a period of transition first, involving an attempt to secure legitimation without the conditions necessary to it. This is the period of elections without free choice: of single parties constructed entirely from above, of plebiscitary votes ('yes' or 'no' to the leader), of experiments in 'indigenous' forms of local democracy which do not affect the centre, and so on (Bienen and Morell, 1976). How long this period lasts depends upon the extent of the pressures, both internal and external, on the one side, and how far the military judge society to have been made safe for electoral competition on the other. In any case they will always be there behind the scenes when the freedoms of speech and association have been restored, to limit the 'excesses' of politicians. Yet the logic of a formal surrender of power is implicit in the character of military rule itself.

Here, in conclusion, lies the key point of difference between revolutionary and military regimes. Revolutionary regimes derive enormous moral authority from the mass mobilisations and popular sacrifices of the revolutionary period. Their institutions embody an acknowledged principle of legitimacy. And they are subject to continued legitimation whether in the electoral or the mobilisation mode, or, more rarely, through a combination of the two. Military regimes, in contrast, at least those that have their origins in a breakdown of democratic politics, can at most possess a temporary or transitional legitimacy. That is to say, their only justification lies in the necessity of overcoming a performance crisis of civilian government, of resolving an impasse which the political system has been unable to resolve, so as to make a return to civilian rule on a sounder basis possible. This is the temporary or conditional legitimacy indicated by the Roman concept of dictatorship, meaning the temporary suspension of constitutional rule in an emergency so that the conditions could be created for its more secure restoration. Of course the military find it necessary to stay much longer than they first intended, or at least they convince themselves that they must. But the longer they stay, the more problematic becomes their lack of any source of authority or any popular legitimation, despite all the 'legitimations' they may themselves contrive.

Conclusion: the dilemmas of political legitimacy

The analysis of the processes of political breakdown, and of the relegitimation, or attempted relegitimation, of revolutionary and military regimes, completes the agenda I proposed at the beginning of Chapter 5. It also reinforces the question I raised there, namely, why is legitimacy so hard to achieve for the contemporary state? By way of conclusion I shall draw together the different elements necessary to an answer.

For all its enormous and evident power, the contemporary state is a highly problematic structure in those respects necessary to its legitimacy. First there is what I have termed the vulnerability of sovereignty: as the supreme law-making and law-enforcing body, which legitimises all other powers within society, there is no higher authority than the state to guarantee its own constitutional rules in the face of intense struggle to exercise and influence its sovereign power. Its rules therefore remain vulnerable unless they are anchored in the most fundamental source of authority acknowledged and agreed within the society. This is the first condition of rule-justifiability to be met.

Secondly, as the power-structure expressly devoted to promoting the public interest, the state has to satisfy the most general societal needs for security and economic sufficiency, and in a way that is not manifestly partial or biassed. It has to do this in a context where, externally, it cannot control many of the forces that affect its security and economic performance, and, internally, the society it governs is divided along class, ethnic, regional and other lines. Whereas all states are equal in the vulnerability of their sovereignty, they vary enormously in their capacity to moderate the external forces to which they are subject, and in the pattern and intensity of their internal societal divisions.

Thirdly, the state has to secure express consent to its power, in a world where all adults are considered entitled to be members of the political community, and therefore to have the right to the minimum political participation necessary to express that consent. This formal equality of political status has to coexist, and be rendered compatible with, inequalities of power in all the dimensions of social life, the political included.

Legitimate political systems comprise legally established and validated rules for the organisation and distribution of power, for appointment to office, and so on, which can meet these three central requirements: which embody an ultimate source of authority acknowledged within the society; which are capable of resolving performance problems and dealing with government failure; which provide for express consent on the part of the population as a whole. These criteria are not easy to fulfil simultaneously, and it is not surprising that there is only a limited number of types of political system capable of meeting them. By way of conclusion I shall distinguish three broad types, each of which has its distinctive strengths and weaknesses.

One is a traditional monarchy, with popular representation confined to a legislative assembly. Jordan and Morocco provide better examples here than Saudi Arabia, whose lack of all popular representation constitutes the most vulnerable point in its political arrangements. This political type combines two key advantages of the traditional order – that the supreme executive office constitutes a focus of social unity beyond competition, and that political power formally reflects the structure of social and economic power – with the minimum requirement for popular consent through elections to a legislative assembly. Such a system cannot be generally replicated, however, for the simple reason that traditional institutions cannot be created; they can only *survive*. Mostly they have not done so, partly because of the disruptions of Western colonialism, partly because the hereditary principle cannot withstand erosion from the principles of equal opportunity and popular sovereignty in the circumstances of the modern world. The remaining monarchies are therefore vulnerable to the assertion of these principles within their own societies, and to agitation on their behalf from without.

Second is the mobilisation regime, whose opening up of careers to those from below and continuous mass-politicisation have their origins in a revolutionary process. A central place in such regimes is occupied by the monopolistic belief system, which, through the agency of a dominant party, defines the collective goal for society and provides the stimulus to mass-mobilisation, as well as the source of authority for the ruling group. The strengths and weaknesses of such regimes cannot properly be identified apart from the specific logic of their respective belief systems, since it is these that provide their distinctive dynamic and trajectory; to treat communism, fascism and Islamic fundamentalism as equivalents would be absurd. Yet we can note common features of their respective regimes. Most important is the way in which the belief system provides for all three criteria of legitimacy simultaneously: as source of authority for the rules of power; as authoritative definition of the common interest or societal goal; as stimulus to consent through mobilisation in the regime's service. Here lies the source of this type's strength and weakness simultaneously: its strength, that the belief system can accomplish all this; its weakness, that, in doing so, it is required to do *too much*. The regime is thus vulnerable to forces making for the erosion of belief; its repression of alternative beliefs and divergent modes of expression, which is necessary to its legitimacy, proves corrosive over the longer term; and its claim to privileged knowledge of society's goal cannot withstand the independent assertion of their interests by the people themselves, once they are sufficiently determined to do so.

A liberal-democratic system, the third type, avoids the weaknesses of both the traditional and mobilisation regimes in the unqualified expression it gives to the principle of popular sovereignty; in the tolerance allowed to a variety of beliefs that is the necessary counterpart to the electoral mode of consent; and in its acknowledgement that the ultimate test of the public good is what the people, freely organised, assert, not what the interpreters of tradition or doctrinal orthodoxy may determine. Its key points of vulnerability lie in the fact that electoral competition for the supreme executive office is liable to intensify societal divisions, and that the tension between formal equality of electoral power and socio-economic inequalities can become unmanageable; how far either becomes critical depends upon the particular institutional forms on the one side, and on the intensity of social divisions on the other. The problems may be moderated, as we have seen, by various devices, formal or informal, for limiting the scope of electoral choice; the corresponding weakness, however, is that this reduces the legitimating force of elections, and their value in removing politicians who have failed, and in restoring governmental authority. These semi-legitimated systems are vulnerable to popular mobilisation outside the framework allowed, in a way that liberal-democracies proper are not.

In contrast to these legitimate types of political system, military dictatorships constitute the limiting case of a non-legitimate political order, in that, however justifiable military intervention may be, they lack the key characteristics of an authoritative source for their power, and popular consent in either the electoral or the mobilisation mode. Their reliance on performance alone explains their typical evolutionary pattern, either towards destructive adventurism, or a gradual return to electoral legitimation. They should thus be seen as an interim, transitional or exceptional type of system, even though the 'transition' may in practice prove long drawn-out.

Now if we compare the three types of legitimate political system analysed above, it is evident that their respective weaknesses and points of vulnerability are not just different, but qualitatively so. The traditional order is vulnerable to demands for popular participation, and for equal opportunity to compete for political office. Mobilisation regimes are vulnerable through their exclusion of the population, not from access to office, but from any influence on policy or the choice of leaders, and through their suppression of independent means of popular-will formation. Both traditional and mobilisation types, that is to say, are vulnerable to the force of popular sovereignty, and to the erosion of the belief system that validates a paternalist definition of the public interest. Liberal democracy, in contrast, is not vulnerable to the erosion of its basic belief system; its problem lies in obtaining the social conditions and institutional forms in which its principles can be realised in a non-conflictual manner. The former types, in other words, are vulnerable to the collapse of their underlying principle of authority; the problem for liberal democracy is to achieve the conditions to enable its principle of authority to be realised.

Such a contrast can only be made sense of by arranging the three types in a developmental series. A mobilisation regime is more advanced than a traditional one in its opening up of political office and its expansion of popular participation. Liberal democracies represent a higher stage than either (although not necessarily a 'final' one) in the extent to which they realise the principle of popular sovereignty, admit a non-paternalist definition of interests, and allow the possibility of consent to the rules of power through their revisability by electoral process. To posit such a developmental series is not to indulge in historical determinism. Traditional systems may develop into liberal-democratic ones, with or without a mobilisation regime as intermediary; each historical transition may in turn take place with or without the interposition of a military dictatorship. The significant point is only that, once a given type of legitimate order is attained, it is impossible to regress to an earlier one.

It follows that both traditional and mobilisation regimes await to be superseded by a further legitimate political order. Liberal democracies, on the other hand, though certainly open to improvement in the extent to which they realise their underlying principles, can only be overthrown by force. This explains why the former are both vulnerable to revolutionary movements from below; the latter only to coups d'état from above. Among the most significant features of the political evolution in the USSR, and of the revolutions of 1989, is the confirmation they provide for such a developmental analysis. Viewed from the historical vantage point of the end of the twentieth century, the legitimation problems of traditional and mobilisation regimes can be seen as problems inherent in a lower stage of development, awaiting to be surpassed; those of liberal-democratic regimes as problems of how the conditions necessary to a higher stage can be attained and consolidated.

One drawback to a developmental analysis such as I have proposed is that it encourages those who live in a secure liberal-democratic order – which is by no means in practice the final realisation of democratic principles – to assume that the failure of other societies to sustain such an order is because their populations are not ready for it, are not 'mature' or 'advanced' enough; that they still require a paternalist definition of their interests. Such an assumption has historically provided all too convenient a legitimation for imperialist and neo-imperialist interventions in other societies. Yet once a people has asserted the principle of popular sovereignty for itself, it is primarily structural or contextual conditions, so I have argued, not cultural ones, that frustrate its realisation in a settled democratic order. Culturalist explanations, besides being themselves paternalistic, provide an alibi to those in the West from acknowledging that they share some of the responsibility for the persistence of socio-economic conditions in the developing world that are adverse to democratisation. For such conditions to be overcome would

require the emergence of a more just and sustainable international economic order as its necessary condition.

8 Legitimacy in Political Science and Political Philosophy

It remains in a brief concluding chapter to draw out the implications of my account of legitimacy for the relationship between political science and political philosophy. In the first chapter I referred to the extraordinary disjunction between the two within Anglo-American departments of politics in their respective treatments of legitimacy, and in the different types of literature that students are expected to read for each. Such a disjunction is symptomatic of a more general separation between the two, that has its intellectual rationale in the distinction between facts and values, and in the different purposes of explanatory and normative theorising respectively. It is a separation that has been progressively reinforced through the twentieth century by the demands of the academic division of labour.

There can be no denying that the activities of explanatory and normative theorising are in principle distinct, since explaining what is differs from exploring the grounds for what ought to be; nor can it be denied that observing the fact-value distinction is a necessary discipline if social scientists are not to intrude their own values into the situation under investigation. Yet such considerations do not entail the separation of the two activities, when they are also closely interconnected. The costs of such separation are evident in the difficulty many social and political scientists experience when it comes to handling the normative dimension of social relations. Either they discount it altogether, as in 'realist' theories of power. Or they treat values in a reductionist way, as deriving their force from psychological or pre-rational motivations. In doing so, they forfeit any under-

standing of the logic of reasons at work when people follow
rules, keep obligations or seek to realise their ideals; and of that
logic of institutional arrangements which derives in part from
the distinctive character and requirements of their legitimating
principles and procedures. Such 'logic' can only be grasped by
an internal analysis of ideas and arguments, of the kind that is
central to the practice of normative philosophy.

On the other hand the work of normative philosophy cannot
proceed in isolation from empirical analysis, for a number of
reasons. We only have the moral and political principles we do
because the world is as it is, and not otherwise. Self-evidently,
if we were invulnerable to a stab in the back or a bullet in the
head, then the prohibition against killing would lose its point; if
we did not need food and shelter for survival, disputes about
the principles by which the social product should be distributed
would lose their force (Hart, 1961, ch.9). Less self-evidently, it
is because we share some capacities as well as needs in common
that democracy can be justified; and because we also have different capacities, and to different degrees, that competitive recruitment to those positions of power that are socially necessary is
justifiable. Moreover, what positions are socially necessary in the
first place is a question that social-scientific evidence is needed to
answer; just as it requires such evidence to identify the conditions
necessary to the realisation of the principles or ideals that we
espouse. In these and other ways empirical evidence is required
for the solution to normative problems (Runciman, 1965). So
the work of normative philosophy and that of social science can,
neither one, proceed in isolation from the other.

If there is anywhere that we might expect the interconnect-
edness of the two activities to be most clearly apparent, it is in
the analysis of legitimacy. Evidence of the connection is provided
by the fact that I set out at the beginning of this book to write
a social-scientific account, and ended up perforce in providing a
philosophical one, not as a deviation from the main enquiry, but
in order to fulfil its explanatory purpose. It will be worth recalling
the different points where this happened, since they suggest a
rather different account of the relationship at each stage.

First was the point in analysing the concept of legitimacy when
I identified a common normative structure underlying the variety
of historically specific legitimations, and explained this structure

in terms of the different ways in which power offends our moral sense, requiring in turn a principle of differentiation, a conception of common interest, and evidence of consent from those qualified to give it. With regard to political power, I argued that its distinctive legitimating requirement of being grounded in the most fundamental source of authority acknowledged within the society, derives from its vulnerable position as final adjudicator and guarantor of positive law. Given this common normative structure of legitimacy, however, social science and political philosophy relate to it in different ways. For the former, I argued, it provides a guide to identifying the specificity of particular historical forms of legitimation, and to making judgements about legitimacy-in-context, as part of an explanatory enterprise. For the latter it provides the framework for elucidating the principles and conditions of an ideal legitimacy that transcends the constraints of given power relations, as part of an essentially normative purpose. For both, the recognition of legitimacy as multi-dimensional should counteract any tendency to reduce it to a single dimension, whether in social science to reduce it to mere belief, or in political philosophy to posit a complete antithesis between social-contract and utilitarian modes of analysis.

Now I must acknowledge at this point that the account of political philosophy I have given above, and previously in the book, is not the only one that can be given. There is, for example, a more limited, conservative definition of political philosophy which lies much closer to the activity of social science, in that it regards the norms and traditions of particular historical societies as constituting the boundary of meaningful theorising. According to this approach, the task of political philosophy is to explore the intimations or implications of a given tradition (Oakeshott, 1962). However, there are substantial problems to limiting political philosophy in this way, which parallel the problems of a social science that is limited to a Winchian programme, and revolve around the same point: how to deal with changes in, or challenges to, established norms of legitimacy, whether from within or without the society. Just as social scientists cannot explain these if they remain confined within the terms of a particular set of society-specific norms or beliefs, so neither can philosophers evaluate them, except from a standpoint which is outside the given tradition, and from which they might prioritise particular elements within it. For this reason I do not see how it is possible to avoid some external or transcendent position altogether in political philosophy, even if it remains implicit and unconscious.

One significant connection, then, between political science and political philosophy with regard to legitimacy lies in their possession of a common concept, with a common structure, which they deploy for different purposes. There is a second level of analysis, however, where they can be seen to share, not only a common concept, but a common standpoint as well. As I argued in Chapter 4, when it comes to explaining, not people's behaviour, but legitimacy itself, and how the beliefs and the consent that comprise it are maintained and reproduced within established relations of power, the social scientist as well as the political philosopher is compelled to adopt a standpoint that transcends these self-confirming processes of legitimation; and to confront the question as to whether there are some conditions or principles in which this self-confirming cycle is less closed than others, and what these might be. In other words, only a comparative analysis from a position outside particular historical power relations will suffice. And this position is identical to that of the normative philosopher who has to stand outside all power relations to establish philosophically valid principles of legitimacy, and to identify the conditions under which consent to power rules is truly voluntary because it is unconstrained by their effects.

This common standpoint shared by explanatory and normative theorising about legitimacy is most evident in the work of Rousseau, who, in his *Discourse on the Origin of Inequality* showed how legitimacy is historically established within pre-existing relations of power and inequality; and in his *Social Contract* demonstrated that the only way to escape this pre-structuring of consent and of the common interest, to the advantage of the powerful, is through a legislative assembly of all citizens, in which power rules are agreed to and revised from a position of equality. Despite the oversimplification in the historical part of Rousseau's analysis, his work is particularly significant for my argument that an explanatory account of how legitimacy is constructed, and a normative account of how it should ideally be so, are logically connected by the common intellectual standpoint they share; and that it is reflection on the empirical processes through which legitimacy is reproduced, that leads to the discovery of the principles and procedures of an ideal legitimacy which is not conditioned by the very power that it validates (Rousseau, 1963).

Rousseau's work is significant in another way, and that is in taking the assumptions of social contract theorising to their logical conclusion, in the institution of the democratic assembly. The importance of his book *The Social Contract* lies in showing that the social contract cannot be conceived of either as a once-for-all agreement on rules of power from a position of equality prior to the establishment of all power relations; nor as a hypothetical device for imagining what rules or principles we would agree to if we were in such a position. Both are ahistorical: the former, because it binds all future generations whatever the change in circumstances that may subsequently occur; the latter, because in seeking to demonstrate what principles people would choose if they were in such an 'original' position, it makes assumptions about human nature that are contestable, and about the human condition that are historically variable (the problem with all such theorising from Hobbes through to Rawls). We cannot anticipate, say, what principles of distributional justice people would agree to in an original position, outside all power relations and in ignorance of their future position within them. What we must do instead is to construct a set of institutions in which the idea of the original or hypothetical contract between equals is as nearly as possible approached in practice, by making all rules of power open to discussion, criticism and revision by the decision of equal citizens. This means that the democratic legislative assembly must have preeminent place in any normative theory of legitimacy; and that theorising about democracy must be logically prior to all other questions in political philosophy (see Beetham, 1987, ch.3).

The problems that confront the ideal of the citizen assembly when it is subjected to the practical requirements of representation and majority voting are not my subject here. Suffice it to say that Rousseau's response to both requirements was inadequate: to the former, because he refused to entertain the idea of representation at all; to the latter, because his concept of the 'general will' notoriously constitutes an evasion of the problem of majority – minority relations, rather than a solution to them. In practice the interests of minorities can only be protected by making the equality of citizenship status that is central to democracy subject to constitutional safeguard; and by devising procedural arrangements that encourage compromise between divergent interests rather than the overriding of some by others. The fuller discussion of such issues belongs elsewhere.

At a second level, then, the activities of explanatory and normative theorising share not only a common concept of legitimacy, but also a common epistemological standpoint. There is a final level, however, where they become effectively one and the same enterprise. This is the point where, in order to explain the breakdown of non-democratic regimes, the social scientist has recourse to an evolutionary account that depends for its explanatory force upon the validity of the normative hierarchy established by the philosopher; and, in explaining the circumstances in which liberal democracies typically break down, the social scientist makes a necessary contribution to the philosopher's exploration of the conditions necessary to the realisation of this political formation. Let me take each of these in turn.

In analysing the different way in which non-democratic regimes break down from the way in which liberal democracies do, so I have argued, the normative philosopher's reasons for the superiority of democratic principles become part of the social scientist's explanation for the vulnerability of non-democratic forms to competition from, and supersession by, more democratic ones. The link between the two is forged by social agents themselves, whose struggle for a more emancipatory principle of legitimacy is one of the key causes of social change. It is here that the analogy Habermas draws with developmental psychology is important, in that it shows how a normative hierarchy can be united with an explanatory account of social change by postulating processes of breakdown as part of an evolutionary process towards a more advanced stage of development (Habermas, 1979, ch.3). It also suggests that such a process corresponds to a developmental potential inherent in the human species itself, which is realised in the course of social and political struggle.

Such an account is similar to that offered by Hegel in his *Reason in History*, which provides a classical example of the integration of normative and explanatory theorising within an evolutionary perspective (Hegel, 1953). To carry conviction, however, such a perspective needs to be freed from the idealist and teleological tendencies to which it is prone. Overcoming the first requires a post-Marxian understanding of the way in which developments at the level of ideas are linked to developments in productive forms, albeit in more complex ways than economic determinism allows. Overcoming the second, teleological, tendency requires a post-Darwinian recognition that the processes whereby new social forms first develop are very different from those that ensure their survival and expansion in competition with others; and that the two require correspondingly different types of explanation. In particular, there is room for all the contingency of a historical account in explaining the original emergence of higher social forms. Yet what validates them as 'higher' is that they prove in practice non-regressive, and able to survive and replicate themselves in competition with other social and political forms; *not* that they are foreordained according to some Aristotelian teleology, whereby all the stages of future development are prefigured in an original starting point, as the oak is in the acorn from which it grows.

Many social and political scientists are sceptical of evolutionary models, for a variety of reasons, some of which I would endorse (see p.241). In the final analysis, however, I have found that the breakdown of non-democratic regimes in comparison with liberal democracies is only intelligible by assuming the validity of an evolutionary perspective. Provided it does not constitute the starting point of enquiry, where it will discourage us from analysing different political systems in their own terms, but only as its culmination, at this point such a perspective offers the means of uniting not only explanatory and normative theorising, but theory and practice also. That this is so will be evident from the final point of connection between the two modes of theorising.

Whereas the breakdown of non-democratic regimes exposes the limitations of a lower stage of development, the breakdown of liberal democracies reveals the difficulties of realising a higher one. (I refrain from saying 'highest' or 'final'.) Here the political scientist's explanation for the breakdown of liberal democracy is but the other side of the coin to the philosopher's account of the conditions necessary to its realisation, since they are one and the same. Among the key difficulties I have identified is the paradox that the principle of popular sovereignty embraces both a universalist criterion of citizenship, and a particularistic limitation of 'the people' to members of a given nation, so that any political conception of the general interest becomes confined to the boundaries of the nation state. It is precisely the commitment of liberal-democratic governments (and their electorates) to realising the general interest within national boundaries that constitutes one of the chief obstacles to generalising the conditions for liberal democracy on a global scale. To be sure, the interdependence of all our interests in securing the conditions for human survival is becoming every day more evident. Yet it may take the institutional embodiment of this interdependence to develop at the global level before liberal democracy can be realised as a universal, and not merely a localised, political form. If that is the conclusion towards which theoretical analysis draws us, then it cannot be a matter of theory alone, but also of practical affirmation.

Bibliography

Abercrombie, N. and Turner, B.S. (1978) 'The dominant ideology thesis', *British Journal of Sociology*, 29, pp.149–70.

Abrahamian, E. (1982) *Iran Between Two Revolutions* (Princeton University Press).

Ahmed, E. (1982) 'Comments on Skocpol', *Theory and Society*, 11, pp.293–300.

Ahmed, I. (1987) *The Concept of an Islamic State* (London: Pinter).

Alavi, H. (1988) 'Pakistan and Islam: ethnicity and ideology', in Halliday, F. and Alavi, H. (1988), pp.64–111.

Anderson, B. (1983) *Imagined Communities* (London: Verso).

Aristotle (1954) *The Nichomachean Ethics* (Oxford University Press).

Aristotle (1962) *The Politics* (Harmondsworth: Penguin).

Bahro, R. (1978) *The Alternative in Eastern Europe* (London: New Left Books).

Bakhash, S. (1986) *The Reign of the Ayatollahs* (London: Allen and Unwin).

Barker, R. (1990) *Political Legitimacy and the State* (Oxford University Press).

Barrett, M. (1980) *Women's Oppression Today* (London: Verso).

Bauman, Z. (1990) 'Communism: a post-mortem', *Praxis International*, 10, pp.185–92.

Beetham, D. (1987) *Bureaucracy* (Open University Press).

Beetham, D. (1991) 'Weber and the legitimacy of the modern state', *Analyse & Kritik*, 13, forthcoming.

Bensman, J. and Givant, M. (1975) 'Charisma and modernity: the use and abuse of a concept', *Social Research*, 42, pp.560–614.

Bentham, J. (1960) *A Fragment on Government and an Introduction to the Principles of Morals and Legislation* (Oxford: Blackwell).

Bialer, S. (1980) *Stalin's Successors* (Cambridge University Press).

Bienen, H. and Morell, D. (eds.) (1976) *Political Participation under Military Regimes* (London: Sage).

Blau, P.M. (1963) 'Critical remarks on Weber's theory of authority', *American Political Science Review*, 57, pp.305–16.

Bloch, M. (1961) *Feudal Society* (London: Routledge).

Borosage, R.L. and Marks, J. (eds.) (1976) *The CIA File* (New York: Grossman).

251

Breuilly, J. (1982) *Nationalism and the State* (Manchester University Press).

Brunner, G. (1982) 'Legitimacy doctrines and legitimation procedures in East European systems', in Rigby and Feher (1982), pp.27–44.

Brus, W. (1972) *The Market in a Socialist Economy* (London: Routledge).

Bush, R. *et al.* (eds.) (1987) *The World Order* (Cambridge: Polity).

Cardoso, F.H. and Faletto, E. (1978) *Dependency and Development in Latin America* (University of California Press).

Chodorow, N. (1978) *The Reproduction of Mothering* (University of California Press).

Clapham, C. (1985) *Third World Politics* (London: Croom Helm).

Clapham, C. and Philip, G. (eds.) (1985) *The Political Dilemmas of Military Regimes* (London: Croom Helm).

Cohan, A.S. (1975) *Theories of Revolution: an Introduction* (London: Nelson).

Cohen, G. (1981) 'Freedom, justice and capitalism', *New Left Review*, 126, pp.3–16.

Cohn, B.S. (1983) 'Representing authority in Victorian India', in Hobsbawm and Ranger (1983), pp.165–209.

Collier, D. (ed.) (1979) *The New Authoritarianism in Latin America* (Princeton University Press).

Connolly, W. (ed.) (1984) *Legitimacy and the State* (Oxford: Blackwell).

Coraggio, J.L. (1986) *Nicaragua: Revolution and Democracy* (London: Allen and Unwin).

Dahrendorf, R. (1990) *Reflections on the Revolution in Europe* (London: Chatto and Windus).

Denitch, B.D. (1976) *The Legitimation of a Revolution: the Yugoslav Case* (Yale University Press).

Denitch, B.D. (ed.) (1979) *Legitimation of Regimes* (London: Sage).

De Sainte Croix, G.E.M. (1981) *The Class Struggles in the Ancient Greek World* (London: Duckworth).

Djilas, M. (1958) *The New Class* (London: Thames and Hudson).

Dunn, J. (1972) *Modern Revolutions* (Cambridge University Press).

Enayat, H. (1982) *Modern Islamic Political Thought* (London: Macmillan).

Feher, F. (1982) 'Paternalism as a mode of legitimation in Soviet-type societies', in Rigby and Feher (1982), pp.64–81.

Feher, F., Heller, A. and Markus, G. (1983) *Dictatorship over Needs* (Oxford: Blackwell).

First, R. (1970) *The Barrel of a Gun: Political Power in Africa and the Coup d'Etat* (London: Allen Lane).

Flynn, P. (1974) 'Class, clientelism and coercion', *Journal of Commonwealth and Comparative Politics*, 12, pp.129–56.

Fox, A. (1985) *History and Heritage* (London: Allen and Unwin).

Freeman, M. (1972) 'Review article: theories of revolution', *British Journal of Political Science*, 2, pp.339–59.

Friedl, E. (1975) *Women and Men* (New York: Holt, Reinhart and Winston).

Friedman, M. (1962) *Capitalism and Freedom* (University of Chicago Press).

Friedrich, C.J. (1961) 'Political leadership and the problem of charismatic power', *Journal of Politics*, 23, pp.3–24.

Friedrich, C.J. (1963) *Man and Government* (New York: McGraw-Hill).

Fukuyama, F. (1989) 'The End of History?', *National Interest*, 16, pp.3–18.

Gellner, E. (1983) *Nations and Nationalism* (Oxford: Blackwell).

Genovese, E. (1970) *The World the Slaveholders Made* (London: Allen Lane).

Genovese, E. (1975) *Roll, Jordan, Roll* (London: Andre Deutsch).

George, S. (1988) *A Fate Worse than Debt* (Harmondsworth: Penguin).

Giddens, A. (1968) '"Power" in the recent writings of Talcott Parsons', *Sociology*, 2, pp.257–72.

Gill, G. (1982) 'Personal dominance and the collective principle: individual legitimacy in Marxist – Leninist systems', in Rigby and Feher (1982), pp.94–110.

Gilsenan, M. (1988) 'State and popular Islam in Egypt', in Halliday and Alavi (1988), pp.167–90.

Grafstein, R. (1981) 'The failure of Weber's concept of legitimacy', *Journal of Politics*, 43, pp.456–72.

Habermas, J. (1973) 'What does a crisis mean today? Legitimation problems in late capitalism', *Social Research*, 40, pp.643–67.

Habermas, J. (1976a) 'Legitimationsprobleme im modernen Staat', *Merkur*, 332, pp.37–56 (revised English version in Habermas, 1979).

Habermas, J. (1976b) *Legitimation Crisis* (London: Heinemann).

Habermas, J. (1979) *Communication and the Evolution of Society* (London: Heinemann).

Habermas, J. (1984) *The Theory of Communicative Action*, vol. 1 (London: Heinemann).

Habib, J.S. (1978) *Ibn Sa'ud's Warriors of Islam* (Leiden: Brill).

Halliday, F. (1979) *Iran: Dictatorship and Development* (Harmondsworth: Penguin).

Halliday, F. (1988) 'The Iranian revolution: uneven development and religious populism' in Halliday and Alavi (1988), pp.31–63.

Halliday, F. and Alavi, H. (1988) *State and Ideology in the Middle East and Pakistan* (London: Macmillan).

Haraszti, M. (1977) *A Worker in a Worker's State* (Harmondsworth: Penguin).

Harris, M. (1977) *Cannibals and Kings* (New York: Random House).

Harris, R.L. and Vilas, C.M. (1985) *Nicaragua: a Revolution under Siege* (London: Zed Books).

Hart, H.L.A. (1961) *The Concept of Law* (Oxford University Press).

Hasek, J. (1973) *The Good Soldier Svejk* (London: Heinemann).

Havel, V. (1987) *Living in Truth* (London: Faber).

Hayek, F. (1976) *Law, Legislation and Liberty*, vol. 2 (London: Routledge).

Hegel, G.W.F. (1953) *Reason in History* (New York: Bobbs-Merrill).

Held, D. (1982) 'Crisis tendencies, legitimation and the state', in Held, D. and Thompson, J.B. (eds.) *Habermas: Critical Debates* (London: Macmillan), pp.182–95.

Held, D. (1989) *Political Theory and the Modern State* (Cambridge: Polity).

Heller, A. (1982) 'Phases of legitimation in Soviet-type societies', in Rigby and Feher (1982), pp.45–63.

Hennis, W. (1976) 'Legitimität', *Merkur*, 332, pp.17–36.

Hinton, W. (1966) *Fanshen* (New York: Monthly Review Press).

Hiro, D. (1987) *Iran under the Ayatollahs* (London: Routledge).

Hobbes, T. (1960) *Leviathan* (Oxford: Blackwell).

Hobsbawm, E.J. and Ranger, T. (eds.) (1983) *The Invention of Tradition* (Cambridge University Press).

Hopkins, K. (1978) *Conquerors and Slaves* (Cambridge University Press).

Hopwood, D. (1982) 'The ideological basis: Ibn Abd al-Wahab's Muslim revivalism', in Niblock (1982), pp.23–35.

Huntington, S.P. (1968) *Political Order in Changing Societies* (Yale University Press).

Joseph, R.A. (1987) Democracy and Prebendal Politics in Nigeria (Cambridge University Press).

Keane, J. (1984) 'Introduction', Offe (1984), pp.11–34.

Keddie, N.R. (1981) *Roots of Revolution* (Yale University Press).

Keddie, N.R. (1982) 'Comments on Skocpol', *Theory and Society*, 11, pp.285–92.

Keddie, N.R. (ed.) (1983) *Religion and Politics in Iran* (Yale University Press).

Keddie, N.R. (1988) 'Ideology, society and state in post-colonial Muslim societies', in Halliday and Alavi (1988), pp.9–30.

Kimmel, M.S. (1990) *Revolution: a Sociological Interpretation* (Cambridge: Polity).

King, D.S. (1987) *The New Right: Politics, Markets and Citizenship* (London: Macmillan).

Kolinsky, M. (1981) 'The nation state in Western Europe' in Tivey (1981), pp.82–103.

Kramnick, I. (1972) 'Reflections on revolution: definition and explanation in recent scholarship', *History and Theory*, 11, pp.26–63.

Krejci, J. (1983) *Great Revolutions Compared* (Brighton: Wheatsheaf).

Lane, C. (1984) 'Legitimacy and power in the Soviet Union through Socialist ritual', *British Journal of Political Science*, 14, pp.207–17.

Lessnoff, M. (1986) *Social Contract* (London: Macmillan).

Lewis, P.G. (1982) 'Obstacles to the establishment of political legitimacy in communist Poland', *British Journal of Political Science*, 12, pp.125–47.

Lewis, P.G. (ed.) (1984) *Eastern Europe: Political Crisis and Legitimation* (London: Croom Helm).

Linz, J.J. and Stepan, A. (eds.) (1978) *The Breakdown of Democratic Regimes* (John Hopkins University Press).

Lipjhart, A. (1977) *Democracy in Plural Societies* (Yale University Press).

Lipset, S.M. (1958) 'Some social requisites of democracy', *American Political Science Review*, 53, pp.69–105.

Locke, J. (1967) *Two Treatises of Government* (Cambridge University Press).

Lomax, B. (1984) 'Hungary – the quest for legitimacy' in Lewis (1984), pp.68–110.

Lowenthal, R. (1979) 'Political legitimacy and cultural change in West and East', *Social Research*, 49, pp.401–35.

Ludz, P.C. (1979) 'Legitimacy in a divided nation', in Denitch (1979), pp.161–76.

Luhmann, N. (1969) *Legitimation durch Verfahren* (Darmstadt: Luchterhand).

Lukes, S. (1974) *Power: a Radical View* (London: Macmillan).

McFarlane, B. (1984) 'Political crisis and East European economic reforms', in Lewis (1984), pp.176–99.

MacIntyre, A. (1970) 'The idea of a social science' in Wilson (1970), pp.112–30.

McQuail, D. (1984) *Communication* (London: Longmans).

Mahdavy, H. (1970) 'The patterns and problems of economic development in rentier states: the case of Iran', in Cook, M.A. (ed.) *Studies in the Economic History of the Middle East* (Oxford University Press), pp.428–67.

Mann, M. (1986) *The Sources of Social Power* (Cambridge University Press).

Marx, K. (1966) *Capital*, 3 vols (Moscow: Progress Publishers).

Marx, K. and Engels, F. (1968) *Selected Works in One Volume* (London: Lawrence and Wishart).

Marx, K. and Engels, F. (1970) *The German Ideology* (London: Lawrence and Wishart).

Merelman, R. (1966) 'Learning and Legitimacy', *American Political Science Review*, 60, pp.548–61.

Milgram, S. (1974) *Obedience to Authority* (New York: Harper and Row).

Mill, J. (1937) *An Essay on Government* (Oxford: Blackwell).

Mill, J.S. (1909) *Principles of Political Economy* (London: Longmans).

Mill, J.S. (1964) *Utilitarianism; Liberty; Representative Government* (London: Dent).

Mill, J.S. (1970) *On the Subjection of Women* (London: Dent).

Millett, K. (1971) *Sexual Politics* (London: Hart-Davis).

Moore, B. (1978) *Injustice* (London: Macmillan).

Morriss, P. (1987) *Power: a Philosophical Analysis* (Manchester University Press).

Mortimer, E. (1982) *Faith and Power: the Politics of Islam* (London: Faber).

Mosca, G. (1939) *The Ruling Class* (New York: McGraw-Hill).

Mouzelis, N. (1986) *Politics in the Semiperiphery* (London: Macmillan).

Nagel, J.H. (1975) *The Descriptive Analysis of Power* (Yale University Press).

Nelson, J.M. (1979) *Access to Power: Politics and the Urban Poor in Developing Nations* (Princeton University Press).

Niblock, T. (ed.) (1982) *State, Society and Economy in Saudi Arabia* (London: Croom Helm).

Niblock, T. (1987) *Class and Power in Sudan* (London: Macmillan).

Nordlinger, E.A. (1972) *Conflict Resolution in Divided Societies* (Harvard University Center for International Affairs).

Nordlinger, E.A. (1977) *Soldiers in Politics: Military Coups and Governments* (New Jersey: Prentice Hall).

Nove, A. (1983) *The Economics of Feasible Socialism* (London: Allen and Unwin).

Oakeshott, M. (1962) *Rationalism in Politics and Other Essays* (London: Methuen).

Oakley, A. (1972) *Sex, Gender and Society* (London: Temple Smith).

O'Brien, P. and Cammack, P. (eds.) (1985) *Generals in Retreat* (Manchester University Press).

O'Donnell, G. (1973) *Modernisation and Bureaucratic Authoritarianism* (University of California Institute of International Studies).

Offe, C. (1984) *Contradictions of the Welfare State* (London: Hutchinson).

Offe, C. (1985) *Disorganized Capitalism* (Cambridge: Polity).

Okin, S.M. (1980) *Women in Western Political Thought* (London: Virago).

Onimode, B. (ed.) (1989) *The IMF, the World Bank and African Debt*, 2 vols, (London: Zed Books).

Pakulski, J. (1986) 'Legitimacy and mass compliance: reflections on Max Weber and Soviet-type societies', *British Journal of Political Science*, 16, pp.35–56.

Parent, W.A. (1974) 'Freedom as the non-restriction of options', *Mind*, 83, pp.432–4.

Pareto, V. (1966) *Sociological Writings* (London: Pall Mall).

Parkin, F. (1974) 'Strategies of social closure in class formation' in *The Social Analysis of Class Structure* (London: Tavistock), pp.1–18.

Parkin, F. (1979) *Marxism and Class Theory* (London: Tavistock).

Parsons, T. (1960) *Structure and Process in Modern Societies* (Glencoe: Free Press).

Pateman, C. (1980) 'Women and Consent', *Political Theory*, 8, pp.149–68.

Pateman, C. (1985) *The Problem of Political Obligation* (Cambridge: Polity).

Payne, G. (1987) *Mobility and Change in Modern Society* (London: Macmillan).

Perlmutter, A. and Leogrande, W.M. (1982) 'The party in uniform: towards a theory of civil – military relations in communist political systems', *American Political Science Review*, 76, pp.778–89.

Philip, G. (1985) *The Military in South American Politics* (London: Croom Helm).

Pitkin, H.F. (1972) *Wittgenstein and Justice* (University of California Press).

Plamenatz, J.P. (1968) *Consent, Freedom and Political Obligation* (Oxford University Press).

Plant, R. (1982) 'Jürgen Habermas and the idea of legitimation crisis,' *European Journal of Political Research*, 10, pp.341–52.

Poggi, G. (1978) *The Development of the Modern State* (London: Hutchinson).

Powis, J. (1984) *Aristocracy* (Oxford: Blackwell).

Randall, V. (1982) *Women and Politics* (London: Macmillan).

Randall, V. (ed.) (1988) *Political Parties in the Third World* (London: Sage).

Rawls, J. (1971) *A Theory of Justice* (Harvard University Press).

Reeve, A. (1986) *Property* (London: Macmillan).

Richter, M. (1982) 'Toward a concept of political illegitimacy: Bonapartist dictatorship and democratic legitimacy', *Political Theory*, 10, pp.185–214.

Rigby, T.H. (1980) 'A conceptual approach to authority, power and policy in the Soviet Union', in Rigby, Brown and Reddaway (1980), pp.9–31.

Rigby, T.H. (1982) 'Political legitimacy, Weber and communist mono-organisational systems' in Rigby and Feher (1982), pp.1–26.

Rigby, T.H., Brown, A. and Reddaway, P. (1980) *Authority, Power and Policy in the USSR* (London: Macmillan).

Rigby, T.H. and Feher, F. (eds.) (1982) *Political Legitimation in Communist States* (London: Macmillan).

Rosaldo, M. and Lamphere, L. (eds.) (1974) *Woman, Culture and Society* (Stanford University Press).

Rose, G. (1983) 'Velayat-e Faqih and the recovery of Islamic identity in the thought of Ayatollah Khomeini' in Keddie (1983), ch.9.

Rothschild, J. (1977) 'Observations on political legitimacy in contemporary Europe', *Political Science Quarterly*, 92, pp.487–501.

Rousseau, J-J. (1963) *The Social Contract and Discourses* (London: Dent).

Runciman, W.G. (1965) *Social Science and Political Theory* (Cambridge University Press).

Ryan, A. (1987) *Property* (Open University Press).

Said, E.W. (1981) *Covering Islam* (London: Routledge).

Saint-Simon, C.H. (1975) *Selected Writings* (London: Croom Helm).

Sanday, P.R. (1981) *Female Power and Male Dominance* (Cambridge University Press).

Schaar, J.H. (1969) 'Legitimacy in the modern state' in Green, P. and

Levinson S. (eds.) *Power and Community* (New York: Random House), pp.276–327.

Schmidt, S.W. *et al.* (eds.) (1977) *Friends, Followers and Factions* (California University Press).

Scott, J. (1982) *The Upper Classes* (London: Macmillan).

Scott, J.C. (1969) 'The analysis of corruption in developing nations', *Comparative Studies in Society and History*, 11, pp.315–41.

Scott, J.C. (1976) *The Moral Economy of the Peasant* (Yale University Press).

Scott, J.C. and Kerkvliet, B.J. (1977) 'How traditional rural patrons lose legitimacy', in Schmidt (1977) pp.439–58.

Semmel, B. (1960) *Imperialism and Social Reform* (London: Allen and Unwin).

Skocpol, T. (1979) *States and Social Revolutions* (Cambridge University Press).

Skocpol, T. (1982) 'Rentier state and Shi'a Islam in the Iranian revolution', *Theory and Society*, 11, pp.239–62.

Smith, A. (1976) *An Inquiry into the Nature and Causes of the Wealth of Nations* (University of Chicago Press).

Spender, D. (1980) *Man Made Language* (London: Routledge).

Steiner, H. (1974) 'Individual liberty', *Proceedings of the Aristotelian Society*, 75, pp.33–50.

Stewart, J.H. (1951) *A Documentary Survey of the French Revolution* (New York: Macmillan).

Stone, L. (1965) 'Theories of revolution', *World Politics*, 18, pp.159–76.

Szeftel, M. (1983) 'Corruption and the spoils system in Zambia' in Clarke, M. (ed.) (1983) *Corruption* (London: Pinter), pp.163–89.

Szeftel, M. (1987) 'The crisis in the Third World', in Bush (1987), pp.87–140.

Szentes, T. (1983) *The Political Economy of Underdevelopment* (Budapest: Akademiai Kiado).

Taylor, M. (1988) *Rationality and Revolution* (Cambridge University Press).

Therborn, G. (1980) *The Ideology of Power and the Power of Ideology* (London: Verso).

Thomas, C.Y. (1984) *The Rise of the Authoritarian State in Peripheral Societies* (New York: Monthly Review Press).

Thompson, E.P. (1975) *Whigs and Hunters* (London: Allen Lane).

Thorpe, F.N. (ed.) (1909) *The Federal and State Constitutions of the USA* (Washington: Government Printing Office).

Tilly, C. (ed.) (1975) *The Formation of National States in Western Europe* (Princeton University Press).

Tivey, L. (ed.) (1981) *The Nation State* (Oxford: Martin Robertson).

Tordoff, W. (1984) *Government and Politics in Africa* (London: Macmillan).

Weber, M. (1956) *Wirtschaft und Gesellschaft*, 4th ed. (Tubingen; J.C.B. Mohr).

Weber, M. (1958) *Gesammelte Politische Schriften*, 2nd ed. (Tubingen: J.C.B. Mohr).

Weber, M. (1968) *Economy and Society* (University of California Press).

Weingrod, A. (1968) 'Patrons, patronage and political parties', *Comparative Studies in Society and History*, 10, pp.377–400.

Whitelegg, E. *et al*. (eds.) (1982) *The Changing Experience of Women* (Oxford: Blackwell).

Wilber, C.K. (ed.) (1984) *The Political Economy of Development and Under-development*, 3rd ed. (New York: Random House).

Willis, P. (1977) *Learning to Labour* (Aldershot: Gower).

Wilson, B.R. (ed.) (1970) *Rationality* (Oxford: Blackwell).

Winch, P. (1958) *The Idea of a Social Science* (London: Routledge).

Winch, P. (1964) 'Understanding a primitive society', *American Philosophical Quarterly*, 1, pp.307–24; reprinted in Wilson (1970), pp.78–111.

Wolin, S.S. (1981) 'Max Weber: legitimation, method and the politics of theory', *Political Theory*, 9, pp.401–24.

Wollstonecraft, M. (1970) *A Vindication of the Rights of Women* (London: Dent).

Wolpe, H. (1968) 'A critical analysis of some aspects of charisma', *Sociological Review*, 16, pp.305–18.

Wrong, D. (1979) *Power: its Forms, Bases and Uses* (Oxford: Blackwell).

Young, M. (1961) *The Rise of the Meritocracy* (Harmondsworth: Penguin).

Zagorin, P. (1973) 'Theories of revolution in contemporary historiography', *Political Science Quarterly*, 88, pp.23–52.

Zubaida, S. (1982) 'The ideological conditions for Khomeini's doctrine of government', *Economy and Society*, 11, pp.138–72.

Index